CW01021160

TOYS · DOLLS · AUTOMATA
MARKS AND LABELS

Marx's Merry Mice by Louis Marx, an animated metal toy by the man who turned out millions of toys and turned himself into a millionaire. Although at the time his toys were the cheapest in the USA this one sold for £70 in 1974.

American 1921 9″ wide

Courtesy of Sotheby's

Toys · Dolls
Automata
Marks and Labels

GWEN WHITE

B. T. BATSFORD LTD
London and Sydney

Written and illustrated by the same author:
Ancient and Modern Dolls
Toys' Adventures at the Zoo
Ladybird, Ladybird
A Book of Toys
Eight Little Frogs
A Book of Dolls
A Book of Pictorial Perspective
A World of Pattern
Dolls of the World
European and American Dolls
Perspective: A Guide for Artists,
   Architects and Designers
Antique Toys and Their Background

First published 1975
Copyright © Gwen White 1975
Filmset by Servis Filmsetting Ltd, Manchester
Printed and bound in Great Britain by
The Pitman Press, Bath
for the Publishers, B. T. Batsford Ltd
4 Fitzhardinge Street, London WIH OAH
and 23 Cross Street, Brookvale
N.S.W. 2100, Australia

ISBN 0 7134 2956 9

CONTENTS

PHOTOGRAPHS

1. SHOPS, BAZAARS, AND THE COMING OF LABELS AND MARKS

Men and women hawked toys at local fairs and markets and some set up stalls. These were temporary affairs and were moved around but gradually shops which were permanent buildings took their place. Since few people could read in the Middle Ages, signs and symbols were hung outside the shops in order to attract customers. These were handed down from father to son and became valuable heirlooms, some actually displaying the date on which they were first used.

Towards the end of the seventeenth century a toy could be a child's plaything or a precious trifle. Amongst the London toymen of the eighteenth century who had addresses in the city in 1738 were William Deard, opposite St Dunstans Church in Fleets, Thomas Wildey in St Pauls Churchyard, and Frederick Deever at Cornhill, all fairly close together. Apart from playthings they sold china animals, scent bottles, etwees and other trifles.

Mrs Chevenix of Regent Street, the noted toy-woman, leased her house to Horace Walpole in 1747. He wrote to his friends, 'This little rural bijou was Mrs Chevenix's, the toy-woman *à la mode*, who in every dry season is to furnish me with the best rain water from Paris, and now and then with some Dresden-china cows'.

Centres for toys in the New World were in New England and Pennsylvania, while the centre for European toys was Nürnberg. Here different villages became known for their specialities, Schalkau for farms and menageries, Eisfeld for rocking-horses, Schwarzberg for polished marbles. Berchtesgaden was famous for its boxes and wooden toys. By 1750 many of the folk toys were produced at Seiffen.

Coles Child was a toyman near to London Bridge in 1754.

The removal of hanging shop signs was enforced in 1762 because they had become so dangerous especially in a high wind. The signs were therefore fixed flat over the doorways, except for the barbers' striped poles and the pawnbrokers' three balls. The numbering of the London shops began in the same year, just as soon as the signs could not be seen when walking along the street.

A decree issued in 1793 suppressed all titles and armorial emblems in France. Actually these had become a menace to personal safety, and royal signs of any kind were obliterated.

1793 was the year when Domenico Pierotti showed his wax dolls at the Old Pantheon Bazaar. This was on a large site with three entrances, one at 359 Oxford Street, another at 8 Great Marlborough Street, and another at 40 Poland Street. The odd number indicates the south side of Oxford Street, and the toy bazaar was in the Upper Gallery, actually the site of the present Marks and Spencer.

A. Loriot of New Bond Street had for sale in 1797, 'Dressed Wax dolls, 8/-, a Regiment of Soldiers 2/6, and conjuring Clowns at 5/-'. In 1803 M. Bremai had a toyshop in the rue St Honoré, Paris. Wooden toys, cheap wax dolls and paper soldiers sold at the various fairs, can now be found in folk museums.

a *1797 A. Loriot, New Bond Street, London. Dolls, soldiers, clowns, etc*

In 1806, 'in London on May-day, the chimney sweepers parade the streets, drest in fantastic finery, and form very whimsical groups. And on August 18th a Fair is held at Camberwell, and on the 21st at Peckham. In this dull season of amusement these two fairs afford great diversion to all descriptions of persons and on Sept 3, Bartholomew Fair begins'. Mention of these fairs and parades is taken from a *Picture of London*.

One of the first London bazaars was in Soho Square. This was opened in the heart of Soho, so called after a hunting cry, in 1816. The square is south of Oxford Street and west of the Charing Cross Road.

The Burlington Arcade was opened in London on 20 March 1819, and the Royal Arcade in Dublin was opened in 1820. In 1832 the St James Bazaar was opened and Austin's had a Toy and Doll counter at the Pantheon Bazaar which was opened in 1834. In 1832 the Queens Bazaar in Oxford Street was burnt down and the Royal Arcade in Dublin in 1837.

The Lowther Arcade in the Strand was opened in 1831 and also the Emporium at 12 Milsom Street, Bath. Here 'the bazaar department contains a great variety of TOYS and almost all the multifarious Articles usually kept in bazaars'. It was owned by Jolly & Son.

At the Manchester Bazaar in 1831, the counters on the first floor were let to males and those on the second floor to the females. Augustus Sala in *Twice Round the Clock* mentions the stalls laden with pretty gimcracks, toys and papier mâché trifles for the table, dolls and children's dresses etc. At the Pantheon there was bargaining, but not so at the Manchester or Soho bazaars for these were considered to be more genteel.

The Industries Fair in Paris, 1844, saw the introduction of many novelties and it was at this fair that the name of Jumeau became known.

By the 1840s there was a toy store in almost every American town. Schwarz's famous toy store opened in Baltimore in 1849. The family consisted of four brothers, each of them going into the toy trade. F.A.O. Schwarz still carries on in New York and his shop is one of the largest for toys in the world. Nowadays it also possesses a department for antique toys.

It has been said that a dagger indicated a wholesale doll and toy manufacturer between 1850 and 1887. I wonder if the sign was really an arrow for there are many arrows included in the trademarks which follow, but not a single dagger. Even the marks for soldiers are indicated by swords.

Cheethan's warehouse for toys was at 212 Pentonville Road, and another maker, E. Tinker, stated that he 'was at 54 Bishopsgate and nowhere else'.

By 1852, Antonio Bazzoni was at 129 High Holborn, maker of wax dolls, John & L. Poole were at 8 Twisters Alley, Bunhill Row, wooden doll makers, and two makers of composition dolls were Joseph Robins, 6 Crown Street, Finsbury Square, and J. W. Wicks at 15 Whitmore Road, Hoxton.

In France, the inscription 'Liberty, Fraternity, Equality' was ordered to be erased throughout the country, and the previous names of streets, public buildings and places of resort were to be restored. Even the trees which had been planted in the name of Liberty were hewn down and burnt.

Makers of wax dolls in 1853 were J. Barton, 2 Constitution Road, and H. Pierotti, 33 Great Ormond Street. Rimmels of 96, the Strand, famous for perfumed gloves, also sold perfumed crackers for balls and parties containing 'Mottoes selected from the best poets and a small metalic tube, filled with best rose-water which may be squirted by mischief-loving maids, even into the eyes of their partners without causing pain'.

In 1854, Joseph Toms in Kensington High Street, opened his 'Toy and Fancy Repository', Mr Toms being in 1862 the Toms of Derry & Toms. The first retail shop of the Singer Manufacturing Company opened at Glasgow in 1856 for sewing machines.

b 1862 Cremer, 210 Regent Street, London. Dolls, toys, games

c 1878 C. Gooch, Soho Bazaar, London. Distributors of dolls made by Charles Marsh

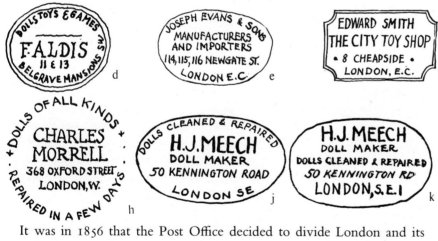

Labels with Marked Districts

d 1865 F. Aldis, 11 & 13 Belgrave Mansions, SW

e 1865 Joseph Evans & Sons, Newgate Street, London. Manufacturers and Importers

f 1880 Edward Smith, 8 Cheapside, London, EC. The City Toy Shop

g 1889 Peacock's, 525 New Oxford Street, London. 'The Beaming Nurse'

h 1894 Charles Morrell, 368 Oxford Street, London. Doll repairer

j & k Two Meech labels, k is after 1917

It was in 1856 that the Post Office decided to divide London and its vicinity into postal districts such as E for East and W for West, and this plan was gradually put into action.

On the 1 March 1857, the letters S E for South East, and W for West were added to the word LONDON. These show in which direction the city had spread and also provide a clue to the dating of the labels which so often appear on the body of a doll or on the boxes containing toys or games, giving the address of the maker or the shop.

In June, W C for West Central was added, N W for North West came in July and E C for East Central in December. The letters W C had no other significance, for at this time water-closets were unknown. Had they been invented, I would imagine that the Victorians would have vetoed these initials. In March 1858 came the single letter E, in May came S W, in September came N and S, and N E came in October.

Years later, in the Spring of 1917, numbers were added to the postal districts of London, such as W 1, S E 2, or S W 10, etc. (This information has been kindly supplied by Miss Coates of the Post Office Record room.)

Notice the label of H. J. Meech. It will be seen in the later label that the figure 1 has been added to the letters S E showing that he was still in production in 1917.

In 1860 there was a small toy department at the Pantechnicon Bazaar in Motcombe Street, Belgravia. Later, when this bazaar concentrated almost entirely on furniture, their vans used the same name and thus came the pantechnicons of today.

The Soho Bazaar occupied 4–7 Soho Square and 6–7 Dean Street. Toy furniture, toy watches, hobby horses etc would be on sale and by 1860 the duty on earthenware goods was removed. There is a coloured engraving in the Westminster archives of the Corinthian Bazaar which was at 7 Argyll Street, Soho, which was Argyll House, now the site of the Palladium.

Two London arcades were demolished during the early sixties, one the Exeter 'Change Arcade, and another which stretched from the foot of the Clock Tower at London Bridge to the South Eastern Railway. An iron trough called a viaduct took its place. It sold tea, bacon, cigars, vesuvians, toys, hot sausages etc. The Royal Arcade, Oxford St sold rocking horses, and the Model Ship Shop had 'every variety of craft and a magic nigger performing double-shuffles in the window'. Other delights are all described in the 'Shops and Companies of London'.

The Lowther Arcade sold dolls and a 'Very curious two-stall stable with a bright vermillion roof and lined with chrome yellow, with our old friends the little bay-horse and the cock-tailed roan. . . . There are some neat little beds too, with pink hangings edged with white fringe with the baby, if possible more pink than the hangings, securely stitched inside the counterpane.

Kitchens with no roof and walls never at right angles, a deal dresser on which repose two gigantic pewter trenchers and two dishes with a papier mâché goose ready for the doll's dinner, while on either side of the fireplace there hangs a pewter gridiron and a warming-pan. Sheep folds containing neatly shaven lemon-coloured sheep with red collars, farmyards with trees each standing on its own pivot, shilling boxes of tools, shilling Noah's Arks, Dutch dolls, ninepins, money-boxes, dominoes, and the magnet and duck, the only scientific toy we can tolerate'.

In France, in 1865, 'a look at the shops in Paris towards the rue de la Paix,

l *1865 Auguste Giroux, Paris.*
This sign registered in 1888

m *1853 A. T. Guillard, rue des*
Petites Champs, Paris.
Jouets

n *1865 Boissier, 7 B des*
Capucines, Paris, Confiseur

the ladies stroll westwards to the famous Giroux, where you may buy toys, an' it please you, at forty guineas each, babies that cry and call "mamma", and automata to whom the advancement of science and art has given all the obnoxious faculties of an unruly child. They walk on to see Boissier, the shining light of the confectioner's art, and also the cots with the babies that were lying in them'.

Spurin's had a full page advertisement headed by the Royal Arms in Lodge's Peerage and Baronetage of the British Empire for the year 1867. 'English and French Toys, Dolls, etc' appeared in heavy type, also 'All the New Games of the Season'.

In 1868, John Edwards at 43–45 Waterloo Road was known for his dressed and undressed dolls, of wax, composition or of rag, including one known as the Exhibition Rag Doll. Lang & Co of 27 Houndsditch made dolls with rubber faces, and Payne & Son at 32 Lowndes Street, SW had foreign and English toys including musical boxes at what had been Miller's Repository. E. C. Spurin was at 37 New Bond Street and W. H. Cremer at 210 Regent Street.

Between 1865–1880, Hyatts at New Jersey made celluloid toys and dolls, heads and bodies, moveable and with real hair. Dolls' trunks (curved-top suitcases) were made by Ewing & Quinn, and bell-toys by the Gong Bell Manufacturing Company.

In 1865, Endymion P. Hidge wrote to Henry Mayhew regarding the shops of America – 'We deont call sech a place as that a shop, we call it a store and we oughterno. A shop tew Americans is a factory, a works whar engynes (frinstance) aar made, likeways rockaways, alser nails. A store is whar you may buy sass, an' dry goods, an' stove pipe hats, and works of art and peanuts'.

Morrell's shop in the Burlington Arcade was opened from 1870 onwards. In this year toy tea and dinner services were made by Ridgway Sparks & Ridgway. They were earthenware manufacturers at the Bedford Works, Shelton, and their impressed mark was a Staffordshire knot with the initials R S R. Other shops at this time were James Izzard, the Juvenile Repository, Upper Brook Street, Bouchets of 74 Baker Street who dealt in miniature print viewers, and Kronheim & Company who were publishers of puzzles.

It was during the 1870s that lithographed paper replaced many of the painted details on toys. The Chromatic Printing Company made paper dolls in Pennsylvania, and Madame Adolphe Goubaud, Rathbone Place, London, had 'a depot for the sale of Berlin wool and needlework patterns in connection with the Paper Model business now so successfully established', indicating paper patterns for dressmakers and for dolls' clothes.

The French shops with marks were mostly in Paris and whereas the London shops specialized in wax dolls, these specialized in bisques. Although the 'Parisiennes' as they were called, were sumptously dressed, they were playthings and contemporary engravings 'depict young ladies playing at

p 1865 E. C. Spurin, New Bond Street, London. The Toy Warehouse

q 1870 Maison Simonne, 1, 3, 5, 7 & 9 Passage Delorme, rue de Rivoli, Paris

r 1890 Mon. Guillard, 4 rue des Petits Champs, Paris. Succ, to Rémond

s 1890 E. Chauviere, Boul' des Capucines 27, Paris. Au Nain Bleu

mothers'. One shop selling dolls and toys was kept by the agent for Bru dolls with the shop label 'Vente Bébés Reparations Girard, 10 R. Lacepede, Paris'.

In 1876 the one shilling store known as 'Paraphernalia' was started. It was a suitable name for apart from toys, games, printed cloth for rag-dolls and stuffed animals, it might sell anything from a clothes-horse to a thimble.

Many of the home-made toys were fitted with iron wheels which were sold in sets of four. Other iron objects were money-boxes known in the USA as banks.

The Royal Arcade connecting Old Bond Street with Albermarle Street was opened in May 1880. In 1881, C. Pierotti was at the Crystal Palace Gallery, Oxford Street, with his Royal Model Dolls. This was no 108 on the north side and not far from Oxford Circus, then known as Regent Circus.

The Deverall Brothers in Cheapside specialized in balls. These well-known toy sellers had their shop, in 1886, where the novelties and knick-knacks in their window would catch the eyes of busy city men. Wind-up toys were sold on the Cheapside pavements, just as in Oxford Street today. Le Paradis des Enfants was a London shop owned by Parkins & Golto in 1886. This was at 54 Oxford Street, where toys, games and dolls were sold. In 1870 a shop in Paris had the same name and it was still selling toys and dolls in 1883.

Emma Susanna Windsor sold games at her stall at 150 Soho Bazaar, and another woman Sophia Mallet at 39 Charles Square, Hoxton, N sold seaside pails, drums and water-cans.

Nankeen dolls, toys and fancy goods were advertised by Stephen Erhard at 2 Aldermanbury Postern EC in 1891 and John Webb had pitch-pine carts and horses at Featherdale Street, Globe Road, E. This is also the year when H. J. Meech is mentioned as being doll-maker to the Royal Family. His addresses were 50–52 Kennington Road, Westminster Road, and 1–2 North Street Kennington Road.

C. Morrell at 368 Oxford Street marketed the wax and the wax-over-composition dolls made by Charles Marsh at 114 Fulham Road.

The Lowther Arcade consisted of a series of small shops, toyshops of every kind, rich expensive toys and automata in some, traditional penny and tuppenny fairground toys in others. Some specialized in dolls, dressed or undressed, with open or closing eyes, rag dolls and wooden Dutch dolls from about half-an-inch to 18 inches high. Toy theatres, lead or tin soldiers, trains, boats, conjuring tricks, and games were all for sale in 1895.

In the early twentieth century, Morrell's had two shops in Oxford Street, no 368 and no 164, the lower number being towards the City end. Indeed, the numbering of the shops running east and west always started with number one at the city end, and continued away from the city in either direction. On the streets running north and south, the lower numbers are always nearest to the river Thames, and this method of numbering is still in existence today.★

Between 1902 and 1911, Lucy Peck, the maker and repairer of wax dolls and toys was at 131 Regent Street. Hamley's toy shops were at 512 Oxford Street, 35 New Oxford Street, 86 & 87 High Holborn and 64 Regent Street. Rose's Toy and Fancy Repository was at 203 Sloane Street and was noted for dolls' furniture.

The grand opening day of Selfridges shop in Oxford Street was on Monday, 15 March 1909. Of the three claimants to be the first customer was a Daily Chronicle reporter, who bought a toy zeppelin for 6/11. In 1908, Selfridges had occupied no 398 to no 422, on the north side of the street. In 1914, numbers 424 and 426 were added, which had formerly belonged to William Ruscoe, a 'Fancy Goods Dealer'.

Lucy Peck label, early 20th Century

New York's famous toy shop, F.A.O. Schwarz, registered a sign in 1914, where at first they had mostly sold outdoor games and sports goods.

Geo. Borgfeldt & Co's address in 1918 was the rue de Paradis, 43, Paris.

★(I first learnt this from 'Farthing' when I was a student at the Royal College of Art)

Makers' Labels

Wax

Wax dolls are marked by stamped labels usually on the doll's cotton tummy or halfway down the thigh. The dolls made by the Pierotti family are not known to have been marked authentically and the written signatures on the dolls by Madame Montanari vary. The one given here is from the front of the little doll shown at the 1851 Exhibition and for which she won a prize. It differs from the one at Bethnal Green, for here the R looks more like a Z.

Augusta Montanari was born in 1818 and would be about 24 when she made portrait dolls of children of the Royal Family. She died in 1864, aged 46.

Unfortunately signatures may be copied in faded brown ink.

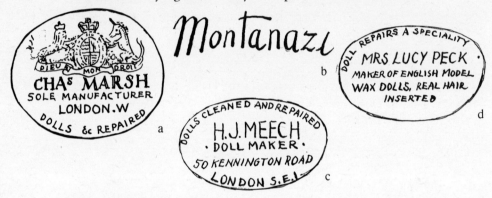

Papier Mâché

Papier mâché, a mixture of pulped paper was much used in the East for toys, many of which were hollow and very light to hold. Tumbler dolls weighted with clay, hollow animals, some with nodding heads, and fragile dolls were made in thousands, many for export, others to be burnt at religious ceremonies. Too delicate to stamp, the papier mâché toys are rarely marked.

The dolls with an elaborate coiffeur and head moulded in one, were known as German Milliners' models, the hair-style being termed an Apollo Knot. These date between 1830 and 1835.

In 1910, Marian Kaulitz won a gold medal for her dolls with their heads of papier mâché and dressed by herself.

Leather

Leather was used for covering toy animals with real skin. Even large rocking-horses have been covered in this manner. Wooden horses, goats and cows have been neatly covered sometimes over the wood base, sometimes over one of plaster. The costly Parisienne dolls had bodies of white or pink kid. In the late 1820s Thomas Anners of Philadelphia made leather dolls with heads of composition.

j 1866 Frank Darrow, Bristol, Conn., USA. Toys, clocks & rawhide dolls

k 1870s Clément (Widow), Paris. Dolls

l 1874 J. Lacman, Philadelphia, USA. Toys, dolls' bodies, dolls' shoes

m 1913 Emil Zitzmann, Steinach. Leather dolls and dolls' bodies, and other 'stuff' material. Registered mark

Fine Bisque

The unglazed heads in the doll world were known as Bisque. Especially fine bisque heads were made between 1860 and 1875, the early Parisiennes having pale blue painted or glass eyes some with a darker rimmed iris. Later dolls had swivel necks, darker blue eyes and extra seams on their well-made bodies. An initial is sometimes found at the bottom of the deep yoke.

n 1862 W. H. Cremer, jnr, Regent Street, London. Wax doll maker

p & q 1863 Simonne, 188 rue de Rivoli, Paris. Dolls of French bisque

r 1862 Aux Rêves de L'Enfance, 40 rue de Richelieu, Paris. Dolls

GERMAN FAIR
a¹

UNIVERSAL PROVIDER
b¹

TOTTENHAM HOUSE
155 SHOOLBRED & COMPY 152
1822
c¹

Grand Bazar National
d¹

e¹

HAMLEYS
64 REGENT ST
W
DOLLS REPAIRED
f¹

THE TOY HOUSE
g¹

LIBERTY
h¹

MAGASIN DES ENFANTS
JOUETS ET JEUX
PASSAGE DE L'OPÉRA·PARIS
j¹

GALERIES LAFAYETTE
k¹

"Incroyable Bazar"
l¹

AU PARADIS DES ENFANTS
m¹

n¹

TOYS 1862
F.A.O.
SCHWARZ
Children's World
p¹

LES GALERIES UNIVERSELLES
q¹

Shops Registered Labels

a¹ *1856 Frederick Waite, Bridge Street, Manchester. Toys*

b¹ *1878 William Whiteley, London. Toys*

c¹ *1878 Shoolbred & Compy, London. Toys, established in 1822*

d¹ & e¹ *1888 Société E. Stein & Cie, Paris. Mark in blue, white and red*

f¹ *1890 Hamley's, Regent Street, London. Toys, games and dolls*

g¹ *1898 Schlesinger, the Toy House, London*

h¹ *1906 Liberty & Co Ltd, 28 Warwick Street, Regent Street, London*

j¹ *1910 Magasin des Enfants, Passage de L'Opera, Paris. Toys and games*

k¹ *1910 Grands Magasin 'Aux Galeries Lafayette', 40 Boulevard Haussmann, Paris*

l¹ *1912 Aron Lévy, 125 Fauberg Saint-Antoine, Paris*

m¹ *1913 Société Anglaise 'Bloch & Behr Ltd, 4 bis et 6 rue aux Ours, Paris. Liquidateur, M. Gordon*

n¹ *1914 F. A. O. Schwarz, NY, USA. Mostly outdoor games and sports*

p¹ *Mark used at present time*

q¹ *1921 Edouard-Paul Malaret, 156 rue de Rivoli, Paris. Jeux, jouets, etc.*

Doll by Herbert John Meech.
Wax head and limbs, stuffed
body with two stamped marks
at base of back, note coarse
stitching. Hair inset, eyes blue.
Meech worked between 1865–
1891.

English *c.*1880 19″ high

*Courtesy of the Horsham Museum,
Sussex*

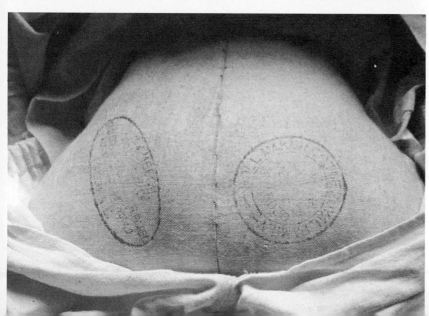

The Need for Registration

When the makers of toys and dolls took their samples to the stall holders at the bazaars, they either stayed with them or handed their goods over for sale. Naturally they would label them and thus we sometimes have the maker's name and sometimes that of the stall holder who was a kind of agent. Anyone could put their signature on the wares which they had made. If a maker sold her goods to a shop there could be some agreement where the name of the shop would be stamped on the toy boxes or on the bodies of the dolls, and they might be exclusive to one shop alone.

In eighteenth-century marks, the initial J is nearly always given as an I. However, written initials sometimes mean nothing more than the initials of the owner of the doll, such as M P for Molly Payne, which is not surprising considering the number of little girls with dolls which went to the making of a Victorian family.

With the increase in commerce it became essential that goods be marked with a name or some kind of a sign. One of the first in England was Roncorone, a maker of beeswax dolls. His address was Summers Town, and his rectangular label was decorated with a border of leaves.

Before marks were registered properly, the early dolls were marked with labels usually stamped on some part of their body. These could belong to the shop owners, dealers or makers. The first registered marks are mainly for porcelain and are found at the base of the porcelain yoke. Sometimes the mark is in cobalt or underglaze blue as in the little tea and dinner sets, marked under saucer or plate.

The words Trademark, Schutzmarke, and Fabrikmarke do not appear in the registered marks during the 1860s. A few makers would stamp their wares with a patent number should they possess one. Among these was Ludwig (sometimes Lewis) Greiner of Philadelphia in Pennsylvania. Between 1848 and 1870 he made toys, dolls and dolls' heads. In the late 1860s they were made by Edward Greiner.

The Merchandise Marks Act of 1862 was passed in order to punish those people who made forgeries of trademarks, but this law was very difficult to carry out. Trademarks with names, letters or devices were often pirated and this became a trade in itself among unscrupulous and inferior tradesmen. This Act still needed a register of marks for until this was made it was very difficult to trace the offender.

An impressed mark seen on toy tea or dinner sets is made from a metal or clay stamp or seal and has a mechanical appearance. It differs from an incised mark which is freer and has a slight ploughed-up effect. On pottery the word Ltd or Limited denotes a date after 1861 and usually much later. The word trademark was used after 1862 but rarely before 1875.

Some French marks include the word *Bis* in an address, but it merely means twice, as in the mark of Gesland which also has the initials S G D G

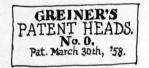

a

a   *1858 Ludwig Greiner, Philadelphia. Pa. Black or gold label found inside doll's head*

meaning *Sans Garantie du Gouvernement*. Madame Rohmer's mark of 1860 also bears these initials showing that the goods were not guaranteed in any way. It was different from copyright for which the French had adequate protection.

b   *1860s Madame Rohmer*

According to the Ministre Plenipotentiare in Paris 'the letters S G D G which were used since the law of 1844 ceased to be applicable as from 31 December 1968. At present two denominations are used, '*Brevet deposé*, or *Demande de brevet en cours*'. The new law will be decided in 1973'. This information I have received from M. A. Rigaillaud, Commercial Counsellor.

The Trademarks Registration Act was passed in 1875 on 13 August. With a register open for examination, the rightful owner of a trademark could pursue the one who had cribbed it. The word Schutzmarke was registered on a trademark by Christian Hacker of Nuremberg, a toy maker who owned a factory. The word Schutz is a kind of safeguard and Fabrik is for factory. The passing of this Act meant that many trademarks which had been in use for years, were now registered for the first time.

The German marks registered in 1875 were mostly for wooden toys though some were of porcelain or of papier mâché. Spielwaaren are toys, Holzspielwaaren are those of wood and Puppenköpfen are dolls' heads. William Simon's sign is for toys and chinaware, Krausz's is for papier mâché, wooden toys and dolls' heads. J. Hagen's sign of an anchor with nine bells is for all kinds of small things including toys and bells: these would be tinklebells for babies' rattles, bells for childrens' harnesses and for Morris dancing etc.

The Holz-masse mark registered by Cuno and Otto Dressel in 1875 belonged to a firm which claimed to be one of the oldest in the toy world. This mark consists of a winged helmet in front of the caduceus. Owing to use and the number of impressions on the back of the dolls' heads, it has become worn and blurred and is not easily recognisable. It has been referred to erroneously as the 'feather mark', or the 'swan' and even likened to a bird flying from a nest full of birds. The drawings show how the original mark was formed.

c   *1875 How the Cuno & Otto Dressel mark arrived*
d   *1885 C. & O. Dressel doll mark*
e   *1910 Jutta mark*
f   *1912 Poppy mark*

19

g   *1878 Charles Bertran*

h   *Deutches Reich Patent mark*

j   *1883 Friedrich Kaestner*

k   *1883 Friedrich Kaestner*

l   *1884 Friedrich Kaestner*

The Dressels made *Puppen, Puppenköpfe, Holz, Glas, Porzellan* etc. *Korbwaaren, Märbel, Schiefertafeln und Griffel. Korbwaaren* were baskets, *Schiefertafin* were slates and *Griffel* were slate pencils.

The words *Marque Déposée* appeared in the Ondine mark of 1878. This was registered by Charles Bertran, 4 rue des Archives, Paris. He was a toy manufacturer and Ondine was a *poupée nageuse*, that is, a swimming doll.

Often the initials D R P are found stamped on the front body of a doll especially those dolls with more than one face. The letters stand for Deutsches Reich Patent, ie. a German patent; when the letters are U S P these are for United States Patent and these are usually followed by the number of the patent.

The Trademarks Registration Act was passed in the USA in 1881. The word *Deposée* appears frequently during the '80s. Déposé in French, Deponiert in German, it can be shortened to D E P and thus appears on both French and German goods. The inclusion of the word England in a mark could be as early as 1880.

Frequently the initials of the maker and of the place name would be included as in the mark of Friedrich Kaestner, where the O is for Ohrdurf and the Z signifies Saxony, pronounced Zaxony in German.

Agents often marked the goods with their own stamp especially when they were acting for some small firm or private person. The section on Character Toys will bear this out.

By the Merchandise Marks Act of 1887, the whole subject of trademarks was placed on a different footing and the forging of a trademark could lead to two years imprisonment, a fine or both, and every chattel or article connected with the offence could be destroyed by order of the court. It was forbidden to make a mark resembling a trademark in order to deceive or to make a false description.

The abbreviation Ste stands for society, firm or manufacturer. Steiner uses these initials frequently which is confusing as they are nothing to do with his name. The letters Fre are short for figure, meaning the number of that design.

Historical events are commemorated, some dolls carrying the mark of the Eiffel Tower which was built in 1889 for the Paris Exhibition. The Eiffel Tower Ascent Game was registered by Ernest de Lima of Peckham in this same year.

It was not until the Tariff Act of 1890 that the country of an article's origin was marked on the toy or the doll itself. The name tariff is derived from the Moorish port of Tarifa where duties were levied on African commerce. Tariffs are concerned with import and export duty but only on certain articles. Therefore after 1890 the country's names gradually appear, the name of the country about 1891, and the words 'made in' about the turn of the century. Toys ready for the market would probably have a tag fixed to them, as would the dolls for it would not have been practicable to add the name to the already fired heads. Often one hears the words 'the doll is definitely before 1890 because there is no name of the country' but take another look because it may be right up under the hair-line at the back of the head.

The single word France is found on a trademark of 1892, that of Germany in 1896 and Made in Germany in 1898. The initials D R G M come on the German toys, standing for *Deutsches-Reichs-Gebrauchs-Muster*, meaning a German registered design. The words *Gesetlich Geschutzt* denote that the article was patented or registered in Germany.

The D R G M on a trademark or label means that the name has been registered. This lasts for three years and after that the makers can apply for an extension for another three years, six years being the limit for the exclusive rights. After 1949, the R for Reichs was replaced by B for Bundes. On the trademark registered in 1919 by Kahn for a board-game, the letters D R W Z appear in the top corner. The W Z is for *Warren Zeichen Gesetz*, that is putting the sign or mark on the merchandise, and are granted for ten years. After that, the exclusive rights may be granted for another ten. This information has kindly been supplied by Mr Porsten Lange of the Legal Department in the German Chamber of Industry.

The letters A:G with two dots between stand for a German partnership or association, ie. *Antien-gesellschaft*, and appear with the names registering marks. Another set, G m b H appear with a place name such as Bremen or Hanover. These stand for *Gesellschaft mit beschränkter Haftung* and mean a German Limited Liability Company. They appear in entries such as that of Tölke in 1922.

It must be remembered that most firms sold both dolls and toys, and the monograms incorporated within the registered marks should be studied carefully, for some toys will be marked with the monogram only.

m *Mark to show patented or registered in Germany*

Porcelain Toys

The early registered marks for porcelain 'toys' are not for childrens' toys but are for the precious trifles and ornaments which were often included in the elaborate table decorations of the eighteenth century. Before 1855, marks are rarely found on dolls' heads but after 1860 well-known names such as Steiner and Heubach appear.

Marks are incised on the dolls' yokes or painted on the inside of the doll's head; whole figures, animals or toy houses are marked on their bases. Some firms list eyes among their items, glass or porcelain eyes for dolls or animals; Max Burghardt of Ilmenau registered eyes under porcelain in the 1920s.

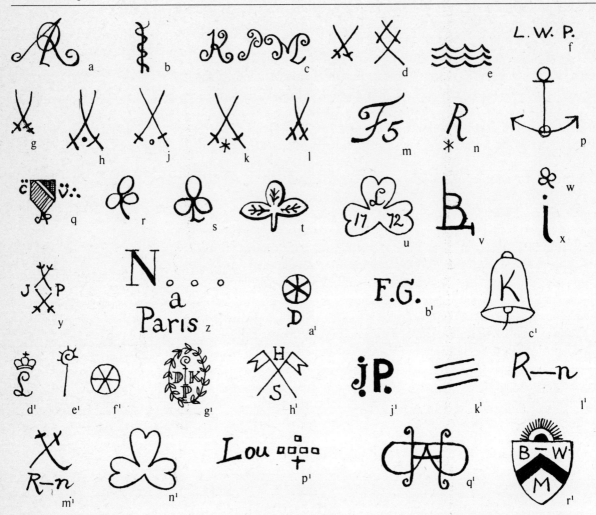

The registered marks of the Königliche Porzellanmanufaktur zu Meissen, Germany

a A R is for Augustus Rex 1709–1726. b 1712–19. c 1720–30. d 1720–30. g 1730–33. h 1733–1763. j 1763–1774. k 1744–1814. l 1814–1875

e 1772, Copenhagen

f, p 1755 Ludwig Wessel, Popplesdorf

m 1760 Fournier

n 1760 Rauenstein

q 1765 Closter-Veilsdorf

r, s, t 1770 Grosbrütenbach

u, v 1772 Limbach, Porzellan Factory. u, This mark was used in 1919, with the words 'Made in Germany' underneath

w, x 1786 Ismenau Porzellan

y 1790 Jacob Petit, Belleville

z 1790 Nast à Paris

a¹ 1827 Damm

b¹ 1829 Gerbing

c¹ 1836 Kling & Co

d¹, e¹, f¹, g¹ 1840 Dressel Kister, Passau, Bavaria. Hard paste porcelain

h¹ 1842 H. Schmidt

j¹ 1843 Jacob Petit, Fontaine-bleau

k¹ 1844–1884 Royal Copenhagen

l¹, m¹ 1855 Rouenstein

n¹ 1855 Grosbrütenbach

p¹ 1855 Limbach, Porcelain factory, Thuringia

q¹ 1859 B. Harratsz of Böhlen

r¹ 1862 Marcus Brown-Westhead, England. Brown-Westhead, Moore & Co, Cauldon Place, Hanley, 1862–1904

Bartholomew Baby & Lambs
Babies of the best,
Babies of the best,
Cradles for their rest.
I'm calling through the town,
Young lambs to sell,
Young lambs to sell,
Red collars as well,
My cry goes up and down.

Long before toys were patented or marked, authentic examples may be seen in pictures. In the collection of the Marquess of Salisbury at Hatfield House there is a painting by John Michael Wright of two children. The boy is holding a beautifully carved horse on a stand with wheels and at his feet lies a toy pistol. This picture was painted about 1658.

Another painting, this time by François Boucher and dated 1749 is of Louis Philippe-Joseph, later known as Philippe Egalité, at the age of two. On his lap he has a toy white kitten on a wooden stand and in his left hand he holds the ribbons of a horse; only the carved head may be seen so it could be a hobby-horse or a rocking horse; on the ground has fallen a pack of cards. This painting is in Waddesdon Manor, now owned by the National Trust.

'Common pressed dolls, carts, chairs, horses for children: fiddlers for children, sorted toys etc.' were advertised in 1764 in the Pennsylvania Journal in the USA. Ivory cup and ball games were made by Charles Shipman of New York in 1767, battledores and shuttlecocks were made by Gilbert Deblois of Boston, and just as in England, there were alphabet cubes, balls and ivory drum-sticks.

By 1791 the traditional toys of Europe were all in production, the butter-churners, the huntsmen, the infants in swaddling clothes and the little carts with birds. The catalogues issued by George Bestelmeier at Nürnberg between 1798–1807 show the toys which were on sale at the time.

Moulds were made for making dolls and toys of papier mâché in 1810 and cheap toys exported from the continent were sold in bazaars, especially toys such as Noah's Arks. In 1814 the animals were mass-produced by the 'ring' method. In 1819 G. Söhlke founded a Berlin firm where they made little toy figures based on fairy tales and also toy trains at the coming of the railways.

Filigree metal had been used for making dolls' furniture and gardens towards the end of the eighteenth century, and at the beginning of the nineteenth century spring-powered cannons were made in the USA.

By 1815 pressed tin-plate was used for making toys in France. The peasants would collect the scrap tin and knock it flat by beating. Shapes were cut and the tin bent into the desired shape. The resulting toys were collected and sold by travelling salesmen.

In Massachussetts a kind of toy guild was formed by William S. Tower, a maker of wooden toys, who had the idea of gathering together other craftsmen. His fellow workers brought him individual toys which they had made in their spare time. At first his project was called the Tower Toy Company but by the late 1830s it was known as the Tower Guild. Samuel Hersey of South Hingham, Massachusetts made wooden toys and became a member. Another was Loring Cushing who made toy furniture, and a doll's wooden cradle has been found with a small label on the base with his name. This would be about 1861. (See the McClintocks' book on American Toys.)

In the early nineteenth century England was getting a name for paper toys such as the paper panoramas of the Thames Tunnel which were on sale in 1843, and for the toy theatres made by Green of London.

From Germany came the majority of building bricks and from France came carnival novelties. In the USA a famous toymaker was Jesse A. Crandall who from 1840 onwards made games, toys and hobby-horses. The USA became noted for toys of iron and tin. J. & E. Stevens made half a ton of iron wheels for children's toy wagons every week, and by 1850 this firm specialized in iron cap pistols. The Philadelphia Tin Toy Manufactory made toys 'superior to any of those imported'. Althof Bergmann made tin and mechanical toys which were on show at the Centennial Exhibition in Philadelphia in 1876. Foreign firms, especially the French ones were much impressed by these low-priced metal toys.

E. I. Horsman of New York sold tennis rackets, baseballs, archery and croquet equipment, also dolls and rag dolls. F. E. Darrow of Bristol, Connecticut, worked between 1866 and 1880, making clocks, toys, rawhide dolls and dolls' heads. Darrow & Peck ran the Darrow Manufacturing Co. The largest toy manufacturers were Reeds of Massachusetts.

Side by side with the new toys remained the traditional ones such as 'the dolls, the bricks, the tea-things, the German farm, the Swiss cottages, the animals, all the dolls' furniture, Noah's ark, horses in the toy stables, and the monkey-up-a-stick' all mentioned by Juliana Horatia Ewing, in the 'Land of Lost Toys' written in 1871.

Wooden horses, waxen dollies, soldiers, wood and tin;
Noah's Ark of birds and beasties; tops that hum and spin;
Little china tea-things and delightful dinner-sets;
Trumpets, drums and baby-houses, balls in coloured nets!

Anonymous

East Hampton, Connecticut, was known as the Bell Town for here the noted bell toys were made, rattles with bells, and horses' harnesses for children to wear which were very popular at this time. In the twentieth century Buster Brown and Tige, his dog, were pictured on bell toys and

The 1870's

a *1872 Althof Bergmann & Co, New York. Jobbers founded in 1867*

b & c *1873 Weintraud, Joyce & Co. He uses the word PROTECTOR also*

d & e *1873 Richard James Secundus Joyce, 18 Aldermanbury, London. Toys*

f *1875 Samuel Krausz in Rodach bei Coburg. Papier-maché und Holz Spielwaaren, Puppenköpfe, etc*

g *1875 Friedr. Robert Krenkel, Nürnberg. Spielwaaren*

h *1875 Wilhelm Simon, Hildburghausen. Spielwaaren und Porzellan*

j *1876 William Meyerstein, 6 Love Lane, Aldermanbury, London. Toys*

k *1876 J. Hager, Nürnberg. Fur all Kurz-Gelanterie-und Spiel-Waaren*

l *1876 Robert Whyte, trading as Whyte & Rydsdale, 73 & 74 Houndsditch, London. Toys and Fancy goods*

m *1876 Barth & Wagner, Rodach bei Coburg. Spiel-waaren*

n *1877 Berthold Eck, Germany. Toys*

p *1878 Ferdinand Rosing, Billiter Square, London. Toys*

q *1878 Hugo Bretsch, Berlin. Kinderspielsachen, toys. (Circle marked 1860)*

r *1878 Edward Henry Vero, Westgate. Dewsbury, Yorkshire. Toys*

s *1879 Julius Dorft, Sonneberg*

t *1879 Ihlee & Horn, 31 Aldermanbury, London. Toys*

u *1879 Merzbach, Lang & Fellheimer, 1 & 2 Snow Hill & 57 St Mary Axe, London. Games & Toys. Their sign is a coat of arms with watches coming out of a cornucopia*

banks. He was a cartoon from the New York Herald and like many another he was made into a cut-out rag doll.

The Panama Canal opened in 1914 and toy dump trucks were made to commemorate this great feat. After the First World War, the German trade took a long while to recover and in the meantime France became better known for her toys and dolls.

The registered marks given here begin at 1872 and include dealers' names besides those of makers, Meyerstein being one of the well-known London agents. Two marks registered by Samuel Krausz in 1875 are interesting because on one he spells his name as it is pronounced, that is Krats.

The marks given here include their date of registration, the maker's name and the address. If a maker has not mentioned what kind of toy or game it is that he is registering, then the mark is listed here under Toys of all kinds, and put in chronological order.

The 1880's

a 1890 Elizabeth Horne, who proposes to carry on business under the Style of the Real Dolls House Female Toy Making Depôt, 9 Greencroft Gardens, South Hampstead, Middlesex, Wife of Frederick Horne. Toys but not including Dolls' Houses	g 1893 Dolffs & Helse, Braunschweig, Germany	Seifenblasenlösungen, that is a game with soap bubbles
	h 1893 Jacob, Leopold Emil, London Wall, London	r 1897 Edouard Ernest Barret, Neuilly. A toy
	j 1893 Ludwig Guhrauer, Hamburg	s 1897 J. N. Reithoffer, Vereingte-Gummiwaaren-Fabriken-Harburg-Wien. Formerly Menier-Harburg
1890 Timm & Schrumpf, Hamburg. 'A dragon on a black ground'. Mark not shown	k 1895 Jean-Herman Boisson-Berrod, fabricant à Dortan	
	l 1893 Antonin Debrieu, négociant à Paris. Jouets de toutes sortes	t 1897 Alphonse Merlin, Paris. Fabricant de jouets
b 1891 A. Goblet, Montroux		u 1897 Thomas Christo. Mohrhardt, Nürnberg
c 1891 Joseph Erdmann, Paris	m 1896 Zeuch & Lausmann, Sonneberg	
d 1891 Paul Denancy, Paris	n 1896 Andr. Müller, Sonneberg	v 1897 Chambre Syndicale des fabricants de jouets et jeux, dont le siège est à Paris
e 1891 Jean Rauly, Paris	p 1896 Auguste Martin, fabricant de bimbeloterie à Moncel-sur-Seille	
f 1892 Pencke & Rascher, Hamburg	q 1895 Nürnberger Spiele Fabrik, Fürth.	w 1897 C. Abel-Klinger, Nürnberg
		x 1897 George Birnbaum, Dresden

LE DÉCOR-EXPRESS a

LA FÉE VAILLANTE b

Converse f

c

Bade zu Hause! d

e

LILLIPUT g

K&B j

FRANCOISE
NOUVELLE ROUE de LOTERIE
Système déposé
W. X. PARIS
m

LA SEULE VÉRITABLE

GRANDE ROUE DE PARIS
LA PLUS EXACTE
LA PLUS FACILE
à Construire
k

Lilliput h

B x F
PARIS
l

TAMANCO

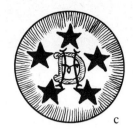
p

Glücksarakel. n

LE GRAND GLOBE CELESTE DE PARIS q

a&b   1898 Charles Auguste
    Watilliaux, Paris
c   1898 Mille Henriette
    Dechancuix, Paris
d&e   1898 Moosdorf &
    Hochhausler, Berlin. Treptow
    Kopenicker Landstr. They
    made articles and toys mostly
    for babies, and registered many
    names
f   1898 Morton E. Converse &
    Son, Winchendon, Mass. Toy

drums, trunks, rocking-horses,
doll houses etc. Claim since
June, 1898
g   1899 Emil Thurnauer &
    Max Neumark, trading as
    'Pabst' Solgerstrasse 16
    Nürnberg
h   1899 G. J. Pabst, Nürnberg
j   1899 Kleinig & Blasberg,
    Leipzig
k&l   1899 MM Bourraux
    frères, négociants à Paris for

designers of toys
m   1899 Watilliaux, Paris. A
    game with a lottery wheel
n   1899 Carl Wernicke,
    Strassfurt, Allemagne,
    Colifichets et jouets, ie
    knick-knacks and toys
p   1899 Erico Mills & Cie,
    Manchester, England. Jouets
q   1899 Edouard Manois, Paris.
    Toys of all kinds

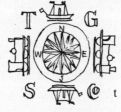
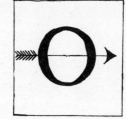

a 1900 G. J. Pabst, Nürnberg

b 1900 Hugo Roithner & Co, Schweidnitz, Sehl. Toys and gymnastic apparatus

c 1900 Emil Wehncke, Altona, Leichstr. Toys

d 1900 Dr E. Lasker, Berlin

e 1900 J. G. Schrödel, Nürnberg. Nürnberger Spielefabrik. Toys of wood and paper

f 1900 Kraus Mohr & Co, Nürnberg

g 1900 Georg Grieszmeyer, Nürnberg

h 1900 Auguste Martin, Moncel sur Seille

j 1900 Otto Maier, Ravensburg

k 1901 Meire et Deberthand, Paris. Designer of toys

l 1901 Dr P. Hunaeus, Linden, Hannover

m 1901 F. Revel père et fils, Lyon. Wood and metal toys of all kinds

n 1901 Fredr. Robert Krenkel, Nürnberg. Kurz and toy exporter, ie Hardware

p 1901 Max Freiherr von Hirschberg, Berlin

q 1901 A.Watilliaux, Paris. A toy

r 1902 W. H. Baker, 98 Gosset Street, Bethnal Green Road, London, E. Toy manufacturers

s 1902 Richter Tschuschner & Co, 2 Falcon Square, London. Toys

t 1902 Globe Supply Company, Islington, London

u 1902 Herbert Edward Hughes, 9 Long Lane, London. Toy dealer

v 1902 Max Polock, Waltershausen

w 1902 David Peck, 9 Pembroke Road, South Norwood, Surrey. Toy maker

x 1902 Regnald-Stansell Williams, Paris. Toys

y 1902 Cathelineau and Bèatrice de Noüe, Paris. Toys

z 1903 Geen, Evison, Stutchbury & Co, 6 Bevis Marks, London

a¹ 1903 Peter Dawson, Glasgow, Scotland

a

b

c

d

Geo M Kelsons e

f

LE PETIT CONSCRIT g

Soll und Haben h

m

MÉZIAN j

MÉMAN k

PARISIANA l

Kalipha n

Hans. p

q

100.000 r

„Buchelero." s

t

u

Nord-Express v

Eissen w

"HUMPTYDUMPTY" x

Alapala y

a   1903 Gebr. Fleischmann, Nürnberg. Schurmmespielwaren

b   1903 Victor Gabriel Pacquet (mechanic), Elbeuf. Une petite grue (jouet) meaning 'a little goose'

c   1903 Frl. Hélène Dutrien, Paris. A moveable push-slide Rutschbahnen mit unterbrochener Fahrbahn

d   1904 Alfred Grombach, Paris. Toys

e   1904 George Mortimer Kelson, Westminster, London

f   1904 Soc des Jeux et Jouets Française, Paris

g   1904 Paul-Toussaint Fourot, Paris. Designer of a toy

h   1904 G. Neiff, Nürnberg. Metal, wood and paper toys

j & k   1904 Louis Borney et Arm and Desprey, Negociants of Paris. Toys, especially those which are safe and harmless

l   1905 Comptoir Géneral de Bimbeloterie à Paris. Toys of all kinds

m   1905 J. Debertrand, Paris

n   1905 Georg Kohn, Hamburg. Toys

p   1905 Walram Derichs-weiler, Dresden. Toys of all materials

q   1905 Rudd & Co, Ludgate Square, London

r   1906 Maurice Schwob, Fabricant of Paris. All kinds of toys, wood, metal except those of rubber

s   1906 Otto Bucheler, Geislingen a. Steig. Toys

t   1906 Emil Thurnauer & Max Neumark, trading as G. I.

Pabst, Solgerstrasse 16, Nürnberg

u   1906 Edouard Sahler, merchant of Montbéliard. Toys

v   1906 Hans L. Zink, Mühlberg i Thur. Toys and birdcages

w   1906 Thomas Izon, Birmingham, England

x   1906 William E. Peck & Co, Bradford Road, London. American merchants

y   1906 H. Müller, Halensee b. Berlin. Toys

KOUSTARI RUSSES

Marsch-Marsch

"Spielwarenhaus Puppenkönig"

PLAYTIME

TINY TOTS

AABA

TWINWIN

ENTENTE   CORDIALE   "LE CAMBODGIEN"

PETER PAN LAYTOYS

a   1906 Oskar Wiederholz, Brandenberg. Toys

b   1906 Léon Snequireff, neg. of Paris. Toys of wood, pottery, etc

c   1906 Martin Winterbauer, Nürnberg. Toys, Christmas snow, etc

d   1906 Ignatz Weiser, Paris. Designer of games and toys of all kinds, machine embroidery, etc

e   1907 Julius Dorft, Sonneberg

f   1907 Lucie Voigt, Tambacher Spielwarenfabrik, Tambach

g   1907 Otto Schäfer, Spielwarenfabrik, Trossingen. Toys of wood, papiermâché, celluloid and similar materials

h   1907 Rouech-Bowden Co, Detroit, Mich., USA.

j   1907 Arthur William James, 69 Gloucester Terrace, Hyde Park, London

k   1907 Henry Mountain, Liverpool

l   1907 Balthaser Paul Birnich u Paul Joseph Birnich, Cöln. Toys

m   1907 Roberts Brothers,

Glevum works, Gloucester

n   1907 Kratz-Boussac, Paris

p   1907 Fernand Gratieux fils, 14 rue Oberkampf, Paris. A toy

q   1907 Müller & Kadeder, Nürnberg. Toys

r   1907 Max Fr. Schelhorn, Sonneberg

s   1907 Jean-Baptiste Guirette, Bajos de Portacoeli à Mexico. Articles coutellerie, mercerie, jouets, passementerie, ie cutlery, haberdashery, toys and lace

JM a

PN b

LAVEUSE ENFANTINE

c

RA d

D ET P e

SUNLIGHT f

 g

"NEW CIRCUS" h

TREPIDUS j

LE ZEBRE m

Vilcar k

„Rekla" l

WIBOLO s

 n

 p

 q

 r

ROLETTO t

„GEOGRO" u

Butzi-Putzi v

„BI-BA-BO" w

VOX POPULI x

DRAKE y

ADAMALIA z

---

a   *1908 Jules Moret, Lyon*

b   *1908 Elsa Beatrice Degen, Finsbury Square, London*

c & d   *1908 Edouard Rogier, Roubaix*

e   *1908 Dannin et Paulet, Paris*

f   *1908 Compagnie Française des Savonneries Lever frères, 263 rue Solférino, Lille. All games and toys of metal, wood, etc*

g & h   *1908 F. Migault & A. Papin, Paris. Designer of games and toys*

j   *1908 Antoine Cardon, Beaulieu-sur-Mer. Designer of toys*

k   *1908 Reinhard Bracht, Dresden. Toys, etc. The Vilcar (Parent) Co Ltd, Portugal Street, London*

l   *1908 Carl Rieboldt, Berlin. Toys, games, etc*

m   *1908 E. Gutenthal, Paris. Designer of a toy*

n   *1908 Michael Haack, Nürnberg. Toys, especially wooden toys*

p   *1908 Offene Handelsgesell-schaft, Leignitz, ie a trading company*

q   *1908 Gebr. Sauer, Nürnberg*

r   *1908 Christof Herbst,*

Nürnberg. Toy maker and toy exporter

s, t & w   *1908 Julius Jeidel, Frankfort. Toys*

u   *1908 Georg Groeszer, Frankfort. Toys*

v   *1908 R. Seelig & Hille Nigr., Hamburg. Toys, import and export*

x   *1909 J. A. Phillips and Co, Birmingham, England*

y   *1909 George Henry Shepherd, Brighton, England*

z   *1909 Constance Clyde McAdam, New Kent Road, London*

"CABINET PICKLE." a

b

c

d

KOMBAK. e

LES JEUX ET JOUETS FRANÇAIS g

WEKO h   L'IDÉAL j

Spilifax k

p

f

P. F. l   PF m

St. & Co.

r

MON-AK n

„Zauberkönig" q

Naches s

Ti Tu t

Im Fluge durch die Welt u

„Kühnert & Co" v

„RETURNO" w

Songo x

a   *1909 Emma Butter Coube, Myrtle House, Warwick Road, Worthing*

b   *1909 Auguste Hannebelle, Paris*

c & d   *1909 Prosper Léve, Paris*

e   *1909 Kratz-Boussac, Paris. Designer of toys*

f   *1909 Migault fils, 15 rue Chapon, Paris*

g   *1909 Soc Levy, Perret, Simonin-Cuny, Alphonse & Alexandre Delhaye, Paris*

h   *1909 Auguste Weiss, Paris*

j   *1909 M. Abrahams, Paris*

k   *1909 Becker & Cie, Mannheim*

l & m   *1909 Paul Toussaint Fourot, Paris*

n   *1909 Carl W. Rolle, Altona-Bahrenfeld. Toys*

p   *1909 Anciens Etablissements Hérold et Cie et Société d'Imprimerie en couleurs. Lavallois*

q   *1909 P. H. Birnich, Cöln.*

Toys

r   *1909 Steinberg & Co, Hamburg. Toys*

s   *1909 Hans Eberl, Nürnberg. Toys*

t   *1909 Otto Maier, Ravensburg. Toys, also pistols*

u   *1909 Egen & Co, Düsseldorf. Toys*

v   *1909 Kühnert & Co, Berlin. Toys of all kinds*

w & x   *1909 C. Abel-Klinger, Nürnberg. Toys and games*

CHANTECLER a

b

KRACKJACK c

WOOLLYBAMBOLLY d

e

KUB f

ODOL g

h

j

k

I.C. A LA PERSÉPHONE l

PERSÉPHONE m

n

p

Antimogelo
q

Jungeweg
r

Scouts Terrier
s

Aërona u

Volafix t

„Aeolus"
w

Dum-Dum
x

Perlico-Perlaco
y

a *1910 A.W. Gamage, Holborn, London*

b *1910 Mary Heaton, Arosfa, Trefuant R.S.O. Vale of Clwyd, North Wales*

c *1910 Herbert Edward Hughes, Goswell Road, London*

d *1910 British Ever Ready Electrical Co Ltd, Theobalds Road, London, WC*

e *1910 G. & J. Lines Ltd, 457 Caledonian Road, London, N*

f *1910 Boissons hygiéniques, Paris. Games and toys of all kinds*

g *1910 Carl August Lingner, Dresden. Toys*

h *Johann Distler, Nürnberg*

j & k *1910 Carlowitz et Cie, Hamburg. Toys and musical instruments*

l & m *1910 Jules Lindauer, Paris. Toys and games of all kinds*

n *1910 Bruno Arthur Meier, Brandenburg*

p *1910 François Puthois, Paris. A toy, the hen sings and lays an egg*

q *1910 Cahen & Schanzer, Düsseldorf. Toys*

r *1910 William Alton Derrick. Berlin*

s *1910 S. D. Zimmer, Fürth. Toys of all kinds*

t *1910 Alex Bener, Nürnberg. Toys*

u *1910 Robert Erlemann, Bergedorf, Hamburg*

v *1910 L. Schirling, Frankfort. Toys*

w *1910 'Aeolus' Gesellschaft, Beim Strohhause, Hamburg*

x *1910 Hermann Brinkhoff & Johannes Meinken. Toys*

y *1910 Fleischmann & Bloedel, Nachf. Joseph Berlin. See Fleischmann and Bloedel*

Der fliegende
Drehwurm

a

b

FLAMIDOR c

MARQUE DÉPOSÉE
S et B
PARIS

d

e

PAP=ER=KRAK f

g

Knall und Fall h

j

k

l

"BRIX" m

EXPORT-AERO n

LE BRAQUET
A·P. t

B R X
MARQUE DÉPOSÉE

p

MARQUE DÉPOSÉE
ARTICLE
FRANÇAIS
No

q

s

u

BOLIDOR r

a *1910 B. Ziegler, Weiszenfels a S. Toys*

b *1911 Eckart & Co, (Hans Engelbert Eckart), 18–20 Barbican, London, EC. Toy Importers*

c *1911 Edouard Husson, Paris. Games & toys of all kinds*

d *1911 Schmeltz et Besnard, Paris. All kinds of toys & games*

e *1911 Hermann Kurtz, Stuttgart. Toys*

f *1911 Edward C. Teuscher, St Louis, Mo. Toys*

g *1911 Bruno Ulbright, Nuremberg. Toys and dolls' accessories*

h *1911 Julius Berhard Pfannenschmidt, Leipzig. Toys*

j *1911 Deutsch-Amerikanische Patent-Industrie Dapi, GmbH Bremen. Toys and household utensils*

k *1911 Taylor & Winchester, New York. Package containing Toys and Dolls*

l *1911 Strobel & Lades GmbH Roth b Nürnberg. Rother Spielwarenfabrik. Kunstmasse gepretztes Spielzeug und Nippfiguren*

m & p *1912 Maurice Gerhardt, Paris. Designer of toys*

n *1911 Albert Bonnet, 37 rue Mouge, Paris. Designer of toys*

q *1912 Chambre Syndicale des Fabricants de Jouets et Jeux, 8 bis, Place de la Republique, à Paris. Renouvellement de dépôt*

r *1912 Julius Berthold*

s *1912 Armand Weill, Paris. Designer of toys*

t *1912 Arthur Pohl, Paris. Toys & games*

u *1912 Hägele & Wendes, Eszlingen*

"Incroyable Bazar."

M. PARIS P. a

b

Surr-Surr

c

Sexta d

e

f

g

TECLA k

l

FABRIK MARKE

j

LE TROTTIN m

HE-RE-AS q

h

n

Oi-Oi p

---

a *1912 Marcel Paquin, Paris. Désigner des jeux et jouets*

b&e *1912 Aron Lévy, Paris. Toys & household articles*

c *1912 Hans Eberl, Nürnberg. Toys*

d *1912 Elizabeth Bollmann, Hamburg. All kinds of toys except those of rubber*

f *1913 Schrener & Co, Nürnberg. Toys*

g *1913 George Howard Hilder, NY. Design for a toy*

h *1912 Ernst Schmidt, München. Toys*

j *1913 Otto Wohlmann, Nürnberg*

k *1913 Société Tecla Ltd, 10 rue de la Paix, Paris. Wood, Metal, etc. Toys of all kinds*

l *1913 Saalheimer & Strausz,*

Nürnberg. Toys

m *1913 Mme Le Montréer (nee Henriette-Joseph), 9 rue Charlot, Paris*

n *1913 B. A. Müller, Dresden. Toys, balloons, picture books, etc*

p *1913 Hans Eberl, Nürnberg. Toys*

q *1913 Eduard Butzmann, Berlin. Toys and games*

AMÉRICAN'S TIR'S-BIEN'S
LA CORDE
LA TRINGLE a

 b

 c

Blue Ribbon d

A.B.F. PARIS e

E. E. Houghton. f

SEA BABY

J. T. Kingsley Tarpey g

 l

LES ALLIÉS m

FRANCE-JOUET h

G M j

JBF k

MARQUE DÉPOSÉE r

 n

Comptoir des Ingéniosités Parisiennes p

CIP q

Masurindenburg s

"Joie des Enfants" t

HARTOLIN u

ANTIBOCHE v

APOLLO w

 a¹

Das Wunder Ei x

 y

PROGALLIA A.C.D.C.E. z

Luftikus b¹

LIGUE DU JOUET FRANCAIS c¹

---

a 1914 Bertrand Toulouse, 69 rue Meslay, Paris

b 1914 Züllchower Anstalten, Stettin

c 1914 Soc G. Fabre et Cie, 26 rue de la Procession, Paris

d 1914 Simon Silbermann, Nürnberg. Toy importer

e 1914 Alcide Breger, 9 rue Thénard, Paris

f 1915 Elizabeth Ellen Houghton, 13 St Peters Square, Hammersmith

g 1915 Jessie Toler Kingsley Tarpey, 33 Buckingham Mansions, West Hampstead, NW

h 1915 Henri Dervaux, 3 rue Mogador, Paris

j 1915 Frédéric Simon, 15 rue Fontaine-au-Roi, Paris

k 1915 Madame Andrée Lesne, 52 avenue de Clichy, Paris

l 1915 The British Novelty Works Ltd, 2–14 Newington Butts, London, SE

m 1915 Gaston Renoir, 5 rue de l'Amiral-Courbet, Alfort

n 1915 Mme Yvonne Detraux, 83 rue Notre-Dame-des-Champs, Paris

p & q 1915 Abel Viard, 25 rue d'Alsace, Paris

r 1915 Chartier, Marteau et Boudin, 54 rue de Lancry, Paris

s 1915 Fritz Block & Co, Breslau

t 1915 Jules Bigot, 14 rue Meslay, Paris

u 1915 Leonhard Wuzel, Nürnberg. Toys

v 1916 Yves Zuber, 36 rue Neuve des Boulets

w 1916 Soc Générale de Coutellerie et Orfeorerie, 31 rue Pastourelle, Paris

x 1916 Arthur Galle, Dresden

y 1916 Mme François De Las Cases, 4 rue Lavoisier, Paris. Fabriqué par des Paysans

z 1916 Soc Progallia, 44 rue des Mathurins, Paris

a¹ 1916 F. Carnot, 8 avenue Montespan, Paris

b¹ 1916 Dr Walter Regbaur, Berlin. Toys

c¹ 1916 Mme Benoist de Laumont, 32 avenue Malakoff, Paris

" ENTENTE MADE " a   POUPÉA b

AU GRAND PÈRE c   Jeu de L'Entente d

 e

 f

 g

 h

CERAMOÏD j

PATRIA k

Tante Lore l

LA BOMBARDE m

Nellfoy r

Le Jouet National Français s

KIDETTE n

 VICTORY q

LEDA. p

PARIS

„Ge + Ro" t

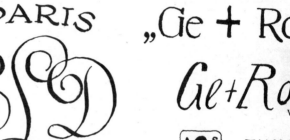 ELD MARQUE DÉPOSÉE x

Ge+Ro v

 JOB u

LE JOUET BRETON w

 y

TANAGRA z

Jouets Artistiques et Français

BIBELOTS GAIS a¹

A L'ALOUETTE b¹

„Strola" c¹   Racker d¹   Schalk e¹   S S Pa f¹

---

a   1916 Mme Germaine Lenoir, 20 rue du marché, Neuilly-sur-Seine

b   1916 Henri Bouquet, 182 rue La Fayette, Paris

c   1916 Paul Dombre, 33 rue de Châteaudun, Paris

d   1916 Gaston Joseph Renoir, Alfort

e   1916 Mme de Gramont, née de Witt, Bordeaux

f   1916 O. & M. Hausser, Ludwigsburg

g   1916 Mille Elen, 13 rue Victor-Massé, Paris

h   1916 Soc La Francia, 16 avenue d'Antin, Paris. (Mark in red)

j,m   1916 Soc Française du Céramoid, 58 rue Taitbout, Paris. Matières plastiques

k   1916 Mme Rachel Stapfer Lebel, 81 avenue de Villiers, Paris

l   1916 Wolgemuth & Litzner, Kunstverlags-gesellschaft, Berlin

n   1917 Speights Ltd, Classic Works, Union Street, Dewsbury, Yorks

p   1917 Thomas Charles Salisbury, 160 Richmond Road, Cardiff

q   1917 Henry Solomon Benjamin, Milton House, 8, 9 Chiswell Street, London, EC2

r   1917 Jessica Borthwick, 55 Church Street, Chelsea, London

s   1917 René Van Godtsenhoven, 24 bis rue Eugène-Sur-, Rosny-sous-Bois

t & v   1917 Gerling & Rockstroh, Dresden

u   1917 M. de Bréville, 25 cours de Verdun, Bordeaux. Toys

w   1917 Mme Ann de Beaufranchet, Rohello en Baden, (Morbihan). Toys

x   1917 Edouard Desrues, 39 rue de la Grange-aux-Belles, Paris. Toys

y   1917 Marcel Soubrier, 78 rue du Faubourg Saint-Denis, Paris. Toys

z   1917 Albert Levy, 14 rue Rougemont, Paris

a¹   1917 Max Martin, 13 rue Hélène, Paris

b¹   1917 Madelaine Girardeau et André Girardeau, 69 avenue de Saint-Cloud, Versailles

c¹   1918 August Schlemmer, Nürnberg. Toys

d¹,e¹   1918 Gans & Seyfarth, Waltershausen

f¹   1918 Leopold Gilbrath, Berlin-Friedenau. Toys

FORGET-ME-NOT a

 b

Sirius c

LIBERTY d

e

f

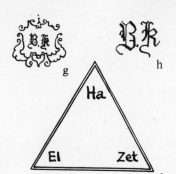

g

h

k

j

l

 DURAX

m

PETSEYMURPHY

n

p

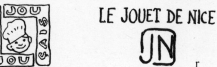

q

LE JOUET DE NICE

JN

r

t

"POUPARD" ART s

Le Joujou Français u

LAFU

v

CAEN

w

MANOTA

x

y

PYGMÉE

z

A la' Marquise de Sévigné a'

„Appelwilly"

b'

Bauer c'

f'

„**Turbo**"

d'

Stratetjusgik e'

---

a   *1918 Samuel Henry Ward, 19 St Dunstans Street, London, EC3*

b   *1918 M. V. Wheelhouse & Louise Jacobs, 64 Cheyne Walk, Chelsea, London, SW3*

c   *1918 Julius Schwarz, Hamburg*

d   *1918 Georges de Roussy de Sales, 22 rue de Levis, Paris*

e   *1918 Joseph Joanny, 6 rue du Marché-Saint-Honoré, Paris*

f   *1918 Elie-Stephane Flachon, et Chauveau de Quercize, 5 rue Chauchat, Paris*

g&h   *1918 Soc Binder et Cie, 11 rue Villedo, Paris*

j   *1918 Edouard-Marcel Sandoz, 2 Villa d'Alésia, Paris*

k   *1918 Hermann Loewenstein, Zürich. Toys*

l   *1918 Rene Dreyfuss, 151 rue du Temple, Paris*

m   *1919 Isobel Dodd, 26 Fitzwilliam Square, Dublin*

n   *1919 John Vincent, 86 St Mary Street, Weymouth, Dorset*

p   *1919 Rene Foucher, rue de Paris, Sannois*

q&u   *1919 V. Lepinay, 22 passage des Petites Ecuries, Paris*

r   *1919 Charles Méreu, 31 rue Rossini, Nice*

s   *1919 Henry Bellet, 50 rue Planchat, Paris*

t   *1919 René Gruet, 75 Boulevard Malesherbes, Paris*

v   *1919 Louis Lapp & Lucien Furcy, Pont de Beauvoisin*

w   *1919 Élie Jean, 76 rue Saint-Jean, Caen*

x   *1919 Mauger et Montera, 19 rue Daguerre, Paris*

y   *1919 Soc Lyonnaise du Jouet Française, 263 rue Garibaldi, Lyon*

z   *1919 André Savary, 11 rue Campagne-Premiere, Paris*

a'   *1919 Soc des Etablissements Rouzard Royat. Toys & games*

b'   *1919 Karl Müller, Dresden*

c', f'   *1919 Richard Bauer, GmbH, Nürnberg. Games & toys*

d'   *1919 Th. von der Linden, Essen. Toys*

e'   *1919 Rigobert Hensinger, München. Amusing toys*

Das tanzende Europa! a

Yak-Yak
Die gackernde Henne
b

Toto-Tip c

K&B
B
e

Hagralu d

Antares f

FLOPSIE g

"GIVJOY" TOYS j

MARKE
k

"LE JOUET SURPRISE" l

Pixat m

Fantanella
SCHUTZ MARKE
n

FS h

KnallFritze p

LINEOL q

BIELEFELDER-SPIELZEUS
M M
r

Nikolo s

BABET t

B-P. GRIMAUD
PARIS
54 RUE DE LANCRY
v

Little Puck w

„Niga" x

› FERLYS ›
u

---

a *1919 Otto Klimke, Dresden. Toys of wood, metal, composition etc & their parts*

b *1919 Hermann Kersten, Schmöckurtz. Toys*

c *1919 Bial & Freund, Berlin. Toys*

d *1919 Albert Rank, Plauen-i B. Toys*

e *1919 Kindler & Briel, Böblingen. Toys & games of wood, metal, wire & iron*

f *1919 Mega-Verlag Hans*

G. Schaefer, München. Toys, games, picture books, albums, etc

g *1920 William Henry Jones, 11 Charterhouse Buildings, London, EC1*

h *1920 Freiburger Spielwaren Fabrik, Freiburg*

j *1920 A. J. Holladay & Co Ltd, 32, 33 Aldermanbury, London, EC2*

k *1920 Anton Laupheimer, Weiszenhorn, Bayern*

l *1920 R. L. R. Murat, 4 rue du Havre, Paris*

m *1920 W. Gustav Voigt, Zwickau*

n *1920 Ernst Vanoli, Freiburg*

p *1920 Edmund Mätzig, Spielwaren*

q *1920 Oskar Wiederholz, Porzellan, Metall, Email, etc*

r *1920 Wolfgang, Meyer-Michael, Bielefeld*

s *1920 Gebr. Patermann, Teltow-Berlin*

t *1921 Mme Cécile Lambert, dite Edmée Rozier, La Garenne-Colombes Seine*

u *1921 Dr Henry Ferre, 6 rue Dombasle, Paris*

v *Chartier, Marteau et Boudin. (Name appears on boxes for toys)*

w *1921 Otto Meinel, Hutmeinel, Klingenthal, Saxe. Toys*

x *1921 Biswanger & Co, Augsberg, Spielwaren*

a

LES JOUETS AMUSANT b

LES JOUETS AMUSANTS c

GILBERT

d

g

FANTASIO f

"S.A.J" h

j

e

k

FRANCE m

l

N V

q

n

ALLEN p

a   1921 Andre Merlino, 8 rue Lamartine, Paris. Toys

b, c   1921 Soc Établissements Gerbaulet Frères, 35 rue de Turenne, Paris. Toys, games, etc

d   1921 A. C. Gilbert Co, 119 Blatchley avenue, ville de New-Haven, État de Connecti-cut, États-Unis d'Amérique

e   1921 Toulet et Cie, 103 rue Lafayette, Paris

f, h   1921 L'Exploitation de Jouets—'S. A. J.', 13 bis, rue Beccaria, Paris

g   1921 Alphonse-Louis-Joseph Martinache, 53 rue Pigalle, Paris. Games & toys

j   1921 Soc Fabrique de Jouets et Souvenirs d'Alsace, 2 fossé des Tanneurs, Strasbourg. Games & toys

k   1921 Paul-Ange-Félix Lebreton, 10 rue Saint-Sébastien, Paris

l   1921 Paul Faral, a la Pomme, banlieue (outskirts) de Marseille. Toys

m   1921 Georges Tranchant, 96 rue Carnot, Montreuil-sous-Bois, Seine. Toys

n   1921 Edouard Le Comte, 20 rue Deguingand à Levallois-Perret-Seine. Toys

p   1921 Mme Anna Juilla, 42 rue Etienne-Marcel, Paris

q   1921 Auguste-Marcel-Ernest Paturel, 13 rue Charlot, Paris

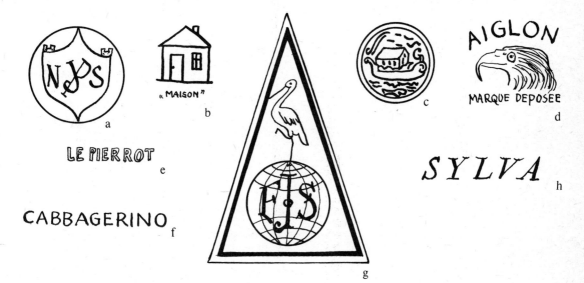

LE PIERROT e

CABBAGERINO f

SYLVA h

a   *1921 Lesné, née J. M. M. L. Bert, 23 rue Pierre Leroux, Paris. Games & toys*
b   *1921 Hutmeinel, Otto Meinel, Klingenthal, Saxe. Toys*
c   *1922 C. H. Müller, junior. Olbernhau*

d   *1922 A. A. Tunmer et Cie, 47 rue Vallier à Levallois-Perret, Seine*
e   *1922 Gaston Lyautey, 59 rue de l'Aqueduc, Paris*
f   *1922 Margaret Ann Dakin, Church Hall, Broxted, Dunmow, Essex*

g   *1922 Fabrique Strasboureoise de Jouets, 59 rue de la Gare, Strasbourg-Schiltigheim*
h   *1922 'Sylva', 66 Grande-Rue-Pontarlier, Paris. Toys*

3. TOYS IN PARTICULAR

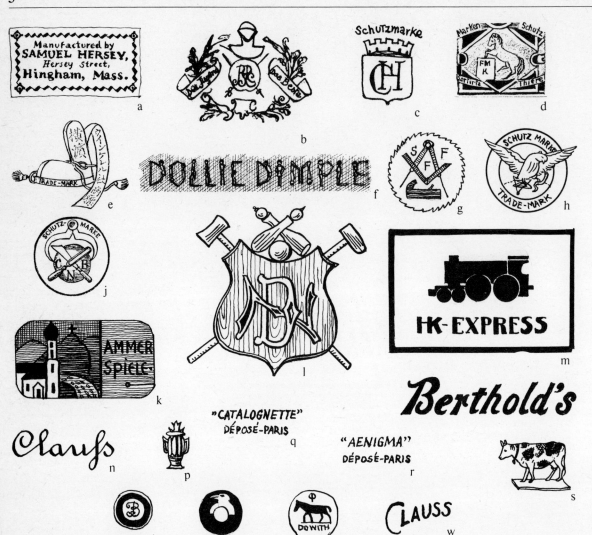

a *1855 Samuel Hersey, Hingham, Mass., USA. Wooden toys*

b *1878 R. Pätzig & Co, Niederneuschönberg. Holzspielwaaren*

c *1875 Christian Hacker, Nürnberg. Holzspielwaaren*

d *1886 Freidrich Meinel, Bad Kissingen. Toy animals and stands of natural white wood. Single and in pairs, and also with wheels*

e *1886 Gebr. Schultze, Hamburg. Lacquered wooden toys*

f *1888 John Lorde Hinde of Hinde Bros, 1 City Road, Finsbury, London. Brush manufacturer. Dolls*

g *1897 S. F. Fischer, Oberseiffenbach, Post Seiffen. S. Wooden toys*

h *1897 Lehnert & Co, Eppendorf. Eppendorfer Holzwaaren und Steinbaukasten-fabrik*

j *1900 C. Baudenbacher, Nürnberg. Wooden toys. Turned wood*

k *1905 George Langsel, Erben, Oberammergau, Bayern. Toys*

l *1903 Nötzel & Drechsler, Niederneuschönberg b Olbernhau. Wooden toys*

m *1903 Hermann Konsbrück, München. Holzernes Spielzeug (Eisenbahnzug)*

n *1908 Robert Geiszler, Zittau-I-Sa. Wooden figures*

p *1909 Jacques Lipatoff, Paris. Toys, Russian bibelots, and all objects of carved wood*

q,r *1910 L'Hoste, Paris. A little toy and a surprise toy of wood*

s *1910 Alfred Berthold, Roszwein i Sa. Unbreakable wooden animals and wooden soldiers*

t *1911 Benner Manu Co, Lancaster, Pa. Wooden games, baby swings etc*

u *1911 Dux Toy Co, Concord, NH. Wooden toys*

v *1911 Caroline L. Pratt, New York, NY. Wooden toys*

w *1912 Robert Geiszler, Zittau I-Sa. Unbreakable wooden figures*

Wooden Toys

It is pointless to hunt for a maker's mark on a homemade doll or toy, but occasionally a label might be found on a wooden toy wagon or doll's cradle. Even the small wooden dolls' house dolls were unmarked but in 1851 they could be purchased from John and L. Poole at Twisters Alley or from Alfred Davis at Houndsditch, a low quarter of London where for years the rubbish of the city of London had been tipped.

The first label for wooden toys is found on those made by Samuel Hersey and his family in the USA. Hersey was a member of the Tower Guild Company. In the 1840s Joseph Jacobs made toy wooden tools, Loring Cushing made dolls' furniture in the 1860s and other members were Crocker Wilder who made wooden toys, Daniel Litchfield dolls' furniture and dolls' clocks and in 1878 there was Ralph Jones making wooden toys and dolls' furniture. The wooden toy industry at Hingham continued into the twentieth century.

In 1870 Henry Jewitt of Kentish Town, a district in London, sent wooden toys to and fro between London and New York. William W. Rose acted as his go-between.

g 1920 Rene Gruet, Levallois
   Perret (Franke). Wooden toys.

Towards the end of the nineteenth century, the Meggendorfer brothers had become known for their intricate cut-outs in their picture books for children in which the pictures were animated by pulling tabs and cords. It is interesting that Lothar Meggendorfer of Krottenmühl registered his signature in 1920 for wooden toys.

The marks shown here are collected from those firms in which the manufacturers especially stated their wooden wares. Boxed wooden toys have labels on the outside or under-surface of the lids, often sliding lids with folded instructions inside. The designs are also registered, the boxes being treasures in themselves.

h 1920 Gebr. Patermann,
   Feltow-Berlin. Wooden toys

45

a

b

FLUFF-FLUFF

c

FLUFFYRUFFLES

d

SCHUTZ-MARKE.

e

f

TEDDY-BEAR

g

Wooden animals

h

HERCULES

j

k

BARNUM'S ANIMALS

l

m

KANDY KIDS

n

MAR-SELL-ENE

p

q

r

s

t

u

a   *1894 Friedrich Meinel, Bad Kissingen. Wood, cane & bamboo toys, assorted animals*

b   *1896 A.W. Fr. Kister, Scheibe. Swimming animals, composition & porcelain*

c   *1902 Henry Cook & John Solomon, Barbican Court, London*

d   *1908 Max Fr. Schelhorn, Sonneberg*

e   *1904 Max Zimmermann, Olbernhau i. S. Toys, also export & import*

f   *1909 Carl Harmus, jr. Sonneberg*

g   *1909 Arthur Baum, Leicester, England. This is an interesting sign for clothing, not a sign for toys*

h & q   *1908 Geffers & Schramm, Hamburg. Toys*

j   *1908 Josef Deuerlein, Nürnberg*

k   *1908 Conrad Sutter, Schlosz Lichtenberg im Odenwald. Toy animals and other figures*

l   *1909 William Strunz, Nürnberg. Stuffed and unstuffed animals, sometimes mechanical*

m   *1910 Martin Winterbauer, Nürnberg*

n & p   *1911 Nonbreakable Toy Co, New York, NY. Toys in animal form*

r, s, t & u   *Leon Rees, London, England. Assignor to Monroe M. Schwarzschild, New York, NY. Three toy dogs and a toy cat*

a   1913 Strauss Man & Co, Rutherford, NJ & NY. Figure toys
b   1913 Samstag & Hilder Bros, NY. Toys
c   1913 William John Bernard Terry, London, England. Assignor to Eisenmann & Co. A toy
d   1913 Grace G. Drayton, New York. A Bunny doll
e   1913 Kate P. Hampton, Washington, DC. Toys
f   1913 Ernst Luckhaus, Drusberg
g   1914 Ethel Elizabeth Mary McCubbin, 3 Boveney Road, Honor Oak Park, London, SE
h   1914 Alfred James Holladay, London. A toy
j   1914   Angèle Laurent, à La Frette, Seine et Oise. (Le Poilu means shaggy, hairy)
k   1914 Jacques Housset, 82 rue de Rivoli, Paris
l   1920 Margarete Martin, Hanover
m   1920 Hahn & Co, Nuremberg. Stoff und Leder Spielwaren Fabrikation, Stoff Tiere und Werf-puppen
n & p   1922 Joseph Sayag, 9 rue Carducci, Paris. (Chien aboyer et canne aboyer)
q   1922 Marcel Pintel, 74 rue de la Folie-Regnault, Paris. Jouets en peluche et étoffes diverses. (Toys of shaggy stuffs, ie fur, plush, etc)
r, s & t   1922 Émile Pagès, 6 rue de Vancouleurs, Paris. Jouets, (toutou, a bow-wow, caniche, a poodle)

Le Dingo

LA COQUETTE

LE COQUET

LE CABOT PARISIEN

LE TOUTOU PARISIEN   LE CANICHE PARISIEN

Animals

Toy animals are among the oldest of playthings and have been made from all kinds of materials. The first registered sign for wooden animals with stands of natural white wood, some with wheels was made by Freidrich Meinel in 1886, who stated that the animals could be purchased singly or in pairs, the latter presumably for Noah's Arks. In 1894 he registered his mark for assorted animals, cane and bamboo toys. Furry animals arrived about the same time as the Teddy Bear, in 1906, but homemade and unregistered animals belong to far earlier periods. Around 1908 names like Fluffy Ruffles appeared, followed by Duckie Doodles, Kwacky Wack etc, names all thought up and registered before the toys were put on the market.

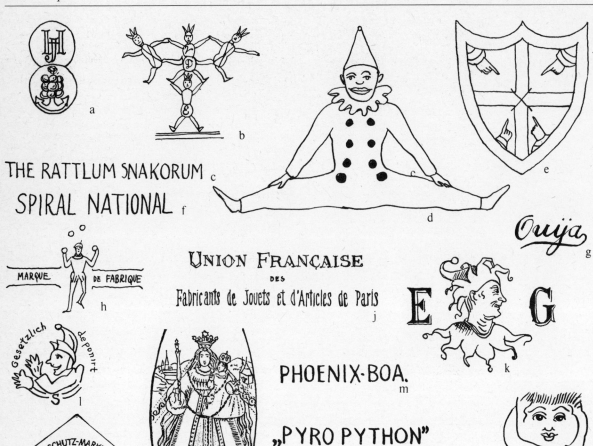

THE RATTLUM SNAKORUM c

SPIRAL NATIONAL f

MARQUE DE FABRIQUE h

UNION FRANÇAISE
DES
Fabricants de Jouets et d'Articles de Paris j

Ouija g

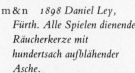

E G

PHOENIX·BOA. m

"PYRO PYTHON" n

MIMOSA·CONFETTI r

a 1875 J. Hager, Nürnberg. Fur all Kurz-Gelanterie-und Spiel-Waaren, bells etc

b 1878 Victor Dürfeld, Osbernhau i.S. Spielwaaren

c 1885 The Economic Electric Supply Co, Wood Green, London. A toy warranted harmless but hideous

d 1887 George Lutticke, Hove. Toys of all kinds

e 1887 The London & Provincial Novelty Co, 24 Great Crosshall Street, Liverpool. Serpents eggs, imitation lightning etc.

f 1893 Georges-Paul Gérard, désigner des rouleaux papier pour fêtes

g 1892 Kennard Novelty Co, Baltimore, Vereinigte Staaten von Americka, Spielzeug

h 1894 Aristide Bernard, fabricant a Saint-Leger-aux-Bois

j 1894 Gùillet, dépositaire a Paris, désigner des jeux de jardin

k 1895 Eugène Gibon, Marseille

l 1895 George Spindler, Sonneberg. Masks and carnival novelties

m & n 1898 Daniel Ley, Fürth. Alle Spielen dienende Räucherkerze mit hundertsach aufblähender Asche.

p & q 1898 Meininghaus & Schulze, Köln. Flags, paper lanterns, flares etc

r 1898 Emile Crémier, architect, Paris

s 1899 Sylvester Smorowski, Landshut. Jokes and Klatschblase, blow-up poppers, crackers & clackers, etc

Hexenkugeln
Magic Balls
Boules MAGiQUES a

FORTLE b

BELLA oder **Wersiegt** ? c

MARKMANN'S
PAPIERSCHLANGEN
BIER SAUGER d

BOLIDE HUMAIN e

LE MATCH g

Pyro-Plomben f

LIEN D'AMOUR

„Liebespfand" h

„Pro Patria" j

LE FLORAL l

CONFETTI-FLEURS m

n

Purgeff p

VESTRIS q

Windikus r

DÉPOSÉ Ⅸ B⁺ᵉ S.G.D.G.
PARIS

Mysto s

ORIOLE t

INDUSTRIE DU RIRE
I.D.R. u

Homunculus.
(Das Menschlein.)

The missing link? w

x

"The Kings of Em All" y

---

a *1901 Richard Renz, Berlin. Toys and games, celluloid balls and blasrohren*

b *1901 Thomas Edward Ivens, Ealing, London. Party toys & entertainments*

c *1902 H. C. E. Leichmann, Untermhaus b. Gera-R. Party games, entertainments, etc*

d *1903 Albert Markman, Langenberg, Rhld. Paper snakes, etc*

e *1904 Eugène, acrobate, Paris. Leaping on bicycles, etc*

f *1905 Gebrüder Welter, Hamburg. Bleigiesgen in der Sylvesternacht*

g *1906 Alphonse Muzet, Paris. 'Ses Gobelets'. Juggling*

h & j *1907 Max Levi, Dortmund. Toys, jokes and cottilon articles*

k *1908 Max Retemeyer, Berlin. Carnival toys*

l & m *1908 Caïus Boirre, Paris. Flower petals, flowers, plants, fruits, animals*

n *1908 Ernest Davot, Paris. A toy 'serpentin extensible'*

p *1910 Arno Fischer, Dresden. Toys and joke articles*

q *1909 Les jeux et jouets Française, 10 rue de la Doriane, Paris. Designers for fêtes, cotillons, etc. The Soc Lévy, Perret, Simonin-Cuny, Alphonse & Alexandre Delhaye*

r *1910 Alfred Caro, Berlin. Geschaftsbetrieb-Metallwarenfabrik, Children's toys and joke articles*

s *1912 Alfred C. Gilbert, New Haven, Conn. Toys and tricks. Magic tricks. The Mysto-Magic Company*

t *1912 Isaac Fald, Baltimore, Md. Toy Pool-tables*

u *1912 Thiry, François, Paris*

v *1913 A. Schoenhut Co, Philadelphia, Pa. Dolls, toy figures, wooden animals, tombolas. Claims used since about March 1887*

w, x *1913 Hatu gummiwerke Hartmann & Tuphorn, GmbH Erfurt. Joke articles*

y *1914 Fair & Carnival trading Co Inc, NY. Dolls & stuffed animal toys*

'Circus' Toys

The eighteenth century puppets were not allowed by law to speak with natural voices, hence the raucous noises made by Mr Punch and his followers. Puppets, clowns and bells are all traditional toys and an early mark for bells was that registered by J. Hager who included hardware among his goods.

In the USA, Alfred Gilbert was well known for his Magic Tricks in 1912, and Schoenhut for circus toys, who, in 1913 backdated his claim to 1887.

a   *1914 B. A. Müller, Dresden. Children's toy horses. A Schaukelpferd is a hobby horse*

b   *1920 Gelma von Hasperg, Frankfort. Besonderen Puppen und Marionetten: especially dolls and marionettes*

c   *1921 Mulius Sperschneider, Sonneberg. Puppenfabrikation*

d   *1921 Georg Schweiger, Nürnberg*

e   *1922 Gustave Billy, 5 rue de Montmorency, Paris. Masques, jouets*

1922 Edi Kallista, Dresden. Theatre puppets

Christmas time

Many Christmas ornaments and decorations for trees were registered from 1895 onwards, particularly in Germany in the early twentieth century. There were so many of them that the marks given here do not go beyond 1910, when it would seem that Christmas snow was included in the 'Chemistry Sets' then appearing in the shops.

a

Gloria-Krippe. b

Kling-Klang e

c

d

Feenglanz f

Silber-Eis-Lametta g

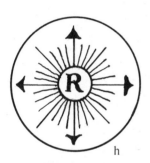
h

j

k

Ave Maria l

Rotkäppchen m

n

„NEUSCHNEE" p

„SCHNEEZAUBER" q

„CHRISTSCHNEE" r

---

a   *1895 Burchard Hoebel, Halle a S. Christmas ornaments and decorations*
b   *1898 Carl Hirsch, Konstanz, Baden. Cribs & their accessories*
c&d   *1904 Metszeler & Co, München. Christmas snow*
e   *1905 Gesellschaft fur Patentverwertung mbH, Leipzig. Christmas ornaments & decorations*

f   *1906 Albert Sebald, Weiden. Christmas goods*
g   *1906 Paul Rieso, Wierdorf b. Dresden. Sächsische Christbaumschmückfabrik*
h&k   *1906 Rehfeld & Backe, Solingen*
j   *1906 Cuno Pohmer, Berlin. Christmas ornaments, etc*
l   *1907 L. Heipcke, Magdeberg. Religious figures*

m   *1908 Kühnert & Co, Berlin. 'Little Red Cap' Christmas decorations, lanterns, light holders, clips and cotillon articles*
n   *1908 Julius Gosda, Danzig-Petershagen h.d. Kirche. Christmas decorations*
p,q&r   *1910 Georg Schnabel, Limbach. Chemistry sets*

Tea sets and food

There was no mention of dolls when Gebrüder Heubach of Lichte, registered his child's tea service in the year 1900. In 1903, E. U. Steiner made children's porcelain tea services, some decorated with daisies and green leaves. Marks may be found under the plates. Sugar cracklings registered by Rehfeld might be eaten off these plates, but what were the 'elastiques' registered by Knorpp from Paris in 1904?

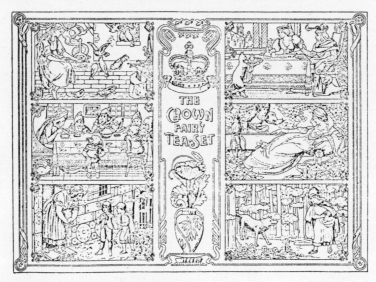

a

b

c

"Le Rigolo"

d

f

„Der kleine Astronom"

e

Zucker-häuschen

j

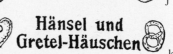

Hänsel und Gretel-Häuschen

k

Hexenhäuschen

l

DAISY g

DAISY TEA SET h

L'INTIME

m

a   *1900 Gebrüder Heubach, Lichte b. Wallendorf. Child's toy tea service*

b   *1901 Sontag & Söhne, GmgH Lettau in Bayern. Porzellanfabrik Lettau*

c   *1901 Henry Ferré, Paris. Toys*

d   *1904 J. N. Knorpp, Paris. Toy sweetmeats, 'elastiques'*

e   *1909 August Baurose, Godesberg. Toys, chocolate & sugar sweetmeats*

f   *1906 A. G. Stollewerck, Cologne sur Rhin. Dolls, toys, chocolate, etc*

g   *1903 Edmund Ulrich Steiner, Sonneberg. Toys, dolls, childrens' porcelain tea-services*

h   *1910 Sontag & Söhne, Bayern. Kinder-service aus Porzellan*

j,k,l   *1906 Rudolf Rehfeld, Solingen. Sugar cottages, witches' houses, sugar cracklings, crisps, etc*

m   *1904 Edmond Person, négociant of Paris. Designer of objects in wood, iron or other materials, wooden horses* a   *1850 D'Autremont, 6 rue de Dauphine, Paris. Rubber toys*

b   *1882 William Warne & Co, 29 Gresham Street, London. Indiarubber goods, games*

c   *1884 The Continental caoutchouc & Guttapercha Co, Hanover. Games & toys*

d   *1884 William Curie. India rubber balls*

e   *1885 Harburg & Vienna India rubber Co, Prussia, Germany. Balls Later, in 1897 taken over by J. N. Reithoffer, Vereingte Gummiwaaren-Fabriken, Harburg-Wein and the initials V.G.F.H.W. added to the sign*

f   *1886 Chas. Macintosh. India rubber manufacturers. Games, rubber balls & billiard balls*

g   *1886 David Moseley, Manchester. India rubber manufacturers, tennis balls*

REX g

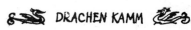

h,k   *1885 The Hanover Caoutchouc, Guttapercha & Telegraph Works, Linden near Hanover, Indiarubber manufacturers*

1893 Heinrich Wilhelm Warmuth, Dresden. Rubber & Guttapercha works

1893 Continental-Caoutchouc & Guttapercha-Compagnie, Hannover

m   *1897 Hermann Kirchner, Chemnitz. Toy figures with elastic cords*

n   *1898 Gaston Edouard Eugene Laurent, Paris. Balloons and bag-pipes of dilatable rubber*

p   *1897 Duquesne et Dockes, Paris. Designer of rubber balloons, etc*

q   *1898 Henry Gavelle, Paris. Balloons of skin etc, toys &*

games

r   *1899 Hannoversche Gummi-Kamm-Compagine Aktien-Gesellschaft, Hannover*

s   *1899 Rheinische Gummi-und-Celluloid-Fabrik, Neckarau-Mannheim*

t   *1899 New York, Hamburger, Gummiwaaren-Compagnie, Hamburg*

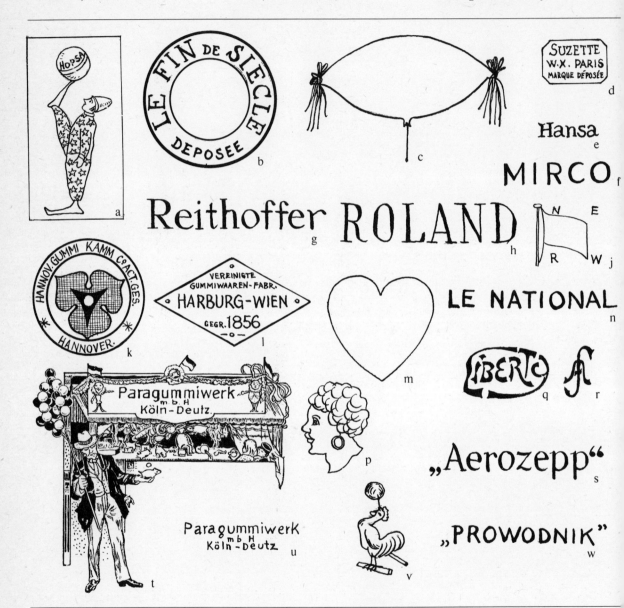

Rubber

Of all playthings made from rubber, bouncing balls would be the most popular, and certainly stronger than the ones of split cane. Next to balls would come balloons, signs for the latter coming in the late nineteenth century, and spongy rubber toys in the early twentieth.

NIHOU a

B & R b

ROYAL c

d

Gut Heil. e

TRËUGOLNIK. g

SCHUTZMARKE f

h

j

RUBBADUBDUB k

L'ÉPONJOUET m

LE JOUET ÉPONGE n

l

MARQUE   DÉPOSÉE p

BABICHOU q

BABIJOU r

BALLE Ste D ÉPONGE s

t

a   1911 M. Nihou, 36 rue de Montmorency, Paris. Rubber toys

b   1911 Behrend & Rothschild, NY. Rubber toys and pacifiers

c   1912 Ste. Ame. pour le commerce & l'Industrie du Caoutchouc, Brussels, Belgium. Rubber dolls, toys, etc, balloons

d   1912 The Star Rubber Co, Akron, Ohio. Toy balloons

e,f 1912 J. N. Reithoffer, Harburg a E

g   1912 Soc Fran for importing and exporting the products of the Russian-American India Rubber Co, Saint Petersburg

h   1913 Elizabeth H. Pusey, New York, NY. A luffa sponge

j   1914 Paramount Rubber Co, Trenton, NJ. Balls

k   1921 J. G. Franklin & Sons Ltd, 17 Colvestone Crescent, Dalston, London. Rubber toys

l   1921 Mme Veuve Blanchard, née Maria Dequittard, Paris. Designer of ballons and toys of dilatable rubber

m,n 1921 André Cullaz et Léon Presberg, 44 rue de Lisbonne, Paris. Toys of rubber & sponge

p,q,r 1922 Charles Rouaud, 45 rue des Petites-Ecuries, Paris. Toys of rubber, sponge, etc

s   1922 B. Delacoste et Cie, 7 rue Notre-Dame-de-Nazareth, Paris. Toys of rubber, sponge, etc

t   1922 J. Lick et Cie, 91–95 rue Mirabeau, Ivry-sur-Seine. Rubber toys

Celluloid

Celluloid bath toys were prettier than those of rubber, especially the pure white swans and the scarlet gold fish which came about the same time as the Kewpie, a tiny doll later to become famous.

a   *1895 Lenel Bensinger & Co, Mannheim. Celluloid toys, washable and watertight*

b   *1909 Paul Hausmeister & Co, Göppingen. Gelatin fabric and dolls' heads*

c   *1912 Jacob Jung, Mannheim. Wholesale toy dealer, toys and dolls of celluloid*

d   *1912 P. Vidal, Vincennes. Celluloid boats*

e   *1913 The Rhenish Rubber & Celluloid Co, 58 Basinghall Street, London, EC. Dolls made of celluloid*

f,g,h,j   *1913 Parson Jackson Co, Cleveland, Ohio. Dolls*

k   *1914 Compagnie Rheinische Gummi und Celluloid Fabrik a Mannheim-Neckarau*

l   *1915 Celluloidwerke Kohl & Wengenroth, Offenbach*

m,n   *1921 Rheinsche Gummi- und Celluloid Fabrik*

p,q   *Two marks used on celluloid heads by Kämmer & Reinhardt, and Simon & Halbig*

4. MOCK BATTLES

LE CHAMPION c

HIRTENBERG d

"STAR" e

CARABINE "LE VOILA" f

"TIR MOUCHE" g

CARABINE "LA PERETTE" h

ELECTRA j

AMORCES GAUFRÉES L.M k

Tir des Apôtres l

Tir des Rois m

TIR OLYMPIEN n

TIR DES PATRIARCHES p

TIR DES GRANDS CHEVAUX r

TIR MÉCANO-ÉLECTRIQUE s

TIR DES PIGEONS t

TIR DES ALOUETTES v

TIR DES BÉCASSES u

TIR DES PERDRIX w

"ÉLECTRA" y

"LE DIRIGEABLE" z

x

AÉROPLANE a¹

e¹

„Freischütz" b¹

Die Faule Grete d¹

AIR-CUSHION f¹

---

a 1861 T. & C. Clark & Co, Shakespeare Foundry, Wolverhampton. Toy cannons, balls, etc

b 1884 J. S. Elmore, 79 Coleman Street, London. Balls of paper pulp, substitutes for glass ball targets

c 1897 V. Maillard, Paris. Shooting toys, targets, etc

d 1903 Keller & Co, Wein. Metal toys, percussion caps, etc

e 1905 Maurice Nicolas, Paris.

Panoplies, shooting, targets, pistols, etc

f, g & h 1906 Maurice Nicolas, Paris. Arms de tir

j 1906 Hugo Kunzel, a Cologne-Lindenthal. War toys

k 1907 Louis-François Mauny, Montrouge. Toy pistols for children

l, m, n & p 1906 Francois Soutoul, Paris. Indoor target shooting

r, s, t, u, v, w 1907 Francois Soutoul, Paris

q 1907 J. G. Schrödel. Ideal sports and toys, Nürnberg. Toys of metal & wood

x 1908 Gebr. Sauer, Nürnberg. Shooting toys of metal and wood

y & z 1908 M. Lochet, Paris. Designer of panels for target shooting

a¹ 1909 Léon-Louis Découan, Paris. Designer of targets, pistols, muskets, and similar toys

b¹ 1908 Gustav Grummt, Annaberg i S. Children's

playthings, shooting ranges, etc

c¹ 1909 Bernard Henné, Paris. Caps for toy pistols

d¹ 1908 Paul Hardegen & Co (KG), Berlin. Means of constructing cannons and cannonades, electrical, etc

e¹ 1913 Abrecht & Traupe, Ata-Schiesszstand-gesellschaft, Hannover

f¹ Parker Bros, Portland, Me. A toy spring-gun

Arrows and Darts

a *1879 Robert Smith Bartlett, Abbey Mills, Redditch. Toys*

b *1888 Samuel Webb Thomas (Clergyman), Southease Rectory, Lewis. A game*

c *1903 Kratz-Boussac, Paris. Arrow with rubber heads and projectiles of the same nature*

d&e *1904 Henri Gustave Poulain, Vernon. Toy arrows and darts*

f *1905 Henri Gustave Poulain, Vernon. A game of swiftness*

g *1904 Albert Deltour, négociant, Tourcoing. Designer of darts with feathers, metal arrows, javelons, shooting, etc*

h *1905 Hippolyte Lallement, Paris. Designer of games with darts, air pistols, lances, etc*

Gottfried Hautsch, the well-known maker of tin soldiers, died in 1703, long before the registration of marks. Andreas Hilpert, in 1780, sometimes signed his famous toy soldiers with his initials A H. Gebrüder Heinrich, a later maker of tin and lead soldiers also signed his toys with his initials G H.

In 1898, Fleischmann made toy soldiers. This was the Fleischmann who, in 1914, became head of the S F B J. Well-known names such as Ernst Heinrichsen, Allgeyer, Lucotte, Gerbaud, and Britain do not appear in these registered marks. There was no need for a maker who used his own signature to register his mark. Lucotte made the solid lead soldiers now in Blenheim Palace, and William Britain was famous for his hollow models. These immediately became more sought after than the toy soldiers made in Germany at that time.

Papier mâché soldiers came from France and stamped tin-plate soldiers with tabs came from Germany.

Iron pistols to shoot caps were made by J. & E. Stevens in the USA from 1850 onwards and air rifles about 1886. The Buffalo Bill gun was made by Milton Bradley in 1885. In 1910 the Daisy Manufacturing Co was known for making toy arms of all kinds, and the craze for playing Cowboys and Indians spread from here to England.

a

FICHE-MARBRE b

EURÉKA c

JAVELOTIN d

JAVELINE GAULOISE e

„FLYING-BALLS" f

FLÈCHES DELTOUR
à Plumes Métalliques
de tous modèles et de toutes dimensions
pour jeux de fléchettes,
tir à l'arc et à l'arbalète, javelots, etc.

g

m

Le Guillaume Tell h AÉROFLÈCHE j

AUTOFLÈCHE k EUREKA l

j&k *1909 Kratz-Boussac*
l *1922 Les Inventions Nouvelle, 14 rue Martel, Paris. Flèches (arrows)*

m *1909 Gebr. Sauer, Nürnberg*

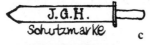

a

b

c

d

e

AMORCES
"AU PETIT CAPORAL"

f

g

M̶eto-P̶last-F̶iguren

h

k

j

l

Montura m    n   **Adol** p

q

a   *1887 Veuve Cocuelle, née Adèle Godard, Paris. Amorces-jouets. Au petit pioupiou qualité supr. (a foot soldier)*

b   *1894 Gebr. Heinrich, Fürth. Tin and lead figures*

c   *1896 Johann Georg Heinrich, Fürth*

d   *1900 Victor Maillard, Paris*

e   *1902 P. Courtès, Paris. Pottery and tin toys, and soldiers of lead and tin*

f   *1905 Auguste Bonvallet et Joseph Boudet, traders, Lyon*

g   *1908 Robert Geiszler, Zittau i S. Toys, wooden soldiers*

h   *1909 Gebruder Heinrich, Fürth. Lead soldiers. Toy figures of composition with cast metal stands*

j   *1909 Pierre Landrieu, 19 Ivy Lane, London. Lead soldiers. Ivy Lane is in SE4 near Deptford Cemetery*

k   *1910 Martin Winterbauer, Nürnberg. Soldiers and figures of tin and lead*

l   *1914 Georg Spenkuch, Nürnberg. Tin figures, lead soldiers, and other tin toy figures*

m   *1914 Gesellschaft zur Förderung von Neuheiten im Handel und gewerbe mbH, Berlin. Soldier figures covered with velour paper or other material*

n   *1915 Emile Merz, 45 rue Sadi-Carnot, Beauvais. A jointed soldier*

p   *1916 Adolf Jacobsohn, Waldenburg. Toys, especially soldiers*

q   *1887 Guillet frères et Cuny-Ra-vet, manufacturers, Lyon. Metal toys*

MARQUE DE FABRIQUE a

b

Wild-West.

DE WET
c

PATRIA
d

Piff-Paff e

LE CANARDEUR f

Eda h Ivo j

Nero k Bruno l Heino m Karo n

Ali p Odu q Titus r „Bim Bum" s

Knick-Knack t

a 1900 A spring-loaded flintlock from Paris. Maker unknown at present
b 1900 Ferd. Wicke, Barmen, Germany. Toy pistols
c 1903 Preute & Brüntjen, Velbert, Rhls. Children's pistols
d 1903 Vve. Chas. Rossignol et Cie, Paris. Carabines and pistols (see automata)
e 1905 Heinrich Kaiser, Hilden, Rbld. Childrens pistols
f 1905 Augustin Pitot, Paris. Automatic repeating toy-pistols
g 1906 Kratz Boussac, Paris. Pistols, carabines

h, j, k, l, m, n, p, q & r 1908 Ewald Nordeck, Velbert. Metal toys, childrens' pistols
s 1913 Paul Hartung, Berlin. Toys, especially pistols
t 1914 Alfons Mauser, Cöln-Marienburg. Toy pistols and metal articles

Ra *Udo* b *Eno* c *Kuno* d *Faust* e

Rudi f *Adro* g *Bey* h *Loki* j *Cid* k *Leo* l

Kastor m *Omar* n *Emir* p *Kunz* q *Leda* r

Top s **Klio** t Luna. u PASCHA v

SULTAN w Amor x Eros y

Reno z **Ikol** a¹ **Bum** b¹ Ruvo c¹

Masi d¹ Ura e¹ Alev f¹ Eiwa g¹

Lodi h¹

a   *1896 Adrian & Rode,*
    Velbert, Rhld. Castles, pistols
    and metal toys
b   *1907 Pistols and metal toys*
1908 c, d, e, f, g, h, j, k, l, m,
    n, p, q, r, s, t, u

1909 Cannons were added to their
    list in addition to pistols v, w,
    x, y, z
a¹   *1910*
b¹   *1911*
c¹, d¹, e¹ f¹ g¹ h¹   *1914*

In July 1914,
  'Schreckschuszpistolen' were
added to their list. These were
pistols to shoot into the air to
give false alarms and to frighten
and intimidate

THE JUBILEE GAME OF SKILL

a

Avant-garde

b

Gordon avenged

Battle of Omdurman Khartoum september 2nd 1898.

c

Victoria!

d

ORION

e

ARTILLA

f

Sans-Sang

g

MARTINICAS

h

"SALTADOR"

j

W – CO – PARIS

k

L'INCROYABLE

l

Kriegs-ABC

Hindenburg
U-boot
Zeppelin

Der Weltkrieg 1914/15
in Knittelversen
als lustiges Kartenspiel
für 2–6 Personen

A·Z

DAISY m

Der
tapfere
Walter

n

p

MARQUE DE FABRIQUE
FORT DES ALLIES

DÉPOSÉ

s

Kriegsspiel Russenfeind q

„Kluczyks Kriegsspiel" r

a   1886 Richard Henry Douglas Hart (gentleman), Tokenhouse Yard, London

b   1896 Johannes Kriszner, Nürnberg. Children's swords. Nbg is for Nürnberg

c   1900 Elias Greiner, Betters Sohn. Lauscha i. Th. Game called the 'Battle of Umdurman, Khartoum Sept 2nd, 1898

d   1900 Gebrüder Arnold, Leipzig-Plagwitz. A war game

e   1904 Adalbert Kempe, Olbernau. Children's toy weapons

f   1907 Oscar Hermann, Pegau

i.S. A game called Artilla

g   1907 Gotthold Lüttge, Oschersleben. Games, particularly war games

h   1908 Marius Magnard, Salaise. Designer of detonating toys

j   1908 Eugène Antoine, Nogent-sur-Marne. The game of 'Lance-balles'

k   1909 Auguste Weiss, Paris. Toys, arms of all kinds, iron-mongery

l   1909 Paul Fourot, Paris. Toys dealing with war, etc

m   1910 The Daisy

Manufacturing Co, Plymouth, USA. Toy arms of all kinds

n   1915 Walter Alperstädt, Berlin. Toys, arquebus toys, etc

p   1915 Züllchower Anstalten, Züllchow b. Stettin. Toys

q   1916 Erich Penndorf, Leipzig. Kriegspiel, ie war-play, Russenfeind, Russian enemy

r   1919 Ignatz Kluczyk, Hombruch-Süd b. Dortmund. Toys

s   1921 Etienne Pouzols, 10 rue Malbec, Toulouse. Désigner des jouets d'enfants

a   b

c

d

l

ACME-SIREN

e

f

THE ACME

g

ACME-THUNDERER   h

m

THE METROPOLITAN j   THE ACME k

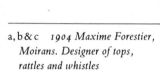

n

a, b & c   *1904 Maxime Forestier,
Moirans. Designer of tops,
rattles and whistles*
d   *1907 Alexandre-Auguste-
Bazin, Paris. Designer of a
rattle*
e, g, h, j & k   *1908 Joseph Hudson,*
*Birmingham, England.
Whistle-calls. Designer of
whistles registered in France,
1908, and in England and the
USA in 1912*
f   *1909 Jean Marie Rouchon,
Lyon. Designer of toy drums*
l & m   *1912 Ernest Rasnesy,
Lyon. Designer of toy drums
made of sheet iron*
n   *1887 André Maglione,
Marseille. A tambourine. The
mark stamped on the boxes*

5. TOYS IN PARTICULAR, MOSTLY OUTDOORS

Of all the toys of mankind the ball is the most popular and new references continually occur. 'The king is extremely fond of tennis, at which game it is the prettiest sight in the world to see him play, his fair skin glowing through a shirt of the finest texture'. This quote comes from the Venetian Calendar of 1519 and the king is Henry VIII. He had a building erected at Hampton Court with a gallery for spectators and from here later on Queen Elizabeth would watch her courtiers at play. According to the privy purse expenses of Henry VIII he lost over £3000 in three years on bets at cards, dice, hunting, tennis and other games. This is from a book by H. S. Nicholas in 1827.

Lawn Tennis, as distinct from real tennis, was played in England in 1870 and 'Garden Party' tennis was introduced by Major Wingfield in 1874.

At Osborne on 7 August 1888, Victor Mallet mentions in his book *On Life with Queen Victoria*★, 'I have been playing lawn tennis this morning with Princess Alex and her Lady in Waiting; they can neither of them get a ball over the net so the game was not exhilarating'.

He also writes that Queen Victoria 'was very amusing yesterday, she thinks football very barbarous and cricket would not be so bad if the ball were softer'. In 1899, in March 'the Prince of Wales has taken to golf, determined not to be behind the times'.

The first Ladies Croquet Championship was held in 1884.

Another quote comes from a newspaper; 'At Newport in the Isle of Wight, 1829, on Tuesday, October 3rd the Society of Archers lately established in this island, held their first public meeting at Carisbrooke Castle, a situation peculiarly adapted, from historical and traditional reminiscences, for the practice of this ancient sport. The meeting was attended by all the rank and fashion of the island; and the picturesque and sylvan dresses on the occasion, particularly those of the ladies, combined with the delightful scenery of the spot, forcibly impressed on the mind the sports and vesture of our forefathers . . . after the amusements of the day were concluded, the assembled company sat down to an elegant repast, prepared by Mr Mew, of the Bugle Inn'.

The game of Netball registered by Laurent in 1907 differs from the game

★ Published by John Murray, being the letters of Marie Mallet between 1887 and 1901.

as we know it in England. This French game was played between two people each holding a square frame of netting in which the ball was tossed and caught.

There were many marks registered for gymnastic and sports equipment during the early twentieth century but only the pictorial ones have been included here. The girl's costume in the Dietrich mark of 1900 is interesting to compare with the children on Pogo sticks in 1921. It is surprising how grown up these earlier young people appear, but that is their costume and not their years.

An interesting piece on the game of diabolo is found in the Commemoration Volume, 1931*, on James Clerk Maxwell. . . . 'During his school days we first hear of a game which he played throughout his life and which all his friends associate with him. One name for it is "diabolo" but it is usually called "the devil on two sticks". The devil consists of a double cone, the narrow part resting on a string, whose ends are attached to the ends of two sticks which are held in the hands of the player; by moving the sticks in opposite directions it is possible to give very considerable rotation to the devil; in fact it is a homemade gyroscope with all the paradoxical properties of that instrument. He attained great skill with it, and no doubt it led him to the construction of his dynamical top, by which he demonstrated in a striking way the properties of bodies in rotation.'

James Clerk Maxwell was born in 1831, his schooldays were between 1841 and 1847. The return of Diabolo and the Great Diabolo Craze took place in 1905 and lasted for four years before retreating once again into oblivion. Skilled players could toss the rotating cone in the air and then catch it again on the string.

Many of the larger outdoor toys came from the United States. Aloys Meisel, one of the first in the USA to register his name, made toys from 1878 onwards. C. W. F. Dare, another maker between 1867 and 1890 made carriages and hobby-horses etc. Christian and Dare of New York made velocipedes from 1868 on. There were rockers of all kinds and sleds – expensive toys, but many boys would be happy with pairs of wheels from cast-off perambulators.

In 1909, the makers of kites registered signs which included toy aeroplanes. Rubber bands had been used by Daudieux in 1880, but the flying craze was in 1909 and 1910. There were cheap copies in tin of early aeroplanes from now on, tin model airships tethered to a pole or gliding along a cord, and construction kits containing bamboo, silk and paper. Japan also participated in the kite and toy aeroplane trade.

1908 Jean Maurice Décamps,
Bordeaux. Game of diabolo

1920 Spielwaren fabrik
Bavaria GmbH München.

*Published by the Cambridge University Press

65

JEFFERIES _a F.H.AYRES _b THAUMA _c CLIMAX _d DRAGON _e

THE DURABLE
Deverell Bros f

 g

LORELEY h

 j

 k

 l

Marque de Fabrique Deposée
ATA
IN HOC SIGNO VINCES

AIGLON

MARQUE DÉPOSÉE m

GRAND DUC

MARQUE DÉPOSÉE n

Gonda p

Ballhei q

„TELLUS" r

KITTY. s

"BOSTON-BALL t

"AERO-BALL" u

Conrex v

 x

SPALDING y

Jetto w

Teddyball b¹

SEMPERIT z

Harras a¹

a   *1855 Jefferies, Wood Street, Woolwich, Kent. Racket balls*
b   *1864 F. H. Ayres, London. Balls*
c, d, e   *1885 Felhausels, 52 Little Britain, London. James Rice, bats, balls, tennis, cricket*
f   *1887 Deverell Bros, 73 Cheapside, London. Balls, toys, etc*
g   *1893 Hannover Caoutchouc Gummi und Telegraph Works. Rubber balls*
h   *1896 G. C. Dornheim,*

Wilh Bitter Nachfolger, Köln. Glass balls & clay pigeons
j   *1899 Max Scherer & Co. Rubber balls, etc*
k   *1901 A. G. Spalding & Bros, New York*
l, m, n   *1904 A. A. Tunmer, Paris. Designers of racquets, balls, footballs, etc*
p   *1910 Paul Behrend, Charlottenburg, Kantstratze 87. Balls and sport-toys*
q   *1910 H. Bierbaum, Berlin. Ballspielen*

r   *1910 Bruno Arthur Meier, Brandenburg. Toys and sportsgear*
s   *1910 Frau Anna Furstin, Lieven geb. Kowalska, Berlin. Toys and outdoor goods*
t   *1910 Sauleau et Rouard, Paris*
u   *1910 Duperrey frères, 19 rue de Paradis, Paris. Toys*
v   *1911 Continental Caoutchouc & Guttapercha Co, Hannover*
w   *1911 Franz P. R. Legener, Berlin. Balls to throw and catch*

x & y *1913 A. G. Spalding & Bros, 124 Nassau Street, New York. Toys of all kinds, bats, sports, etc*
z   *1913 Oesterreichisch-Amerikanische-Gummiwerke Aktiengesellschaft, Vienna. Balls for children*
a¹ & b¹ *1914 J. N. Reithoffer, Vereinigte Gummiwaaren-Fabriken Harburg-Wien. All kinds of balls*

66

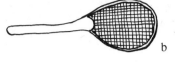 a

 b

 c

 d

OPTIMUS e

SHUTTLE TENNIS f

"PIM PAM" g

 h

 j

The Genteel "*Gem*" *Younglady* Tennisa

k l m n

C. LILLYWHITE & CO. p   THE WOOD STREET BALL s   JOHN BULL u

 q

 r

 t

 v

a   *1850 Pascal Tasso, 14 rue Lefort, Paris, Rackets*

b   *1879 Frederick Henry Ayres, 111 Aldersgate Street, London. Rackets. A lop-sided bat. Registered name Fellkoropalon*

c   *1884 Slazenger & Sons, 56 Cannon Street, London. Games*

d   *1884 Frank Bryan, 38 Charterhouse Square, London. Games*

e   *1886 Charles Fotherley Bagley, Barbican, London. Tennis etc.*

f   *1888 A game played during this year*

1886 Hyman Abraham. Abraham's tennis. Sign, a spider on a web

g & h   *1901 Delhaye Frères, Paris*

j   *1906 Abel Lonquet, trader, Bords*

k, l, m   *1908 Tissages d'Angers, Angers. Tennis raquets for young ladies*

n   *1910 Wolff & Co, Berlin. Ball throwing and catching games*

p   *1881 C. Lillywhite & Co, Frederick Ough. Cricket bats, etc*

q   *1886 William Salmon, 5 Clayton Street, London. Cricket*

r   *1886 Harry Woodham, 109 London Road, Tunbridge Wells. Cricket bats*

s   *1886 Charles Malings, 18 Cockspur Street, London*

t   *1886 Richard Daft, 1 Lister Gate, Nottingham. Football, etc*

u   *1886 William Howard. Footballs*

v   *1913 William Sykes Ltd. The Yorkshire Athletic Goods Manufactory. Horburn*

ROCKET - BALL

a

b

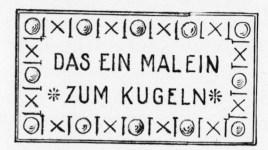

DAS EIN MALEIN
ZUM KUGELN

e

NET-BALL

d

NET-BALL

LA FUNDA

f

g

MAN, Y BAL,
F R
MARQUE DÉPOSÉE

j

BILBO

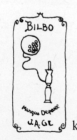

Marque Déposée
J.A.G.E.

k

BILLY POSSUM

BUMBLE PUPPY

l

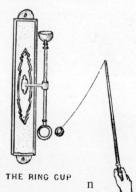

THE RING CUP

m   n

a   *1888 Eliza Jane Fairless (spinster), Brixton Road, London. An outdoor game*

b   *1891 Dorothy Annie Garner, West Kensington, London. A cup & ball game*

c   *1905 Fernand Reyaud, Paris. A game*

d & h   *1907 G· Laurent et Cie, 4 rue Halévy, Paris. Designer of articles for games*

e   *1907 C. Kobrow, Hamburg. Toys, furniture. Kugeln are balls*

f   *1908 Armand d'Abreu, Paris. A toy*

g   *1908 Deutsche Spitball-gmbH Cöln-Ehrenfeld. Spitballspiele*

j   *1908 Charles-Marie-Joseph-Léon Richard and Georges-Bertrand-Alphonse Faireau, Paris*

k   *1907 M. Casadessus, Paris. A toy*

l & m   *1909 Max Illfelder, Fürth, Bayern*

n   *1912 Charles-Louis Valentin, Neuilly-sur-Seine. Designer of a game*

a

QUILLETTE b   CROBILLE c

CROCKET·BALL d

USE THE "CHICK" GOLF BALL
g

P

PEG GOLF
e

ZODIAC f

Fabrik-Marke
h

Trade Mark
j

TURNERS LAWN SKITTLES
k

Kaiser Wilhelm II
Deutsches Kugel-Roulette
schwarz-weiss-rot l

BOOMERANG
m

BALLING GULL
GULLING BALL
BALL GULLING n

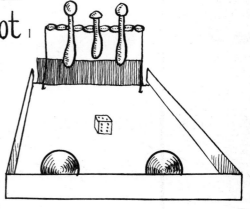
p

Clubs and Mallets

a   1883 Thomas Murray Gardiner, Hoddesdon, Hertfordshire. *Games*

b   1887 John Thomas, Clerk in Holy Orders, Manorbier, Pembrokeshire. *An improved game of skill, analgous to croquet*

c   1889 Jaques. *An outdoor game*

d   1909 Paul Fourot, Paris. *Designer of 'jeux de maillets'*

e   1912 The Peg Golf Co, New York, NY. *Toy golf games*

f   1913 Martins, Birmingham. *Play balls and golf balls*

g   1913 North British Rubber Co, Berlin. *Rubber balls*

Billiard Balls

h   1884 Wilhelm Schutz, Dusseldorf. *Für künstliche Billiardbälle*

j   1886 Compagnie Générale de Chromolithie à Paris.

Billiardkugeln. *Many marks were registered for billiard balls.*

Skittles

k   1882 John Turner, Albert Villa, Tiverton-on-Avon, Somersetshire. *An outdoor game*

l   1905 Wolf Kronheim, Hamburg. *Skittles and ninepins*

m   1910 Compagnie-Brunswick Française, Paris. *Games of skittles, bowls and the like*

n   1910 Victor Gervais, La Garenne-Colombes. *A game in which balls are thrown at silhouettes or mannequins until they fall down flat.*

p   1921 Francisque-Philibert Grandjean, 6 rue de la Loire, Le Havre. *Games*

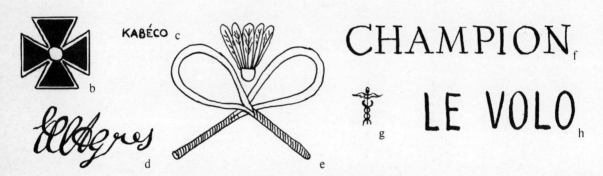

Mark for Rubber Ball Syndicate

a *1917 Deutsches Gummi-ball-Syndikat GmbH, Harburg. Rubber balls*

Bat and Shuttlecock

b,d *1885 F. H. Ayres, London. Shuttlecocks, balls, raquets*
c *1887 Kirby Beard & Co, London. Shuttlecocks, raquets*
e *1888 Thomas Hardman (artist), Liverpool.*

Battledore & shuttlecock

f,g *1905 Pierre Jean Geisler, manufacturer, Paris. Shuttlecocks*
h *1908 Jules Berger, Neuilly-sur-Seine. A shuttlecock*

JACULUM a

COUNTY b

 c

LE DISCOLO d

 e

LE DISCOBOLE f

"LE PAMPA" g   "SALTADOR" h

 j

Daisy k

Whitely. l

LE SPORT INCASSABLE
Celluloid
A. & F
PARIS p

DÉPOSÉ
★ E. H. ★ n

m

POGO
APPAREIL A SAUTER q

LA COMÈTE r   CLIMBO s

a   1879 William Beale, Ravenstone House, Farquhar Road, Upper Norwood, Surrey. Games

b   1883 Frank Bryan, 38 Charterhouse Square, Aldersgate, London. A game

c   1903 J. G. Schrodel Nürnberg, Schweinau. Sports and games

d   1908 Jules Moret, Lyon. A game of 'graces' to play alone

e   1887 Richard frères, Paris. A roundabout game entered as 'Le Nouveau jeu de bagues Japonais'

f   1908 Paul Fourot, Paris. A game of sport, for outdoors or indoors

g   1908 Lucien Dulphy, Paris. A game with balls

h   1908 Eugène-Antoine Hamm, Nogent-sur-Marne. A game with balls

j   1909 Jules Moret, Lyon. 'Le Cerf Volo', a game similar to 'Le Discolo'

k   1891 Thomas Farrar, Manchester. Skipping ropes

l   1899 Chs. Lavy & Co, Hamburg. Gymnastics & sports

m   1900 Julius Dietrich & Hannak, Chemnitz i S. Balls, gymnastic toys of all kinds

n   1901 Mme Eugénie Herrmann, Paris. A hoop, and other toys

p   1907 Anel et Fraisse, Paris. A sporting game

q   1921 Isolabella Italo, Paris. The game of Pogo

r   1909 M. Dechaux, Paris. An outdoor game

s   1914 C. Abel-Klinger, Nürnberg. A climbing game

TIP ♡ a

LA FUREUR
M. P.
TOUPIE DU NORD DEPOSÉE c

ÉQUILIBRE EUROPÉEN
QUESTION DU JOUR
Nouveau Jeu
DÉPOSÉ. PARIS. d

Tipple-Topple e

NATIONAL LUFTKREISEL
„FANGOLO" f

Melodien Kreisel „Kirch" g

TIP-TOP h

TippLe ToppLe j

"TOUPIES TURF" k

KAKO l

NEO m

---

a,b *1886 Hale Bros, Sheffield*
c *1887 Mordacq Plamont, Lille.*
  Sign, a spinning top, printed in
  violet
d *1888 Jules Paquet, trader,*
  Paris. Sign stamped on the
  boxes containing the toy
e *1906 Georg Kohn, Hamburg.*

Toys of all materials
f *1909 Adolf Cahen,*
  Düsseldorf. An air top
g *1910 Heinrich Kirch, Mainz,*
  Mombach. A humming top
h *1910 Hector Amanieu,*
  Bordeaux. A toy for the open air

j *1916 Pfeiffer, Emil, Wein,*
  Austria
k *1922 Odhams Press Ltd, 93*
  Long Acre, London. Tops, toys
l *1922 Alfred Tebbitt, Paris.*
  A top
m *1922 M.Watris, Paris. Tops*

DIABOLO b

Diabolo Tennis
Diabolo Club
Tennis
Club
Diabolo Amateur
Populaire
Diabolo Scolaire
Scolaire Sportif
Scolaire d

J H PARIS e

Le "DIABLE à QUATRE" g

LE MENUET
LE CRI-CRI
LE BENGALI
LE JOUJOU
THE DEVIL
LE DÉSIRÉ f

BOBINO h

DIABLE-VOLANT j

.. LE PRÉFÉRÉ l

.. LA PRÉFERÉE m

CAMBO n

LE PETIT POUCET k

Diabolo Populaire q

DIABLE-CAMBODGE r

a 1905 Fernand Reynaud, Paris. A toy

b,q 1905 Gustave Philippart, Paris

c 1906 Fernand Gratieux, Paris

d 1907 Nine names registered by Philippart

e 1907 J. Hausmann et fils, Paris

f 1907 Six names registered by Hausmann

g 1907 E. Maupin et R. Ducase, Paris. Designer of a toy

h 1907 Georges Krieg, Paris

j 1907 Casimer-Adrien Gout, Paris. Bobines-toupies

k 1907 Ernest, Frènot, Paris

l,m 1907 Georges Abrahams, Paris. An extendable bag to carry the top etc

n 1907 Emile Vuillaume à Saint-Gilles, Bruxelles (Belgium)

p 1907 Brunessaux et Gratieux, Paris. A toy composed of two tops united at their extremities. Cyrano de Bergerac (1619–1655) was a Gascon playwright, hero of Rostand's play, who fought many duels to avenge insults to his enormous nose

r 1907 François Delvoye, Paris. A toy worked by means of rubber or elastic

"FLYER" **JB** TRADE MARK a

LE VRAI DIABLE SEUL INCASSABLE F.J.S. PARIS MODÈLE ET MARQUE DÉPOSÉS b

LE DIABLOTIN MODÈLE & MARQUE DÉPOSÉS c

LE BLANCO DIABLE CELLULOÏD DÉPOSÉ d

DIABOLO SPORT ★ DÉCAMPS & RUBICHON ★ Bté S.G.D.G. ★ e

DIABOLO-DOPPELKREISEL D.R.P. 171983 · 131872 f

LE SOLEIL MARQUE DÉPOSÉE g

h

L.E MÉPHISTO.S DÉPOSÉ j

SATANAS k

MÉPHISTO - SCOLAIRE
MÉPHISTO - SPORTIF
Méphisto-Game
Le Méphisto l

LE DEMON m

a *1907 Jules-Alfred Boudin,*
   Paris, Diable
b & c *1907 Jean-François*
   Janssens, Paris. A 'jeu sportif'
d *1907 M. Bernhold, Paris*
e *1907 Jean-Maurice Décamps,*
   Bordeaux. Diabolos
   ornamented with leather
f *1907 Gustave Philippart,*
   trader, Paris
g *1907 Auguste Fouché, Paris*
h *1907 Félix Giradin, Paris.*
   Designer of a toy

j *1907 Louis Sauleau, Paris.*
   A toy
k *1907 Le Jouet de Paris, 23*
   rue de Reuilly, Paris
l *1907 Four names registered by*
   Sauleau
m *1907 Fernand Crötte, Paris*

a

b

DIABOLOPHONE c

DIABLOPHONE d

Rocket-Diabolo-Ball e

ROCKET-BALL f

g

DIAVOLANT h

DIABOSIRENE j

"PHONODIABLE" m

k

l

a&b   *1907 Rémy et fils, Saint
       Denis. Toupie-double, ie a
       double top*
c,d,e,f *1907 Philippart, Paris.
       Double-tops*
g   *1907 L. Berlan fils, Paris*
h&j   *1907 Paul Valter, Paris*

k   *1907 Ferret et Livet, Paris.
     A double-top called Diable*
l   *1907 Pitel-Reffay, Molinges*
m   *1907 Gutmann & Schiffee,
     Nürnberg. Musical diabolo*

"LE RONFLEUR" b

LE DEMONIO c

d

LE POSTILLON
DIABLE—GRELOTS e

"LE FÉLIXB" f

LA "PRESTO" g

"DIABLO-BALL" h

VOLO k

DIABOLO l

j

LE FASCINATEUR m

"PARISIEN" n

DIABOLO-EURÉKA p

LE ROBUR q

M.C. s

LE DIABLE SANTOS

r

t

a 1908 Jean-Maurice Décamps, Bordeaux	g 1908 M. Pezard, Paris. Small bags for diabolos	m 1908 Jean Jary, Colombes
b 1908 Peillon frères, Oyonnax	h 1908 Delvoye et Pasquet, Paris. A game of sport and skill	n 1908 Albert J. B. Jacquier, Paris. A pliant diabolo
c 1908 Henri Thiéry, Paris		p 1908 Philippart, Paris
d 1908 Rodolphe Carpentier, Paris	j 1908 G. Perron, Paris. Designer of the filins for diabolo, filins are the cords	q 1908 M. Peyrot, 107 rue Oberkampf, Paris
e 1908 Cyrille-Pierre-Joseph Bonnet, Paris. Grelots are little bells	k 1921 Little Frères, Paris. Designers of double-top toys called diables	r 1908 Paul Prezkowski, Paris. Designer of games & toys
f 1908 Felix Boulleau, Paris. Pouches or satchels for diabolos	l 1921 Les Inventions Nouvelles, Paris	s 1908 Machinal et Chaufray, Paris. Diabolos
		t 1909 Li and Tsu, Paris. Musical diabolo

In the 1870s dolls' prams in which the doll could lie down appeared about the same time as the ones for real babies. By 1883, the prams made of wicker and with four wheels, had the doll facing the child instead of with its back to it. About this time the real ones made by the Army & Navy Stores were called the 'Sociable Vis-à-Vis'.

a

b

c

d

e

f

g

a *1876 Louis Schmetzer & Cie, Rothenburg. Toys and childrens' waggons*

b *1877 Chr. Nemmert, Nürnberg. Children's, dolls', and invalid carriages, wickerwork and basketwork*

c *1885 E. A. Näther, Zeitz. Children's, dolls' and invalid carriages, dolls' furniture, etc*

d *1896 Wunsch & Pretzsch, Zeitz. Doll carriages, folding seats, etc*

e *1914 W. Baumann et cie, Colombier-Fontaine. Dolls' prams, waggons, wheels etc*

f *1921 Manufacture Française de Jouets à Beaurepaire (Isère). Toys, prams, wooden articles, etc*

g *1922 Juliette Girodot, 69 rue Alexandre-Dumas, Paris. Toy prams*

'TALLY-HO' b

'CHILD'S BENEFACTOR' c

Kinderfreund
d

MONOPLANE e   KayDee f   Sleepy Hollow g

HORSEMOBILE h   CRANBERRY j   CHEROKEE k

l

Schwungmaxe n

p

m

AUTOPEDALES q   AUTO-PÉDALES r

AUTOPÉDAL s   Eile mit Weile. t

u

v

w

x

a 1870 Paris Manufacturing Co, Paris, Maine, USA. From 1861 on, toy wagons, sleds & wheelbarrows

b 1878 Charles W. F. Dare, Brooklyn, USA. Carriages & hobby horses

c 1878 J. A. Crandall, Brooklyn, USA. Hobby horses, velocipedes, etc

d 1902 Karl J. Krause, Finsterwalde. Finsterwalder Holzwaarenfabriken, Childrens' sportswaggons, etc

e 1912 York Novelty Co, York, Pa. Children's sleds

f,g 1912 Herman L. Hohlfeld, Philadelphia, Pa. Hammocks & children's rockers

h 1912 The Horsemobile Toy Co, Oshkosh-Wis. Hobby horses

j,k 1912 C. M. McClung & Co, Knoxville, Tenn. Toy wagons

l 1912 Adolf W. Pressler, Keene, NH. Design for a rocking-horse

m 1913 Henry William St Denis & Walker St Denis, Ottawa, Ontario, Canada. Rocking or hobby elephant

n 1919 Oskar Schulz, Dresden. Toy swing

p 1913 William R. Newton, Ingleside, Ill. Rocking toys

q,r,s 1904 Soc du Louvre, Paris

t 1915 G. J. Pabst, Nürnberg. Eile mit Weile, speed with leisure

u 1921 Toulet et Cie, 103 rue Lafayette, Paris. Jouets et Auto Skiffs

v 1912 Auto Specialty Manufacturing Co Inc, Indianapolis, Ind. Toy vehicles

w 1922 Clauduis Mondon, 13 rue Saint Joseph, Saint Etienne. Jouets

x 1921 Manufacture Française d'Ameublement, Saint Étienne. Toy propelled by the arms & legs

a

OLGA – PATIN
Breveté S. G. D. G
GARANTI INCASSABLE

Skatometer

b

san

risk

MARQUE & MODÈLE

DÉPOSÉS

d

G. F.
2

c

RINK CROQUET e

RINK CURLING f

CURLING STONES

g

"FEARLESS FLY"

j

LE PETIT NAVIGATEUR

h

FLUVIO

k

UNSERE ZUKUNST.

LIEGT AUF DEM WASSER

l

L·S

m

LE

YÉ-YÉ

...

MARQUE DÉPOSÉE

n

---

a *1878 George Gibson Bussey, Museum Works, Rye Lane, Peckham. Roller Skates*
b *1899 Louis Jacobshon, Freien-Walde a.D. Skatgeber*
c *1920 Gerbaulet frères, 35–37 rue de Turenne, Paris. (A patin is a skate)*
d *1922 Laurent Peyron, 2 rue Jacquard, Saint Etienne. Patins à roulettes, (roller-skates)*

e,f *1886 Hugh Dalziel. Games and toboggans*
g *1887 Ayreshire curling stones*
h *1903 Paul Toussaint-Fourot, Paris. Boats and marine accessories*
j *1904 F. V. M. Bressoux, trader, Paris. An 'attraction nautique'*
k *1908 G. Philippart, Paris. Nautical toys, fishing, etc*

l *1909 L. Uebelacker, Nürnberg. Toys for in the air and in the water*
m *1921 Louis Simonet à Saint-Amand (Cher). Pêche, fishing toys*
n *1921 Felix Tabariès, 57 avenue Gambetta, Béziers. Sacs de chasse, (hunting satchels, toys)*

a

PANOPE b

CERF-VOLO c

d

"AIGLOPLAN" g

"AIGLEPLAN" h

"TORPILL'S" j

"AIGLEPLANEUR" k

"LA SPORTIVE" l

e

Phil-hô f

AEROPALLA n

CHANTECLAIR s
CHANTECLER t
AIGLOPLAN u
AVIOPLAN v

LE ZODIAC p

CERVOL-HÔ q

L'ANTOINETTE r

m

"VICTORIA" w

LABOR y

x

AIGLO BLANC
EAGLE BLANC
EAGLO BLANC

AIGLON BLANC
AIGLE BLANC
EAGLON BLANC

z

a 1879 Carl August von der Meden, 4 Jeffreys Square, London. Toys and paper kites

b 1892 Sir George Strong Nares, a kite

c 1907 Jules Moret, Lyon. Désigner d'un jeu d'anneaux

d 1909 Eugène Adeline, Biarritz. Kites & aeroplanes

e 1909 A. Pelliccioni, L. Paulhan, J. Riber, Paris. Designers of toys

f 1909 P'e-se-tsong, and Rene & Marcel Philippart, Paris. Kites, aeroplanes & aerial toys

g,h,j,k,l 1909 Sauleau & Rouard, Paris. Toy aeroplanes, kites, etc

m 1909 Li and Tsu, Paris. Designers of toys

n 1909 Goldmann & Co, Offenbach. Offenbach Celluloid und Hartgummi, etc. Air & ball toys

p,q,r 1910 Sauleau & Rouard, Paris. Kites

s,t,u,v 1910 Sauleau & Rouard, Paris. Aeroplanes & kites

w 1910 R. & M. Philippart, Paris. Toy aeroplanes & kites

x 1910 Henri Oudet, Paris. A winged flying toy

y 1910 Maurice Clèves, Neuilly-sur-Seine. Automatic toy

z 1911 Charles Rouard, Paris. Kites & aeroplanes, six names

BLÉRIOT   EURÉKA   "SKI AÉRIEN"   "ZEPHYR"
b   c   d

a

"LIBELLULE"   "MOUETTE"   L'AVIOPLANE
e   f   g

"SIMPLEX"

"LA CHOUETTE PARISIENNE" j

"LE GOELAND APPELANT" k

"LE CERF-AEROPLAN" l

h

"L'AERO-PHOTO" m

"L'INTREPIDE" n

p

q

LE VIROPLANE

AÉRO CIRCUIT
AÉRO CIRCUIT DES AVIATEURS
AÉRO CIRCUIT DES CAPITALES
AÉRO CIRCUIT DES NATIONS

LE ZIGOMAR t
L'IBIS u
LE ZIG v
LE ZÉNITH w

r

s

Bleriotplane

x

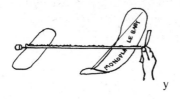
y

z

---

a   *1909 Gabriel de Lapeyrouse, Paris. Toys*

b   *1909 H. O. Kratz-Boussac, Paris. Toy aeroplanes*

c   *1909 Louis Santa-Maria, Paris. Toy aeroplanes*

d,q   *1909 F. Migault fils, Paris. A toy aeroplane*

e,f   *1909 Maurice Nicholas,*

Paris. Toy aeroplanes

g   *1909 Georges Parmeland, Paris. An aeroplane toy*

h   *1909 Henri Durand, Paris. Designer of a toy aeroplane*

j,k,l,m,n,p   *1909 José Vines, Roda, Paris*

r   *1910 Jean Fieux, Harfleur. Toys*

s   *1910 Henri-Claude Soudan. Games manoeuvring aeroplanes*

t,u,v,w   *1910 Sauleau et Rouard, Paris. Aeroplanes*

x   *1911 Joseph Auge, Neuilly-sur-Seine*

y   *1911 Gaston Bonnot, Paris. 'Monoplan Le Baby' etc*

z   *1911 S. D. Zimmer, Fürth*

a

b

MOTOPLANE c

AVIETTE d

VÉLOPLANE e

M N

AÉRO-PUZZLE

MARQUE DE FABRIQUE
DÉPOSÉE

f

g

AIRSHIP j

BALLON CAPTIF AUTOMATIQUE
"LE PETIT AÉRONAUTE" h

a   *1912 Otto Ackermann,*
   Leipzig. Toys to fly, planes to
   build
b   *1912 Julius Bernhold, Paris.*
   Designer of toys
c,d,e   *1912 Jules Laurent,*

Asnières. All kinds of toys,
excepting those entirely of
rubber
f   *1912 Serge Mignot et William*
   de Noé, Paris. Designer of toys
g   *1910 William Rode, Steglitz.*

Gliders & other toys
h   *1909 François-Marie-Auguste*
   Puthon, Paris. A toy called
   captive balloon
j   *1912 Gaston Viguié, Nanterre.*
   Flying toys and kites

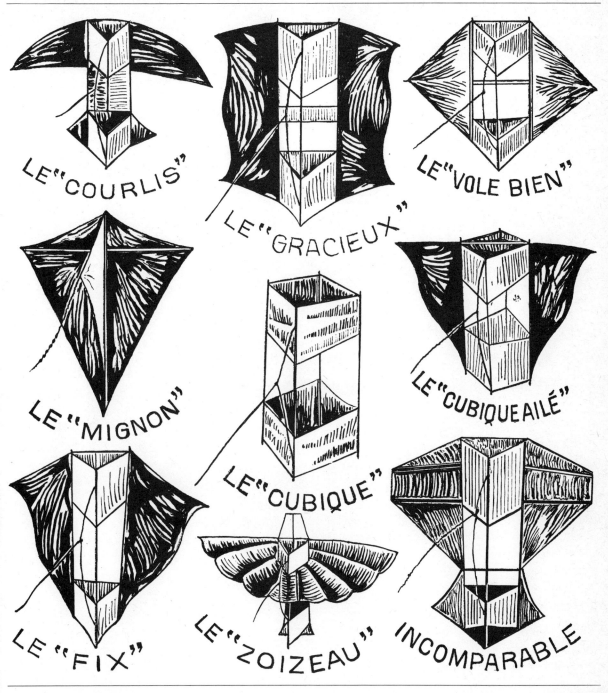

LE "COURLIS"

LE "GRACIEUX"

LE "VOLE BIEN"

LE "MIGNON"

LE "CUBIQUE"

LE "CUBIQUE AILÉ"

LE "FIX"

LE "ZOIZEAU"

INCOMPARABLE

1921 Edmond Biermé Van Oye,
17 rue de la Lys, à Halluin.
Designer of toys & games

Gramophone, with trade plaque of Parkins & Golto. Probably made by Kämmer & Reinhardt and with six 5″ records and horn of papier mâché.

German *c.*1893 Gramophone base 14″ × 7½″ horn 11″ by 6½″ diameter

Courtesy of Christie's

A Racing Game by Ayres of
London. Heavy leather board
with embossed gilt numbers
and pictures. Six metal horses,
two metal fences, mirror water
jump, and book of instructions
for playing the 'Game of Race
or Steeplechase'.

English   1909   Board 16 × 32″
Horses 3″ long, 1½″ high

*Courtesy of Miss Ruth
Wainwright*

a   *1849 Jaques, London. Publishers of games and chessmen*

b   *1876 Pears, Games of all kinds*

c   *1870 Henry Jewitt, Toys and Games. The R is for William Rose, USA*

d   *1872 Chapman, Son & Co, 2 Charterhouse Buildings, Aldersgate, London. Games*

e   *1876 De la Rue. Games of all kinds*

f   *1876 Salford & Irwell Rubber Co, Fenchurch Street, London. Games*

g   *1876 Bovril. Games of all kinds*

h   *1876 Reason, Mann Co Ltd, Brighton. Toys and games*

j   *1876 Robert Whyte, trading as Whyte & Ridsdale, 73 & 74 Houndsditch, London. Games, toys and fancy goods*

k   *1877 Frank Bryan, Bartholomew Close, London, EC. A game*

l   *1878 William Farini, 74 St James Street, Westminster, Middlesex. Games*

m   *1878 Alfred Bird & Sons, 69 Worcester Street, Birmingham. Games*

n   *1879 John S. Elmore & Co, 77 Coleman Street, London. Games*

p   *1882 William Meyerstein, 6 Love Lane, Aldermanbury, London. Games and toys of all kinds, paper Chinese lanterns*

q,r   *1884 Caroline Manby, Oakhill, Bath, Somerset. Two games*

s   *1884 La Soc Meiffre, Neveu et Cie, 82 rue Hauteville, Paris. Games & toys*

t   *1885 Davidson & Co. Games*

u   *1885 Deverell Bros, 73 Cheapside, London. Games*

v   *1885 Slazenger & Sons, 56 Cannon Street, London. Games*

'The Court amused itself with the ordinary recreations which we have in winter, and in most solitarie times busie our minds with, as Cards, Tables, and Dice, Shovel-board, Chesse-play, Shuttlecocks, billiards, musicke, masks, singing, dancing, yule-games, frolicks, jests, riddles, catches, purposes, questions, and commands, merry tales of Errant Knights etc.' All this happened on 20 January 1563, in Scotland, and is taken from the *Anatomie of Melancholie* by Burton.

These were the indoor games of the time and, except for 'purposes' one can imagine all of them, especially the 'frolicks'.

'Emblematical Cards for the Amusement of Youth' were produced by Wallis in 1788. Cards and printed cut-outs often bore the name of the maker but rarely the date. This would be because people were always searching for something new as a gift and not 'last year's old things'.

At Balmoral in 1896, the guests of the Queen played the new game of

w   *1885 Oscar Moenich, Coleman Street, London. Toys*

x   *1885 The Tobogganing Co. Domestic engineers, Palace Chambers, 9 Bridge Street, Westminster, London SW. A game*

Whist and the younger ones played Happy Families. Card games in Bohn's Book of Games were Whist, Solo Whist, Poker, Piquet, Ecarté, Euchre, Bézique, Cribbage, Loo, Vingt-et-un, Napoleon, Newmarket, Pope Joan, and Speculation.

The card game of Rook was played in the USA in 1911, and the trade name of 'Linoid' was registered by Doherty, this being a method of finish on the surface of playing-cards. Donkey, Old Maid, Snap, and Spin were popular games and there were several others which did not require specially designed picture cards.

All through the Victorian and Edwardian days parlour games were popular for there was plenty of time to play in and plenty of maids to do the work. Other games listed in Bohn's Handbooks, published in 1902 were Billiards, Chess, Draughts, Backgammon, Dominoes, Solitaire, Reversi, Go-bang, Rouge-et-Noir, Roulette, E O, Hazard and Faro.

SQUAILS a

 b

KANGAROO c

PATCHESI h

DÉPOSÉ J.M n

C. TERNISIEN j

 k

PRESIDENT f

PARLOUR THE GRACE CRICKET g

BRITTON'S SETOW l

NAVAL BLOCKADE m

TESSELLA ROYALE p

TIDDLEDY-WINKS q

LADY BLOWAWAY'S VISIT TO THE ZOO r

MINIATELLE s BILLIATELLE t SPINNAKER u FLITTERKINS v

 w

THE EIFFEL TOWER ASCENT GAME x

COZARI y

PALMERETTO z

QUOITAC & ALSO SLIDIT a'

a 1884 John Jaques, 102 Hatton Garden, London, EC. Publishers of games

b,c 1866 Chas. Macintosh, Manchester & London. Games

d 1886 Thomas Blenkarn, 62 Fenwick Road, Peckham. Games and toys

e 1886 Co-op Wholesale Co, Balloon Street, Manchester. Games but no dolls

f 1886 Frank Bryan, 36 Charterhouse Square, London. Games

g 1886 Mowbray Fitzroy Bailey, Gracechurch Street, London. A parlour game

h 1887 John Jaques, 102 Hatton Garden, London. A game

j 1887 Cléophas Ternisien, Paris. Name stamped on the dominoes

k 1888 Thomas Lidster (Pattern maker), Hull, England. Games

l 1888 Canonbury (Professor of Music), a game

m 1888 Henry Chamberlain (Lieutenant, Royal Navy), Greenwich. Games

n 1888 Jules-Denis Marc, Paris. Stamped on the game of dice

p 1888 R. G. Powell, Manchester. Toys. A game

q 1889 Joseph Assheton Fincher (gentleman), 114 Oxford Street, London

r 1889 Emma Susanna Windsor (Manufacturer & Saleswoman), 150 Soho Bazaar, Soho Square, London. A game

s,t 1889 The Toy Manufacturing Co, 5 Oxford Street, London

u 1889 Henry Glanville Barnacle (Clergyman), The Vicarage, Holmes Chapel, Cheshire. A game of skill

v 1889 Jaques, London. A game

w 1889 Henry R. Hughes, Long Lane, London. Games

x 1889 Ernest de Lima Bird, Peckham

y 1889 James Morrell (Engineer). A game

z 1890 Emma Barker, Gwendyr Road, Kensington. Games

a' 1890 Edward Mortimer. Ten table games

FLICKEM b   LABYMAZE c   BOOMERANG d

FLIPPERTY FLOP e

KAN HOOPLAR f   JAQUITTA g   BUFFALO JACK h

COZZARE j   BASILINDA k   PLIFFKINS l

KHANOO n

JEUX

MULTIPLES r

LA BALLE AU BOND t

ZANZI-PIQUET u

Les Nouveaux Jeux
DU
XXeme Siecle v

Chemin roulant w

Timo x   *VIGORO* y   BUHURT z

LE PLUTUS a¹   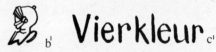 b¹ Vierkleur c¹

---

a   *1890 Ménard & Moss, Greenock. Péronnelle games*

b   *1890 Hildesheimer & Faulkner. Games*

c   *1890 Jules Pierre Cavallier (Accountant). A game*

d   *1890 Robert Owen Allsop (Architect), Strand, London. A game*

e   *1891 Oppenheimer & Sulzbacher, Nuremburg, Germany. A game*

     1890 Games played in 1890 f, g, h, j, k, l

m   *Goodalls sign, used since 1885*

n   *1893 W. H. Wilkinson, BA. Published by Charles Goodall & Son*

p   *1898 The Laripino game. This name comes again and is registered by Spear in 1912*

q   *1892 Ephriam Samson (collector), Houndsditch, London. Games*

r   *1898 Kratz-Boussac, Paris. A box of various games*

s   *1898 Eugène Sinoquet fils, Dargines. A game*

t   *1898 Eugène-Alexandre Ouachée, Paris. Jeu de Société*

u   *1899 Benjamin Allemand, trader, Marseille. A new game*

v   *1899 Charles Rambour, Paris*

w   *1900 George Dreyfus, trader, Paris*

x   *1901 Alfred Thieme, Leipzig. Social games*

y   *1901 John George Grant, Hampstead, London. Games for indoors and outdoors*

z   *1901 Gebrüder Heinrich, Fürth. A social game*

a¹   *1902 Eugène Rambour, Paris. 'Game of Société'*

b¹   *1902 Soehlin et Bailliart, Paris. Designers of games*

c¹   *1902 Ewald G. Schultze*

a

b

PUNTA c

e

PIPIFAX d

"POLYGLOTTE" g

Chronos' Stop f

Chit-Chat. l

LE TACTICIEN h

STOPP-STOPP k

LE TACTITIEN j

HUMPTY-DUMPTY n

TROLLEY m

NEIGEOBOUL p

LE CHAMPION r

MIXED PICKLES q

„Togo" s

LEIBENGER t

w

Alpina u

LA BOÎTE MAGIQUE v

DER KLEINE COHN x   „Kehr' zurück" y

Daheim z

a, b   *1902 A. Sala, Berlin. A floor game*

c   *1902 Emil Lauterburg, Berne, Switzerland. Games*

d   *1903 Johannes Paul Gerhard Wolf, Leipzig. Toys*

e   *1903 E. Couerville, Levallois-Perret. 'Jeu de Société', ie played with others*

f   *1903 Ferdinand V. M. Bressoux, trader, Paris. A game of skill*

g   *1903 Kratz-Boussac, Paris*

h, j   *1903 C. E. L. Regnard, Paris. 'Jeu de Société'*

k   *1903 Gustav Eisele, Leipzig. A game*

l   *1903 Jean Fliesz, Kattowitz D-S Friedrichstr. A game*

m   *1903 Le Jouet de Paris. A game of skill*

n   *1904 H. E. Twining, Paris. Designer of games for grown-ups & children*

p   *1904 Georges Loyer, Paris. 'A foreign game'*

q   *1904 John Jaques & Son Ltd, London. A game*

r   *1904 E. Champion, Neuilly-sur-Seine. Engineer, designer of a 'game of société'*

s   *1904 Friedrich Ruppel n Theodor Kämpfer, Wiesbaden. A game 'Marine-blockade'*

t   *1905 Prof George Leibenger, Nürnberg. Spielen u. Blatter und Karten als Vorlagen hierzu*

u   *1905 Michel Baum, München. Games and the parts for them*

v   *1906 Kratz-Boussac, engineer, Paris. Games of all kinds*

w   *1905 Emil Hausotter, Treuen i V. Games and parts for them*

x   *1906 Leopold Hochstein, Mannheim. A money-lending game*

y   *1905 Graff & Co, GmbH, Berlin. Games*

z   *1907 Heinrich Heller, Leipzig-Neudnitz, and Hugo Ziegler. Games, playing-cards, toys, etc*

LE PRÉCIEUX FRANCE c

Nèige de Riz b

U·S·A LOTTO a

Glück-Auf d

„Union" e

RAIL BALL g

LE TOURBILLON f

MODÈLE DÉPOSÉ.

"LE VIRTUOSE" h

VINGT-ET-UN

"LES GUGUSS" j

L'OCTOGONE INTERNATIONAL l

L'OCTOGONE NATIONAL m

BOLOTO n

BOUCLONS LE CIRCUIT p   AVIA q

Le "RÉJOUI" r

a   *1907 J.W. Spear & Söhne,*
    Nürnberg-Doos. Paper & toy
    factory. The game of Lotto
b   *1907 Douglas Farquhar*
    Glennie, Knightsbridge,
    London
c   *1907 Anel et Fraisse, Paris.*
    A game
d   *1907 Hermann Wielers,*
    Bocholt Westf. Amusing games
e   *1907 Wilhelm Bethke, Berlin.*
    Amusing games

f   *1908 Mme Lonquet (Anne*
    Huet) and Mme Veuve
    Rouquaré (Eléonore Strady),
    Paris. A game
g   *1908 M. Déchaux, Paris. A*
    game of skill
h   *1908 Albert Grossaint, Paris.*
    Musical dominoes
j   *1909 Charles Daniel*
    Alexandre Pasteur, Paris. A
    game of skill
k   *1908 Charles Heitmann,*
    Hamburg. Games with dice

l, m   *1908 Gouttebaron et*
    Dutel, Saint Marcel-de-Félines.
    Designer of games
n   *1909 Louis Mandrillon,*
    Saint Claude. Toys, especially
    games of Loto
p   *1909 Adolphe Milliaud,*
    Paris. A game
q   *1909 Albert Pujol, Paris.*
    Designer of games
r   *1909 Lucien Bisman, Lille.*
    An automatic game of skill

TAP-TAP b

JEU DES PUISSANCES c

a

d

CAHIN-CAHA e

f

"LE NIBÉ" g

SALTA h

„BELLUM" k

l

BILBOLA
m

LOTO MOBILE
n

Domino-Musical p

Rätsch-Ratsch
q

Elearenspiel
r

MINORU
s

GLOBE TROTTERS t

PIRATE AND TRAVELER
u

SCRAMBOLO
v

---

a   *1909 Auguste Lebourdais, Paris. 'Un jeu de toton'*

b   *1909 Alfred Giraudet, Paris. Designer of games of skill and toys*

c   *1910 Léo Deglesne, Paris. A game or toy. Puissances means power*

d   *1910 Zero–Spiel-vertriebs. Gesellschaft mbH, Frankfort*

e   *1910 André Lombard, Paris. Designer of a 'jeu de société'*

f   *1910 Pierre-Louis Mansuy, Paris. Designer of a game*

g   *1910 J. Leischener, Paris. Designer of a game*

h   *1910 Henri-Othon Kratz-Boussac, Paris. A 'jeu de société'*

j   *1910 Ernest Génault, Châtellerault. Designer of a pleasant game for recreation*

k   *1911 Vinzenz Vacek, Berlin. Games & toys*

l   *1911 J.W. Spear & Söhne, Nürnberg*

m   *1911 William Lloyd Derning, Salem, Columbia, Ohio. Games*

n   *1911 Jules Levy, Nanterre. Toys & games*

p   *1911 Mille S. J. Ruffier de Marqueron, Paris. A game*

q   *1911 J. H. Mähl, Hamburg*

r   *1911 Johann Ad. Klein, Troppau. A game*

s   *1912 John Jaques & Son Ltd, London, England. A game*

t   *1912 Harry Thompson, South Hampstead, London, England*

u   *1912 New Idea Game Co, Oakland, California. A game*

v   *1912 Strobel &Wilken Co, New York, NY. A game*

SMIP a

"FIXO" b

Pantheon c

HOP! HOP! d

HOP! HUP! e

PONIES f

TIT
TAT
FINGER g

MOSAÏQUE h

H P j

TREE THE POSSUM k

„Katz im Sack" l

RAKAFORCE m

OSPREY n

YOO PLĀ p

HomeRun q

Pan-Puz r

SUMRUN s

Parabello t

MAKU Doppelspiel z

JEU DES DÉCORATIONS u

NIP AND TUCK v

ABRACADABRA w

MANIFESTO x

GET MY GOAT y

---

a   1912 Jean Hardy, Paris. Toys & games of all kinds

b   1912 André-Barbey Graves, Paris. Toys & games of all kinds

c   1912 Paul Langguth, Deutsche Steinholz-Werke, Berlin. Designer of games

d,e   1912 Adolphe Welfling, Paris. Designer of games

f   1912 Milton E. Moss, Hartford, Conn. Games

g   1912 Rustico, Wheeling, W. Va. Games

h   1912 Kratz-Boussac, Paris. Games of Loto of all kinds

j   1912 Mme Angèle Pècheur, Paris. Designer of games

k   1912 Hermann W. Fachmann, Indianapolis

l   1912 Otto May, Chemnitz. Puppen etc

m   1912 Summers Brown, London, England. Games

n   1912 Louis J. Eppinger, Detroit, Mich. Games

p   1912 O. Newman Co, Los Angeles, Cal. Games

q   1912 Albert E. Lenz, Perth Amboy, NJ. Games

r   1913 Francis C. Wallace, Drummond, Md. A game

s   1913 The Pastimes Novelty

Co Inc, New York, NY. Games

t   1913 William Krause, Wittenberge. Social games

u,w   1914 Madame Angéline Rousselet, 132 rue de Rivoli, Paris. Designer

v   1914 Einer L. Grondahl, Seattle, Wash. Games

x   1914 John Jaques & Son, London, England. A game

y   1914 William H. Huff, Los Angeles, Cal. Games and puzzles

z   1914 Martin Kuërs, Berlin. 'Doppel-Spielzeug' = Backgammon

Minetto b

Feldzugsspiel Asakir. d

Blockato e

Riba j

„Rauten-Spiele" k

"LE ZANZINET" JE SAIS TOUT n

COIN-COIN r

SELECT 'ZANZI s

LE TOUT-VA! t

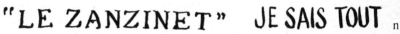

a 1914 A. Sala, Berlin. Games to delight the hearts of children
b 1914 Adolf Ulshöfer, Frankfurt. Toys & games
c 1915 J. Rotschild, Offenbach/Main. Toys
d 1915 Fritz Schubert, Würzberg. Toys & games
e 1916 Adam Nette, München. Games
f 1916 Heinr. Zahren, Frankfurt. Toys
g 1919 Emil Hartmann, Hermsdorf. Games

h 1917 Edward Bilz, Radebeul-Oberlosznitz, Games
j 1919 Richard Bauer GmbH, Nürnberg
k 1919 A. Thurnauer Sen, Burgkundst, Bayern
l 1920 Julius Blasz, Wisman. A game with dice
m 1921 Alphonse-Louis-Joseph Martinache, Paris. Games & toys. A game
n 1922 Les Inventions Nouvelle, 14 rue Martel, Paris. Games & toys

p 1922 Louis Beutier, 11 rue Saint Ambroise, Paris. Games
q 1921 Soc Roevens Père et Fils, 36 avenue Jean-Jaurès, Paris. Games
r 1922 A. F. P. de Donats, 5 rue Vaucanson, Paris. Games & toys
s 1922 Paul-Ulysse Tellène, 82 rue Chevallier, Lavallois-Perret. Games
t 1922 Harry Bernard, 122 Quai Jemmapes, Paris. Games

7. INDOOR GAMES AND PASTIMES

The majority of marks collected for building bricks belong to the end of the nineteenth century and the first ten years of the twentieth and come from Germany. Stone building bricks were made from ground stone, the powder being mixed with other ingredients to form bricks which were made in moulds. Cubes, rectangles, triangles at first, and later on arches for making bridges. These are shown in the mark registered by Fleischmann & Bloedel in 1901. Richter's firm became the most well known in the toy world, but the cut-out chimney brick to fit over a roof at 45° was devised years later by Lott of England.

Among bricks with pictures were 'Scripture' bricks, small oblong pieces of wood with a Biblical incident on one side and a text on the other.

The construction outfit known as Meccano was made in England in 1908, and contained strips of metal perforated with holes and packets of nuts and bolts, together with a few wheels, depending on the size of the outfit. By 1911, Meccano was registered in England, by 1912 in Berlin, and much later in 1921 in France.

Erector sets were made by Alfred Gilbert in 1913, and many of the construction kits when assembled could be made to work with steam engines.

The firm of Pellerin in eastern France was well known for printed sheets with plans, elevations etc. for the making of three-dimensional models in paper. The celebrated printing works were at Epinal at the end of the nineteenth century. Pantins, Hampelmänner and figures for the Théatre Guignol were produced in 1880 and during the next ten years their cut sheets became famous. Amongst these were villages, stations, locomotives and later on were ships, battleships and submarines, and some cut-outs which could be worked by sand. The flat sheets came first, then the three-dimensional models and the name Planches d'Epinal became connected with cut-outs.

Lothar Meggendorfer's animated books with threads and tabs were between 1847 and 1925, thus he was 78 when he died about 50 years ago. Talking picture books and peep-box pictures known as Guckkastenbild were made by Schreiber of Esslingen, Scholz of Mainz and by Pollock in England.

Paper patterns were made by W. Payne & Son, dolls' paper clothes by Raphael Tuck, and Dean & Son put out Dolly's Wardrobe. Decalcomania, that is transfers, known as Chromos in France and Scraps in England were collected and stuck in albums by the late Victorians and by Edwardian children.

Friedrich Fröbel established his first school near Rudolstadt, the home of the Richter Building Bricks. The Fröbel method of teaching led to toys which were made especially to encourage children to use their hands. The first 'Kindergarten' was opened in Germany in 1837 and the equipment included cut paper, wooden blocks, raffia, cane, and simple puzzles. Soon other Kindergartens opened.

In the USA Milton Bradley became interested. He had made a board game called the 'Checkered Game of Life' in the 1860s which became popular owing to its high moral tone and now in the 1870s he became involved in the Fröbel movement and produced a 'Kindergarten Alphabet'. Other toys were building blocks with numerals and animals, painting and crayon outfits, and sheets of lithographed paper. These lithographs were for cutting into three-dimensional villages or to cover wooden trains. The jig for cutting jig-saws appeared in 1872.

The most famous of numbered boards for playing board games was the French Game of Goose, and many others followed. Some were played with dice as in Snakes and Ladders, and there were other games without numbered boards such as Ludo and all the variations of Chess and Halma. In 1904, Parker Brothers of Missouri, were awarded a gold medal for a board game with dice at the World's Fair at St Louis.

The Richter company is one of the oldest in Europe, supposedly founded as long ago as 1508. The first registered sign was in 1879, an anchor, and this device has been used in some manner ever since. The building bricks of F. Ad. Richter were patented in 1880 and on the boxes containing them was this label 'Caution, – Beware of quicklime imitations, and see that each box bears the Trade-Marks, the Anchor and the Squirrel'.

The address in London was 1 & 2 Railway Place, Fenchurch St EC and in New York it was at 30 Broadway, NY. In the nineteenth century there was a branch factory in Brooklyn and medals were awarded for their Ankerbaukasten in Paris in 1900 and also at St Louis in 1904.

Just before World War One, the American side of the Richter Blocks was purchased by Alfred C. Gilbert, owner of the Erecto Sets and the Mysto-Magic Company. This was in 1913. Although Richter's name is firmly associated with building bricks and 'mosaic' outfits, they had other commodities, not the least surprising being a sugar factory with chocolates, gingerbreads and fancy edibles, a far cry from stone bricks. Porcelain was also mentioned and by 1922 dolls were added to their list: leather and stuff dolls and separate doll's bodies.

1919 Kann & Co, Cöln. A board game. Note DRWZ

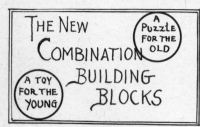

THE NEW COMBINATION BUILDING BLOCKS

A PUZZLE FOR THE OLD

A TOY FOR THE YOUNG

a

TESSELLA ROYALE b

UNIVERSAL

d

THE BROWNIE BLOCKS c

Feen-Glas-Baukasten e

FABRIKS-MARKE

f

GESETZL. GESCHUTZT.

·SCHUTZMARKE·

g

SCHUTZ-MARKE TRADE-MARK

h

Imperial Toy Building Bricks

j

ARCHITECTEN-KASTEN- MUNDUS k

Stella m

Diamant n

Le Castor

F & B PARIS

l

FABRIK MARKE

p

KREUZ-STEINBAU-KASTEN

q

Simplicissimus r   **Münchener Kindl** s   Der kleine Schwede. t

a   *1886 William Richardson, Poultry, London*

b   *1888 R. G. Powell, Manchester. Toys*

c   *1889 Palmer Cox (artist), Broadway, New York. Registered in England*

d   *1894 J. W. Arold, Nürnberg. Toys and wooden bricks*

e   *1898 Bernhard Pfretzschner, Dresden. Glasbaukasten, Baukasten mit Glassteinen*

f   *1897 Louis Engel, Blumenau*

i.S. Building bricks and toys

g   *1899 Leipziger Steinbaukasten–Fabrik Richard Zeife, Leipzig. Stone building bricks*

h   *1900 Edwin Feilgenhauer. Sächsische Dachsteinwerke und Steinbaukasten Fabrik, Lausigk. Stone bricks and stone dominoes, roofing stones and other little things*

j   *1901 Hamburger & Co, New York, with Zweigniederlassung in Berlin. Toys, dolls and other*

things for children

k   *1902 Wolf Kronheim, Hannover. Building bricks and wooden toys*

l   *1901 Fleischmann et Bloedel, Paris*

m   *1903 H. Fiedeler Commanditgesellschaft, Döhren vor Hannover. Stella Baukasten Fabrik. Toys, building bricks, etc*

n   *1903 Gebr Keller, Rudolstadt. Rudolstädter Steinbaukasten Fabrik. Childrens' playthings*

p   *1903 Carl Brandt jr Gösznitz, Sachsen. Building bricks, etc*

q   *1905 Sächsische Dachstein n Schamotte- Werke GmbH, Lausigk*

r   *1904 Harzer Werke 'Gluck Auf' Dr Rudolf Alberti, Eisenhütte. Toys and building bricks*

s   *1905 Xaver Sepp, Munchen. Baukasten*

t   *1908 S. F. Fischer, Oberseiffbach. Baukasten*

b

d

c

e

f

g

a   *1909 Edmund Hopf, Suhl i
Thür. Boxes of bricks*
c   *1910 Franz Sander, Cöln.
Steinbaukasten*
b,f   *1910 Max E. Werner,
Reichenbachi.V. Bäukasten*

d   *1912 Domusto Gesellschaft
mbH Oppurg. Steinbaukasten*
g   *1919 Chronoswerk GmbH
Schwenningen a N. Wooden
building bricks, wood and
earthenware bricks, metal, etc*

e   *1920 L. Kleefeld & Co,
Fürth. Toys, picture cubes, etc*

NOUVEAU JOUET UNIVERSEL

L'INNOCENT

Jeu de Constructions et de Combinalsons

(DÉPOSÉ)   e

SCHUTZ - MARKE

B.   Sch.

MARQUE   DEPOSÉE

TRADE - MARK   c

EURÉKA   d

MECCANO   f   „RAUHREIF"   g   RAYLO   h

BANGAROO   j   SIK-EM   k

ARTS & MÉTIERS   l

STRUCTO

m   TINKERTOY   n

LES ORIGINO'S   p

a   *1898 Wattilaux, Paris.*
'C'est la mere Michel, qui a
perdu son chat, qui cris par la
fenèt, qu'est-t-qui le lui
tendra?'
b   *1901 Marie Mackensen geb.*
Spilcke, Hannover. 'The Little
Dachdecker' meaning slater,
tiler or thatcher
c   *1900 Bernhard Karl Emil*
Scheer, tinsmith, Burgstädt.
Zerlegbare Metallspiel-
baukästen. Metal toys to take to
pieces
d   *1902 Kratz-Boussac, engineer,*
Paris. Construction games of all
kinds

1904 Alfred Rank, Wien-böhla.
Constructions for miniature
gardens. (Sign not included here)
e   *1905 Daniel Quintin,*
Pavillons-sous-Bois. Toys
f   *1908 Meccano Ltd, England*
g   *1909 Georg Schnabel,*
Limbach. Gardens of Paradise,
cribs, chemistry outfits, etc
h   *1911 Meccano Ltd, England.*
Mechanical Toys
1912 Meccano Gesellschaft,
Berlin
j   *1908 Alfred James Bartlett,*
Gloucester, England. Detached
pieces to join together

k   *1912 Sik-Em-Novelty Co,*
St Louis, Mo. Mechanical toys
l   *1911 Julius Bernhold, Paris.*
Construction toys
m   *1912 Thompson Manufactur-*
ing Co, Freeport, Ill. Building
material for mechanical toys
n   *1914 Charles H. Pajeau,*
Chicago, Ill. Games, toys and
children's building-blocks. A
construction toy with rods &
spools
p   *1912 Henri Twichet, à*
Antony. Découpages en bois,
voitures, animaux
q   *1913 Hermann Tietz, Berlin.*
Toys

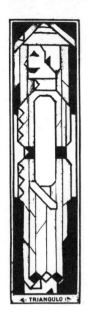

a

b

c

Combinator d

g

h

MECCANO f

Blumenfee j

k

e

l

a   *1913 Johann Korbuln, Berlin. Bauspielzeug, ie building toys*

b   *1914 Bill Deezy Co, Boston, Mass. Construction members*

c   *1914 Francis A. Wagner, Dayton, Ohio. Mechanical toys*

d   *1914 Adolf Schuhmann, Nürnberg. Toys, metal building bricks, construction toys*

e   *1916 Fernando Hace, Berlin.*

Toys and games and everything dealing with them

f   *1918 Märklin, Germany*

1921 Meccano (France) Ltd, 5 rue Ambroise-Thomas, Paris

g   *1922 Paul Schroeder Fabrikation von Modellspielwaren*

h   *1921 S. Gunthermann, Nuremberg. Mechanische Blechspielwarenfabrik*

j   *1922 Paul Reuter et Cie, Hertigswalde à Sebnitz. Scientific toys*

k   *1922 Soc Belasco Mechanics Corporation, 342 Madison Avenue, NY*

1922 Alfred James Bartlett, Gloucester, England. Detached pieces to join together

l   *1920 Martin Peter Anton Lorentzen, Hamburg. Toys*

a STENOCHROME *

b R

c

Lisette

LA FAVORITE d

LA PETITE MERCERIE e

„Era" f

RONDO g

POLLY'S PAPER PLAYMATES h

S.L.F.J.T. l

MARQUE DÈPOSÉE P.Y j

k

m Sharp-Shooters

n LITTLE FOLKS

s Bull in a China Shop

p TURN OVER

q LITTLE BOWLER

r *Tru-Life*

a,b 1876 Carl Heinrich Otto
Radde, Hamburg. Toys
c 1881 Dorn & Crandall. A
folding box toy, not a registered
mark
d 1901 Victor Bois, Lyon.
Playing cards, and cardboard
letters
e 1902 E. C. Laboureyras,
Paris. Haberdashery, paper
patterns, sewing, etc
f 1910 Rudolf Apel, Oberlind

S M. Toy paper animals
g 1910 Adolf Voglmayer,
Wien. Paper toys, etc
h 1911 Joseph P. Schiller
Syndicate, Baltimore, Md.
Paper dolls
j 1922 Yvonne Lelievre, 23 rue
de Constantinople, Paris.
Designer of dolls of very fine
materials & tissue paper
k 1921 Raphael Tuck & Sons
Ltd, Raphael House,

Moorfields, London. Toys,
especially of paper & card
l 1922 E. Rau et Cie Soc.
Lyonnaise pour la Fabrication
de Jouets en Tissus, 33 rue de
Vendôme à Lyon
Games by Milton Bradley
Milton Bradley, Springfield,
Mass, USA
m 1913 a game
n,p,q,r,s 1914 games. See also
Optical Toys

TOM TIDDLER'S A₉ B₉ C₉ AND 1₉ 2₉ 3₀ a

ENDLESS PUZZLE b

BIG BEN BANK E. A. Tice c

Heimchen am Herd d

PLASTO e

f

Hopp! Hopp! g

"ALRÉ" k

SCHUTZ-MARKE l

h

j

a   *1884 Louisa Hammon (spinster), 3 Sudeley Terrace, Kemptown, Brighton. A toy*

b   *1887 Perry & Co, Birmingham. A puzzle*

c   *1888 Edward Albert Tice, Middlesex. Toys*

d   *1897 C. Abel-Klinger. Toys, etc. Globes and picture-books of the World*

e   *1900 Plastographische Gesellschaft Pietzner & Co, Wien*

f   *1902 Bernard Keilich, Berlin. Toys, chalk and crayon manufacturers*

g   *1904 Gesellschaft für Patent Verbvertung mgH Leipzig. Instructive toys*

h   *1905 Société du Louvre, Paris. 'Jardin Botanique', an instructive toy*

j   *and 'géographie enfantine', also instructive*

k   *1905 Ad. Lee-witz, Paris. Alphabetic cubes, blocks of wood, etc*

l   *1905 Carl Throll, München. Toys for schools, etc*

NEVADUN
a

Jeu de Composition „Bubi"
b   c

LE TETRAGLOTTE
NOUVEAU JEU DES QUATRE LANGUES
d

Le Pratique
Méthode de Lecture
AVEC LETTRES MOBILES EN COULEURS
e

Das schwarze

Dreleck

f

" Artistique

Paris

Puzzle "
g

ZAG-ZAW
h

LES "PUZZLES" CB
j

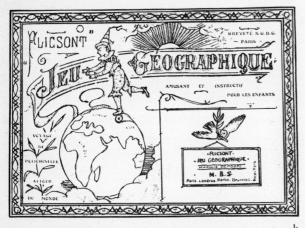

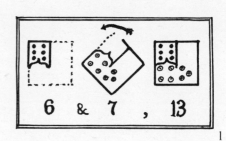

k

l

Nummerato
m

SILHOUETTE PUZZLE
n

---

a   *1907 Arthur Worsnop, 25 Union Street, Halifax, England*

b   *1906 Mathilde D. Leibenger, Bâle (Swisse). Alphabetic et dessin, for use in schools*

c   *1907 Berlinen Kunstanstalt, etc, Berlin. Steindruckerei, an earthenware printing outfit*

d   *1907 Passerat et Radiquet, 117 rue Michel-Bizot, Paris*

e   *1907 Celestin Arnaud, 178 Chemin des Chartreux, Marseille. A toy*

f   *1909 Rudolf Commans, Cöln. Educational toys. The wording around is Hochinteressantes Figuren-Spiel für jung und alt, ie for young and old*

g   *1910 Chevrel et Pied-chevrel, Paris. Designer of puzzle games*

h   *1910 Raphael Tuck & Sons*

Ltd, GmbH, Berlin. Games that can be put together or composed with patience

j   *1910 Georges Pinget, Paris*

k   *1909 B. Silisteanu, Paris. 'Un jeu géographique Flicsont'*

l   *1910 Adrien-Gédéon Gory, Paris. An instructive game*

m   *1911 Josef Fendt, München. Toys*

n   *1911 Pierre Landrieu, Paris. 'Jeux de Société'*

a

THE LITTLE MIND BUILDER b

c

Die ganze Welt im Sack d

e

f

Rollmops g

HAPPYNAK h

HARMONIE j

SPIELEND LERNEN – LERNEND SPIELEN k

MANIP l

Die kleinen Kästchenschmücker m

Zetes n

p

q

---

a *1912 Gilbert Wiart, Paris. Designer of a toy*

b *1913 Baker & Bennett Co, New York. Children's letter blocks*

c *1913 Forsheim & Konigsberg, NY. Puzzles*

d *1913 Waldemar Wendland, Berlin. Toys*

e *1914 Joshua Jerome Nordman, Wexford & Pittsburgh, Pa. Games*

f *1913 Tiernan Walton, Philadelphia, Pa. Toys*

g *1914 Wilhelm Lönholdt, Berlin. Toys & instructive games*

h *1915 The Matchless Metal Polish Co, Old Swan, Liverpool, England. Toys & instructive toys*

j & k *1918 Orion-Verlag GmbH, Leipzig. Mosaik games, Legespiele, and building bricks*

l *1919 G. Cottray, rue de Pierrefitte, Saint Denis. Boîtes de chimie, Chemistry outfits*

m *1919 Melitta Bentz geb. Liebscher, Dresden. Toys, cut-outs, papers, gums, etc*

n *1919 Zocher & Semmler, Leipzig-Connewitz. Toys, boxes, etc*

p *1920 Fernand Nathan, 16 rue des Fossés-Saint-Jacques, Paris. Educational games*

q *1920 Association pour la rééducation professionnelle des Mutilés, 102 rampe Magenta, Paris. Toys to help maimed children*

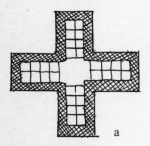

a

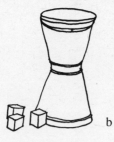

b

ROMETTE

d

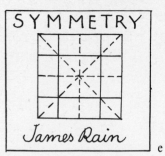

SYMMETRY

James Rain

e

REVERSI f   "REVERSI" g   *Jeu des Dames* j

HALMA

h

k

l

LAZARUS

m

Steeple
LAZARUS

n

Fortuna p

De Wet. q    *Würfel=Piano* r   **AHEP** s

---

a   *1876 James Asser, England. Manufacturer of games*

b   *1878 John Lilley, Manchester. Games*

c   *1883 Edward Falkener, Carmarthenshire. Game of the Bowl, Senet & Tau*

d   *1887 Edwin Leworthy (gentleman), Bromley, Kent. A game for board and pieces*

e   *1885 James Rain (mathematician), 1 Napier Villas, Waldegrave Road, Upper Norwood, Surrey. Games*

f   *1887 Lewis Waterman, Bristol. Boot and shoe manufacturer. A game similar to draughts*

g   *1888 Lewis Waterman, Bristol. The original game of Reversi for the Chessboard*

h   *1888 F. H. Ayres, London.*

j   *1891 Eugène Lavignac, Négociant à Bordeaux. The game of draughts*

k   *1898 Kölner-Stoffwäsche-Fabrik, Ehrenfeld, Köln*

l   *1899 August Wasmuth, Hamburg. Board games*

m,n   *1899 Jaques, London.*

Lazarius is the name of his agent in Paris. A game with dice

p   *1900 Richard Scholze, Dresden. Zahl & Spielbrettern. Number & gaming boards, games of chance*

q   *1901 August Scheel junr, Hamburg. Board games and with figures belonging to them*

r   *1901 Joseph Schindler, Berlin. Würfelspiele, ie games with dice*

s   *1901 August Hermann, Emil Peter Wehucke, Altona, Leichtstr. Board games*

SALTA SPIEL

Harras · Saletto · Saladin
Saletto Weltmeister · b

Salo · Sala · c
Salta-Spiel · d

ARCHIMEDES · e

Salta-Spiel
der Zunkunft · f

Salta
Saltanella · Saltadonna
Saltino · Sal · ta · santa · Saltone · g

Treis kai deka
13 · 13 · h

SNAKES AND LADDERS · p

Octo
8 · 8 · j

Ahoi · k

WIG · l

Delarey · m

Maha Rajah · n

L'INDISPENSABLE COMPTE-POINTS DE TOUS LES JOUEURS

q

---

a, b, c, d, e, f, g
1900 Salta-Versand von August Wasmuth, Hamburg. Board games
and
1901 Salta Spiel der Zunkunft, Salta Spiel etc games with chess boards

h, j   1902 Curt Sauer, Konigsberg i. Pr. Board games with cards and draughtboard games

k   1903 Henry Jacob, Berlin. Gesellschaftspiele and board games

l   1903 Theodor Heymann, Grosz-Olberdsorf i.S. Board games and their parts

m   1902 Ewald G. Schultze, Hamburg. Board games

n   1903 Christoph Thurnau, Dresden. A board game

p   1904 Snakes and Ladders

q   1904 Ernest Loriot, Marseille, designer of games especially those to do with counting and reckoning

105

STEEPLE-BILLES

Bilanz. Favorit „Hidda"

JE SAIS TOUT G. R.

Auf Leben und Tod.

Wyn-Kah

VAUEN

„Zepplin" Kombino

Arena

AERO CIRCUIT INTERNATIONAL AERO CIRCUIT NATIONAL
AERO CIRCUIT DU TOUR DE FRANCE AERO CIRCUIT D'EUROPE
AERO CIRCUIT DU TOUR DU MONDE Hus-sah

---

a 1904 Louis-Georges Degrange, Paris

b 1904 H. Rehse, Bukoba am Victoria Nyama (Deutsch-Ostafrika). Board games and dice

c,d 1904 Otto Heppe, Moschelmühle, Pfalz. A board game

e 1904 Dr Jacob Loevn, Graudenz. A board game

f 1906 Kratz-Boussac, Paris. A board game

g 1907 Auguste Robinot, Paris. Designer of a method of replacing the dice in the game of jacquet

h 1908 Jos. Süszkind, Hamburg. Toys, games, especially board games

j 1909 Gebhard Ott and Ziener & Ellenberger, Nuremberg. Games of chess and dominoes

k 1909 Emil Biersohn, Strasburg. A game with dice

l 1909 Hugo Rosenfeld, Nürnberg. Board games with coloured stones or pieces, counters, draughts, etc

m 1909 A. S. Milliaud, Paris. Designer of a game

n 1910 Theodor Klob, München. Board games & chessboards

p 1911 Tixier-Chauveau, Reuilly. Leather boxes for dice

q,r 1910 Henri Claude Soudan, designer of games with aeroplanes & other similar games

s 1910 Alfred Köhler, Berlin. Board games and novelties

Râmanâ
a

Krokonol
b

Fendt's
Schach-Mühle.
c

TEMCO
d

Lasca
e

f

TOY TOWN
g

h

Isch-Ga-Bibbel
k

Fehde
l

Zwei neue Spiele und zwei alte Spiele

Feldgrau   Dame

und   Oder   AZ   Marke   und

Schwarzweißrot   Mühle

auf jedem Dam- und Mühlbrett zu spielen.

j

m

a   *1910 William Buron, Berlin. Ringbrettspiel, a game played on a board*

b   *1911 Nieskner, Holzindustrie GmbH Niesky O/L. Dice and tossing games*

c   *1912 Josef Fendt, München. Games, chess, draughts, etc*

d   *1912 Tower Manufacturing & Novelty Co, NY. Dice, Dominoes, Cribbage boards, etc*

e   *1912 Hans Joseph, Schöneberg, Germany. A game,*

square boards with divisions, squares or spots in rows, played with discs or round pieces

f   *1913 Frank K. Atkins, Philadelphia, Pa. A gameboard*

g   *1913 Parker Bros, Portland, Me. & Salem, Mass. Children's Toys and Games, board games and card games*

h   *1914 Tower Manufactory & Novelty Co, New York. Dominoes etc*

j   *1915 Züllchower Anstalten, Züllchow. Games. Mühle is draughts*

k   *1914 Parker Bros. A spinning game*

l   *1916 Walther Knoop, Cöln-Ehrenfeld. Board games*

m   *1922 Manufactures Française d'Ameublements, 20 rue Saint-Joseph, Saint Etienne*

 a

SPOOF b

 d

 e

 c

JABE f

 g

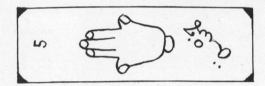 h

 j

 k

Gummoid l Lithoid m

 n

Padischah p

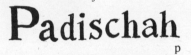

Flotte q "TRUST" r

GOLLIWOGG u

L'ARCHE DE NOÉ v

 s

 t

---

a 1866 Jaques, 102 Hatton Garden, London

b 1889 Ayres. The new game of Spoof

c 1893 Louis Gervais, Médicin à Rouen. Sign stamped on the playing cards for use of blind people

d 1899 A. Camoin et Cie, Marseilles. Playing cards

e 1899 Vereinigte Stralsunder Spielkarten Fabriken A–: G. Stralsund

f 1899 M. Arnodin, constructor, Paris. A game of cards

g,h 1900 Fossorier Amar et Cie, Paris. This mark goes on the cards & on their other games & toys

j 1900 Léopold Tourel, Avignon. Playing cards

k 1900 G. J. Pabst, Nuremburg. Cards and table-games, etc

1900 Emil Zipper & Co, Hamburg. A card game called Double Heads

l, m 1901 Nockler & Tittle, Schneeberg. Playing cards

n 1901 Joh. Pet. Bürger, Cöln. Playing cards. Bürger Kölnische Spielkarten

p 1904 Steidtmann & Nagel, Hamburg. A card game

q 1905 Otto Blank, Hamburg. Playing cards

r 1905 G. Laurent et Cie, Paris. A card game

s,t,u,v 1905 Thos de la Rue et Cie, traders in Paris for designers of illustrated card games. Printed in all colours

L'ENFANTIN
b

c

POPINTAW
(Prononcez Popineto)
d

SIAOSI
f

g

DÖRWALDS GESELLSCHAFTSSPIEL h

PIT k

j

l

a   1905 Curt Sauer, Konigsberg.
A social game

b   1906 Louis-Albert Grossiant.
Professor of Music, Paris. A
game of musical cards

c, d, e, g   1908 Landrieu, Pierre,
19 Ivy Lane, London

f   1910 David Morrison,
Gisborne, New Zealand.
Card games

h   1908 Richard Dörwald,
Stadthagen. Playing cards

j   1908 Soc des Politiques et
Littéraires, Paris

k   1908 Parker Bros, Portland,
Maine, & Salem, Mass.
Card games

l   1911 Charles-Joseph-Jules
Boespflug et Henri Allaire,
Paris. Designer of illustrated
cards with separate pieces to
form the game of patience

a *1912 Chas. Gilbert Shaw,*
   Bloomington, Ind. A parlour
   game of cards
b *1912 Askyo-Deler-Vantage*
   Co Inc, Baltimore, Md. Playing
   cards
c *1912 Peter D. Keim,*
   Kalamazoo, Mich. A card game
d *1912 Flinch Card Co,*
   Kalamazoo, Mich. Games
e,j *1912 Parker Bros, Portland,*
   Me. & Salem, Mass. Card
   games

f *1912 Standard Playing Card*
   Co, Chicago, Ill. Playing cards
g *1912 The Check Game Co,*
   Hiram, Ohio. Playing cards
h *1912 Watson W. Ayres,*
   West Allis, Wis. Combined
   numerical card & die games
k *1913 Lucy D. Wheelock,*
   Weedsport, NY. A game of
   cards
l *1913 Milton Bradley,*
   Springfield, Mass.

m *1913 Allen L. Peckham,*
   Chicago, Ill. A card game
n *1914 Louis Rodney Berg,*
   NY. A playing card
p *1914 John A. Phillips,*
   Englewood, NJ & NY. A
   card game
q,r *1914 Parker Brothers,*
   Portland, Me. & Salem, Mass.
   Card games

a

 b

 c

 d

Anchor⚓Box e

Pythagoras f

Nicht zu hitzig g

Zornbrecher h

Quälgeist j

Kreuzspiel k

Sternrätsel l

Kopfzerbrecher m

Blitzableiter n

Ei des Columbus p

Grillentöter q

Geduldprüfer r

Komet s

⚓ t

Sphinx u

Kobold v

Alle Neune w

Ruhig Blut x

Triumph y

Märchen. z

Anker-BrückenbauKasten a¹

Rudolstädter Anker-SteinbauKasten b¹

Richter's Rudolstädter Brückenbaukasten c¹

Rudolstädter BrückenbauKasten d¹

Volksfreund f¹

Meteor g¹

Saturn h¹

 e¹

 j¹

a 1879 F. Ad. Richter & Cie, Nürnberg. Toys and toy blocks

b 1879 F. Ad. Richter & Cie, Königl, Landgericht zu Nürnberg

c 1886 Children's games, instructive games, building blocks, thinking games, the inlaying and arranging of things of different sizes, shapes and colours

d 1886 Boxes of assorted bricks

e 1888 Building stones in three colours

1894 Registers his elaborate label as a surround for his box lids

f–q 1895 Ten registered names for Legespiele, games in which the aim is to win, played with counters and dice, usually on a board

r 1896 Another Legespiele

s 1896 Steinbaukasten. Building bricks

t 1896 Building bricks

u 1899 Legespiele, ie winning games, counters, etc to go with them

v 1899 Winning games and viewing apparatus. A kobold is a goblin

w, x, y, z 1899 Games

a¹, b¹, c¹, d¹ 1901 Building bricks, including blocks for arches and bridges, etc. Kindergarten games, but not lead pencils or colour pastels

e¹, f¹, g¹, h¹, j¹ 1902 Pattern making etc, arranging of coloured balls in cardboard holes, etc

Freya

c

Karola

Mosaikspiel für junge Mädchen

d

a

b

Jugendfreund

e

Richter's SteinbauKastenfabrik

f

Imperator

j

Richter's SteinBauKasten g

Richter's SteinbauKasten h

k

n

p

l m

Das Wunderei

q

r

s

t

u

v

w

x

y

a,b *1902 Dolls and mouth harmonicas*

c *1903 Mechanical musical instruments and imitation stone bricks*

d *1903 Arranging of mosaic stones for young girls*

e *1903*

f,g,h *1903 Building bricks, stein meaning earthenware*

j *1905*

k *1906*

l *1907*

m *1914*

n *1914*

p *1912 The Magic Egg*

q *1917*

r,s,t *1917*

u,v,w,x,y *1918*

a

b

c

d

Dürer Steinbaukasten e

Richter's Ankerbaukasten Dürer g

f

h

j

k

l

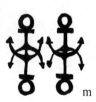

m

n

a   *1916–1918*
b,c,d   *1918 Variations of the original anchor sign*
e,g   *1917 Building bricks*

f   *1917 Construction outfits*
h,j,k,m,n   *1918 More anchor signs*

l   *1919 Building bricks. Registered as usual by F. Ad. Richter & Co, Rudolstadt i Müir*

Doll by Alice Couterier (and opposite). Bisque head, fair hair wig, unpierced ears, blue eyes. Mark on waist front. In original silk gown trimmed with real lace, hooped petticoat and drawers. Purse, handkerchief, fob watch and gloves. Elastic-sided boots with soles marked C C.

French *c.*1860 Doll 17½″ tall Shoes 2⅛″ long

From Newbury Museum

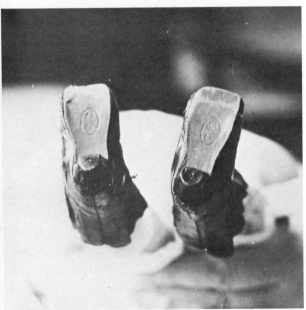

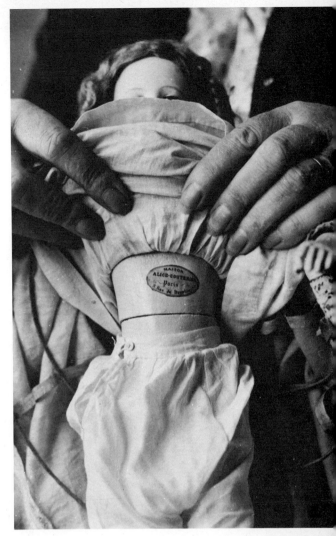

Not many of the 'Queen Anne' dolls were actually made during the reign of Queen Anne, 1701–14. They were hand carved and unmarked, and later were made by settlers across the Atlantic. Sometimes turned on a lathe and home-dressed, no two are alike, the features on the ladies being highly carved whereas those of the children are more rounded. Eyes were set in grooves, sometimes of enamel, sometimes of glass, with or without pupils. The child ones were definitely playthings but the 'ladies' could have been miniature fashion models or even figures for a crèche.

Dolls, carts with cupids etc were used for table decorations in the eighteenth century, and later put on the actual cakes for weddings and christenings – made of unglazed china, they exactly matched the icing sugar, and later became known as *sugar-bisques*.

8 February 1753. 'The last branch of our fashions into which the observation of nature has been introduced, is our desserts . . . jellies, biscuits, sugar-plums and creams have long given way to harlequins, gondoliers, Turks, Chinese, and sheperdesses of Saxon china. But these, unconnected, and only seeming to wander among groves of curled paper and silk flowers, were soon discovered to be too insipid and unmeaning. By degrees whole meadows of cattle, of the same brittle materials, spread themselves over the whole table: cottages rose in sugar, and temples in barley-sugar; pigmy Neptunes in cars of cockle-shells triumphed over oceans of looking-glass, or seas of silver tissue . . . confectioners found their trade moulder away, while toymen and china shops were the only fashionable purveyors of the last stage of polite entertainments.'

Dresden porcelain was first made in 1709 by J. F. Böttger at the Royal Factory, but in 1710 it was transferred to Meissen, not very far away. The child's head of 1770 is rather like that of a doll. Copenhagen ware has been produced since 1772.

Dolls lend themselves to being made in moulds whether it be papier mâché, porcelain, pottery or wax. This is because the heads and limbs are made separately and then joined by materials such as leather or linen which is firmly stuffed before being assembled.★ The early wooden dolls before-mentioned had their limbs joined in this manner.

★Later figures were joined by wire or elastic

Stuffed bodies could be of coarse linen, but calico was expensive – 'In 1776, Thomas Duxbury of Rishton, near Blackburn sold to Messrs Peel, Yates & Co Church Bank, two common-fine pieces for £5, 9s, 8d. These were the first calico pieces ever manufactured in this kingdom. Pieces of the same description are now sold for about 5s. 6d, or 6s each'. (Morning Post, 5 October 1829.) By the 1760s many large wooden dolls were fitted with ball-joints.

Most pottery wares could be produced in a simple two-part mould but a detail which should not be overlooked is that the original former is usually made over-size to allow for shrinkage during firing. Therefore in a reproduction from a finished head, where the mould has been taken from the copy, the result will be a slightly smaller article.

Napoleon III married Eugénie de Montijo in 1853 and for many years she was a favourite subject for dolls with parian heads and those with hair and head moulded in one. Her own hair was of a reddish tinge. They both visited London in 1855 and in August Queen Victoria and Prince Albert visited Paris for the French Exhibition.

In 1862 the word '*bébé*' was used for the first time in the doll marks. This was by Jules Steiner for a doll which could talk and was named *Bébé Parlant*. It must be remembered that whenever the word *Bébé* is incorporated in a mark it will be for a *child* doll and not for a curved limbed baby doll. The latter did not arrive until about 1909 or 1910.

Not many of the French Parisiennes are marked. It points to the fact that the dolls were probably made before 1875. There is a beauty in Hatfield House with the initials C C on the soles of her shoes and the Alice-Couterier stamp marked on her body.

The letters F G within an oval with two spirals at either end belong to the mark of Gesland. Although the entry in the Patent Office mentions A Gesland which might be mistaken for an initial, it is really a Gesland without a full-stop. The French entries, for example, read 'A Maelzel' or 'A Girard' just as one might say a Brown when referring to Mr Brown. The full entry is 'A Gesland, Fque de Bebes & Tetes Incassables Bte S.G.D.G. Reparations en tout genres, 5 & 5 Bis rue Berangeren Boutique, Paris'.

A novelty was a double-faced doll patented by Bru Jne & Cie in 1873. The face on the front was awake, the one at the back was asleep. Another doll with more than one face is the well-known one patented by Fritz Bartenstein of Huttensteinach. He describes his thus 'Whereas in Checkeni's invention the doll-head turns on a horizontal axis pivoted in the sides of the wig-frame, the doll-head herein turns on a verticle spindle secured to the body of the doll'.

Dolls had become more and more intricate and it is interesting to read in the Journal of Beatrix Potter that Mrs Gladstone would actually buy dolls just to see the way in which they were made.

Axel Munthe, in 1898, remarked that 'the German doll manufacturers,

a¹   *Label on doll's tummy. A fashion doll of about 1870 in the Newbury Museum*

b¹   *Shoes worn by Couterier doll. Label found on the sole*

c¹   *A Gesland mark*

d¹   *Another Gesland mark*

e¹   *Carl Bergner. His mark on body of doll with two faces*

incapable themselves of producing pretty and expressive doll faces, buy their doll heads by retail from the porcelain factories of Montreux and St Maurice, where they are modelled by first-rate artists, such as Carrier-Belleuse and others'.

Separate bisque heads and yokes were joined to soft, sawdust-stuffed bodies of pink material. These dolls were cheaper than the ones with jointed composition bodies, but were certainly not to be despised. The little Princess Beatrice had one in her room at Osborne, the advantage being that they were soft to hold and they stayed put whether sat up on a chair or laid down in bed, and their black-stockinged legs looked well with black shiny shoes and buckles.

It was in 1904 that Charles Bergner patented his changeable faces on one head, the initials C B appearing on the yokes of some of these dolls.

Although the flirting eyes had been on the market for a few years, at the Paris Exhibition of 1907 they were one of the attractions. Celluloid dolls became popular about 1908.

By 1918 children began to wear their frocks much shorter in length and to show their knees. This meant that dolls in the fashion had to have their legs better finished, therefore the joint was placed well above the knee instead of below as in the days before the First World War.

The 1870's

a

b

c

d

e

POUPÉE NANA f

a 1870 Clarke, Nicholls & Combe, Hackney Wick, Middlesex, England. Dolls, toys and edible figures

b 1876 Louis Schmetzer & Cie, Rottenburg. Toy manufacturers, playthings, dancing dolls etc.

c 1876 Scheller & comp, auf der Bohrmühle bei Schmalkalden. Dolls

d 1876 Berthold Eck, Unternenbrunn, Thuringia. Dolls & Christening dolls

e 1879 John Wheeler, 15 Newgate St, London. Toys, dolls & dolls' dresses

f 1879 Gregori-Olivier, France. A doll

a   1880 Emily Dorcas Godfrey, Sarah Godfrey, and Catherine Maria Godfrey, 30 George Street, Croydon, Surrey. Doll manufacturers

b   1881 E. Escher jun, Sonneberg. Dolls, etc

c   1881 Fleischmann & Craemer in Sonneberg. Toys, dolls, etc

d   1883 Gebhard Ott, Steinbühl

e   1883 John Batt & Co, London, England

f   1884 Paul Sevette aîné, Paris. Maker of toys

g   1884 Müller & Froebel, Sonneberg. Toys

h   1884 L'Union des Fabricants de Jouets, France

j   1885 Carl Geyer & Co, Sonneberg. Dressed dolls

k   1885 Benoit fils et Romain, Paris. Jouets

l   1885 A. Nörregaard, Hamburg. Spielwaaren

m,n   1885 Adolphe Falck, Paris. (Falck Roussel). Mark stamped on the dolls & on the boxes containing them

p   1886 Jacques-Adolphe Sommer, manufacturer à Paris

q   1886 Gebrüder Haag in Sonneberg. All kinds of dolls in imitation biscuit & washable

s   1887 Louis Neumann, Germany

t   1887 Théophile Lanagnère, Paris

u   1887 Carl Hauser, Leipzig

r,v,w,x,y   1887 Henry Delcroix, manufacturer à Montreuil. Mark engraved on the dolls' heads

z   1887 A. & J. Isaacs, 33 Houndsditch, London. Wholesale doll importers and Dressers. Dolls dressed and undressed

a¹   1888 Francois Emile Marseille, fabricant a Maisons-Alfort. Unbreakable jointed dolls

b¹   1888 Frédéric Rémignard, négociant, Paris

c¹   1888 Gebrüder Schelle, in Bohrmüle bei Schmalkalden

d¹   1888 La dame veuve Leredde (née Leonie Alphonsine Monnet) & Charles Eugène Sonnet. Mark incised or raised on the doll's head

e¹   1888 M. Leconte, rue Charlot 35, Paris

f¹   1889 Saunier & Caux, Paris

a

b

c

d

H&C 55
e

BÉBÉ MASCOTTE f

g

h

j

k

l

m

n p q

AI r A1 s

MARQUE DÉPOSÉE

BÉBÉ-SOLEIL t

u

v

marque déposée a¹

Bébé le Favori w

Bébé Favori x

y

z

MÉNAGE PARISIÉN b¹

BÉBÉ FRANÇAIS c¹

Bébé Loulou d¹

BÉBÉ PETIT PAS e¹

a 1890 Marie Dégenetais Legros, Saint-Maur-les-Fossés

b,c 1890 B. Harratz, Böhsen

d 1890 Albéric du Val, Paris

e 1890 Hinrichs & Co, New York, NY. Dolls. Makers & Importers

f 1890 May Brothers, merchants, Paris, designers of jointed dolls

g 1890 J. F. Pflaumer & Co, Weitzenberg, Germany

h 1891 Hugo Fehr, Hamburg

j 1891 Victor Tuckmann & Co, Invicta Works, London. Toys and dolls

k 1891 E. A. Grimm & Co, Hamburg

l 1891 Otte, Janns & Co, Hamburg

m 1891 Rösing Brothers & Co, London

n,p,q,r,s Achenbach & Co, Hamburg

t 1891 Jean Marie Guépratte, maker, Paris. Mark stamped on the dolls & on their boxes

u 1891 Gobillot et Samson, Paris

v 1891 Oscar Blank, Hamburg. Toys

w,x 1891 Cosman Frères, Paris. Designers of dolls & other toys

y 1891 Jules-Joseph Jeanson, Paris

z 1891 Charles-Auguste Watilliaux, Paris. Maker of toys

a¹ 1891 Germain Rousseaux, France

b¹ 1891 Gaston Monteux, Paris

c¹ 1891 Danel et Cie, manufacturers a Montreuil-sous-Bois. At one time worked with Jumeau

d¹ 1891 Wannez et Rayer, Paris

e¹ 1891 Paul Girard, France. Agent for Bru

a

b

c

d

LE PARISIEN e

BABY RUTH h

BÉBÉ LÉGER j

f

g

Splendide Bébé k

BÉBÉ MODERNE l

BÉBÉ PHÉNIX n

POUPÉE FRANÇAISE p

m

BÉBÉ FAVORI q

POUPÉE-SATIN

s

IDÉAL BÉBÉ t

r

u

v

w

x

y

a *1892 Paul Perret, Paris*

b *1892 E. Pelletier, Marseille. Stamped on the boxes containing the dolls & toys*

c,d *1892 Wedeses & Co, Hamburg. Dolls*

e *1892 Amédée-Onesime Lafosse, Paris. Designer of dolls (both poupées & babies)*

f,g *1893 P. Franken, 35 rue N.D. de Nazareth, Paris*

h *1893 Craemer & Heron, Sonneberg*

j *1893 Chalory (Widow). France*

k *1893 Cosman Frères, Paris*

l *1893 P. H. Schnitz, Paris*

m *1894 B. Harrasz, Böhlen, Thuringia*

n *1895 Madame Marie Lafosse, fabricant à Paris. Designer of dolls (poupées)*

p *1894 Toulouse, rue Saint Merri 24, Paris. A jointed doll*

q *1893 Clément Catusse, Paris*

r *1894 Carl Adam, Konigsberg*

s *1894 Marignac, rue Oudinot 6, Paris. Doll-unbreakable*

t *1894 Bortoli Frères, négociants à Marseille. Designer of dolls (bébés)*

u *1895 Hermann Landshut & Co, Waltershausen. Dolls and doll parts (bébés)*

v *1895 Emil Bauersachs, Sonneberg. Dolls (bébés)*

w *1895 Max Dannhorn, Nürnberg*

x *1895 Heinrich Weisz, Sonneberg. Dressed dolls (bébés)*

y *1895 Hamburger & Co, New York*

BÉBÉ OLGA a

JL PARIS b

Trade.Marks c

LA CHARLOTTE d

AMOUR–BÉBÉ e

Cinderella Baby f

W. X. PARIS g

Cinderella Baby Nº
Eyes...... a girl with dwarfs Hair...... h

Trade-Mark Fabrik-Marke
Germany. m

FABRIKS-MARKE j

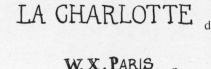

C. & S. k

Globe Baby n

LE RÊVE DE BÉBÉ
Montre à Remontoir
DÉPOSÉE t

BÉBÉ ARTICULÉ p

PHÉNIX-BABY q

BÉBÉ-LIÉGE r   BABY s

BÉBÉ MONOPOLE.V.G. u

BÉBÉ MÉTROPOLE.V.G. v

BÉBÉ LE SELECT.V.G. x

BÉBÉ EXCELSIOR.V.G. w

---

a *1896 Ernest Ballu, commissionnaire of merchandise, Paris. Designer of dolls (poupées)*

b *1896 Delhaye Frères, Paris. Designers of games & toys*

c *1896 E. Escher, Sonneberg*

d *1896 Madame veuve Soulard, rep. by Good, rue de Rivoli 70, Paris*

e *1896 Louis Guillet, Paris. Designer of dolls (poupées)*

f,h *1897 C. M. Bergmann, Waltershausen. Dolls*

g *1896 Charles–Auguste Watilliaux, manufacturer, Paris*

j *1898 Louis Engel, Blumenau*

k *1898 Curner & Steiner, Sonneberg & New York*

l *1898 Carl Hartmann, Neustadt b. Coburg. Dressed dolls of all kinds*

m *1898 J. Franz, Sonneberg i Th. Dressed dolls of all kinds*

n *1899 Carl Hartmann, Neustadt b. Coburg. Dressed dolls*

p *1899 Friedr. Edmund Winkler, Sonneberg. Doll manufacturer, jointed dolls*

q,r,s *1899 Jules Mettais, Paris. Dolls, both poupées and bébés*

t *1899 Albert Migault, Paris*

u,v,w,x *1899 Verdier et Cie, manufacturers, Paris. Designer of dolls (bébés)*

BÉBÉ MODÈLE

a

b

c

d

POUPÉE MERVEILLEUSE e

"LA PARISIENNE" f

"BÉBÉ MODÈLE" g

Salta h **Dewey Doll** j **Gummoid** k **Lithoid** l

Dornröschen m

Little Sweetheart. n

p

q

r

s

t

u

OLD GLORY v

a   *1900 Madame Caroline Rivaillon à Argenteuil. Dolls*
b   *1900 Sylvian Thalheimer et Cie, Paris. Dolls*
c,d   *1900 Carl Geyer, Sonneberg. Dolls*
e,g   *1900 Jules Mettais, Paris. A doll*
f   *1900 Auguste Martin, Paris. A doll*
h   *1900 Auguste-Louis-Martin-Albert-Wasmuth, merchant, Hamburg. A doll*

j   *1900 Gebrüder Süszenguth, Neustadt, Coburg*
k,l   *1901 Nockler & Tittel, Schneeberg, Germany. Material for dolls' heads*
m   *1902 Otto Krampe, Schalksmühle*
n   *1902 Max Illfelder, Bayern. Dolls*
p   *1902 Klen & Hahn, Ohrdruf, Thuringia. Doll manufacturers*

q   *1902 Franz Schmidt & Co, Georgenthal, Thüringia. Dolls, etc*
r   *1902 Bernhard Richter, Cöln*
s   *1902 Heinrich Steiner, Schalkau*
t   *1902 A. Wislizenus, Waltershausen. Jointed dolls*
u   *1902 Carl Geyer, Sonneberg*
v   *1900 Hamburger & Co, New York. Dolls*

POUPÉE·SANVER'S a

BÉBÉ LE PETIT FRANCAIS c
BÉBÉ LE GLORIEUX d

BÉBÉ LE RADIEUX e

BÉBÉ LE SPÉCIAL f

BÉBÉ L'UNIQUE g

L'HEUREUX l

h

Puppe der Zukunft m

Rosebud b

ETOILE BÉBÉ j

PALADIN BABY k

Poupon Parisiana n

Poupée Parisiana p

Bébé Parisiana q

American Queen r   GENTIL BÉBÉ s   Noris t   "Y-Do-I." u

Das süsse Trudelchen v   "LITTLE SWEETHEART" w

L'Idéal x   **L'AIGLON** y    d¹

z

BÉBÉ MONDAIN a¹   Baby Violet b¹   Princess Royal e¹

DOLLIT c¹   The Princess Doll f¹

---

a   1903 P. Vercasson et Cie, Paris

b   1903 Max. Illfelder, Fürth, Bayern. Dolls

c,d,e,f,g   1904 Claude-Valery Bonnal, Vincennes, France. Dolls

h   1904 Emil Pfeiffer, Wein. Vertr. Dolls

j   1904 Bernheim & Kahn, Paris. A doll

k   1904 Carl Hartmann, Neustadt, Germany. Dolls

l   1905 Louis L'Heureux, Paris

m   1904 Gebrüder Süszenguth, Coburg, Germany

n,p,q   1905 Soc Anonyme du Comptoir General de la Bimbeloterie à Paris

r   1905 Otto Morgenroth, Sonneberg

s   1905 Hippolyte Naneau, Paris. A doll

t   1905 Carl Debes & Sohn, Bavaria

u   1905 Cole Ackermann Co, Cleveland, Ohio, USA

v   1905 Johannes Kriege, Magdeburg. Toys and doll parts, etc

w   1905 B. Illfelder & Co, New York, NY, USA. A doll

x   1906 Mille Blanche Fouillot, Paris. Dolls

y   1906 Kratz-Boussac, Paris. A doll

z   1906 Leon Snéquireff, Paris. Dolls from Russia

a¹   1906 Bernheim et Kahn, Paris. A doll

b¹   1906 Abraham & Strauss, Brooklyn, New York. A doll

c¹   1906 Annie Alice Ivimey, Manor Road, East Molesey, Surrey

d¹,e¹,f¹   1906 Strawbridge & Clothier, Philadelphia, Pa. Dolls

a

b

J.J. c

LE BEAU D'ABLE d

Angelo e

BABY f

BÉBÉ g

h

'Bébé l'Avenir' j

„Spielwarenhaus Puppenkönig" k

l

m

n

p

Mausi s

M P t

ALB q

r

Merry Widow u

L'IDÉAL v

BÉBÉ ORACLE y

w

z

LA FÉE AUX TRÈFLES x

LA FÉE AU TRÈFLE a1

LA FÉE AU GUI b1

BÉBÉ PROPHÈTE c1

LA FÉE BONHEUR d1

a   1907 Walter Edward Christie, 41 Charterhouse Square, London EC. Dolls

b   1907 Aubert & Papin, Vésénet, Versailles. Dolls, mechanical toys, etc

c   1907 Joseph Joanny, France

d   1907 Maurice Nicholas, Paris

e   1907 Charles Kendrick Gibbons, Surbiton, Surrey

f,g   1907 Gustave Philippart, France. Agents for dolls & toys

h   Rubbing from back of bisque dolls with cloth body

j   1907 Gutmann & Schiffnie, Nuremberg. A doll

k   1907 Balthasar Paul Birnich, Cöln

l,q   1908 Adolf Landsberger, Magdeburg. Dolls

m   1908 Anne Huet Lonquet et Eléonore Strady, Paris. Dolls

n   1908 Hermann Hachmeister, Sonneberg. Toys & dolls

p   1908 Marie-Félicienne Gosse, à Clefs. A doll

r   1909 Paul Hausmeister & Co, Göppingen

s   1908 Robert Carl, Köpplesdorf. Dolls & their parts

t   1908 Migault et Papin, France

u   1909 Max Illfelder, Bavaria

v   1909 M. Abrahams, Paris

w, x, y, z, a1, b1, c1, d1   1909 Madame E. Cayatte, née Marie Mommessin, Paris. Designer of dolls & bébés

 a
 b
 c
 d
 e
 f

 g
 h
 k
 l

j

Little Snookums
The Newlywed's Baby
m

 n

 r

PERSÉPHONE p

JOLI BÉBÉ q

LA PARISIENNE s

Tuff-A-Nuff t

 Buporit u

 w

 Marke: Harzwald x

 y

EUREKA z

VELVOKIN v

CHANTECLER a¹

a,l   1910 Klen & Hahn, Thuringia
b   1910 Catterfelder Puppenfabrik, Catterfeld, Thuringia
c,m   1910 Max Fr. Schelhorn, Sonneberg
d   1910 Franz Schmidt & Co. Georgenthal
e,f   Marks on dolls by Martin Winterbauer
g   1910 'Au Bébé Rose', Paris

h,j   1910 Sauleau et Rouaud, Paris
k   1910 P. R. Zierow, Germany
n   1910 Gans & Seyfarth, Waltershausen
p   1910 Jules Lindauer, Paris
q   1910 Jules Damerial et Charles Damerial, Paris
r   1910 Gerbaulet Freres, Paris
s,z   1910 Henri-Othon Kratz-Boussac, Paris
t   1910 Ad. Ernst Schuldt, Hamburg

u   1910 Baer & Proeschild, Thuringia
v   1910 Chatanooga Medicine Co, Chattanooga, Tenn.
w   1910 Hermann Hende, Dresden
x   1910 William Rohde Clausthal, Oberharz. Note there is no bugle on the tree
y   1910 Bawo & Dotter, East Orange, NJ & New York
a¹   1910 Aetna Doll & Toy Co

QUEEN
b

a

c

d

h

e

f

Mein Sonnenschein
j

g

"BÉBÉ-COIFFURE"
k

BURGESS
l

The Fairy Kid
m

BÉBÉ-OLGA
n

TWEE DEEDLE·
p

q

A. P.
r

s

MARY ALICE

Sixth Race
t

Yankee
u

Marceline
v

Pat-a-cake Baby
w

---

a,b   *1910 A. Wislizenus,*
Waltershousen

c   *1910 C. M. Bergmann,*
Walterhausen

d,f   *1911 Ernst Winkler,*
Sonneberg

e   *1911 Klen & Hahn,*
Ohrdurf, Thüringia

g   *1911 Gans & Seyfarth,*
Walterhausen

h,k   *1911 Gutmann et*
Schiffnie, à Nüremberg

j   *1911 Catterfelder Puppen-*
fabrik, Thüringia

l   *1911 P. Couturier et Cie,*
9 rue Saint-Ambroise, à Paris

m   *1911 Peter Scherf, Sonneberg.*
Dolls

n   *1911 Ernest Ballu, 76 rue*
Saint Denis, Paris

p   *1911 A. Steinhardt & Bro,*
NY. Dolls and their apparel

q   *1911 Edmond-Louis L'hotte,*
9 rue des Carbonnets à
Bois-Colombes

r   *1912 Arthur Pohl, 6 rue*
Notre-Dame-de-Nazareth,
Paris

s   *1911 Lena M. Scurlock,*
Kansas City, Mo. The portrait
and name being that of Mary
Alice Chipps. Dolls

t   *1911 James N. G. Singleton,*
Orlanda, Fla. Dolls

u   *1912 Mitred Box Co, New*
York, NY. Children's Dolls

v   *1912 A. Steinhardt & Bro,*
NY. Dolls

w   *1912 A. Luge & Co,*
Sonneberg

„Baby Betty" a

b

c

B.4.L d

e

LOOPING-BABY f

KONIGSKINDER g

Rönigskinder h

j

m

NINI KASPA k

LE PETIT HUMORISTE l

n

Cellunova p

s

FLINTEX q

r

w

„Jing-Go-Ring"
Doll t

HUG ME KIDDIES u

v

„Dotty" x

Ursula y

---

a   *1912 Butler Brothers GmbH, Sonneberg. Exporter of toys, dolls & games*

b,c   *1912 Madame Alexandre Delhaye, 12 rue du Chemin-de-Fer, à Villemonble*

d   *Rubbing from doll by Fred Britain*

e   *1912 Fred Britain, 6 rue du Delta, Paris. Designer of games & toys*

f   *1912 Louis Maillard, 18 rue du Château, à La Garenne-Colombes*

g   *1913 H. B. Claflin Co, New York. Dolls & Toys*

h   *1912 Koenig & Rudolph, GmbH, Walterhausen. Doll factory, especially Puppen*

j   *1913 Joseph G. Kaempfer, NY. A doll head*

k   *1912 Julius Bernhold, 9 rue des Petites-Écuries, Paris. An unbreakable, jointed, artistic bébé*

l   *1913 Albert Crétois, 30 rue d'Armenonville, à Neuilly-sur-Seine*

m,s   *1913 Ravenaz et Tabernat, 3 et 5 rue des Haudriettes, Paris*

n   *1913 Butler Bros GmbH, Sonneberg. A doll*

p   *1913 Klen & Hahn, Ohrdruf*

q   *1913 Northport Novelty Co, Northport, NY. Dolls*

r   *1913 Ernst Hofmann, Chemnitz. Manufacturer of material for making dolls & dolls' clothes*

t   *1913 Fritz Lutz, Sonneberg. Doll merchants, dolls and dolls' bodies*

u   *1913 Samstag and Hilder Bros, New York. Rag dolls*

v   *1913 Bernard H. Tompson, London, England. Toys*

w   *1913 Arthur Schoenau, Sonneberg. Doll*

x   *1913 Geo. Borgfeldt & Co, Berlin. Dolls*

y   *1913 E. W. Matthes, Berlin. Toy merchants, dolls, doll parts, wigs, clothes, furniture, etc*

THE SOLDIER'S BABY a

BABY COTTAGE b

The „Wide-Awake" Doll. c

GOSS d

DOLLY MINE e

TOTTIE g

Herka h

Dolly Pat travels j

SPORTFREUND m

"LE BÉBÉ„ k

"MONA LISA" n

p

s

TRÉSOR q

MON TRÉSOR r

t

Boy=Scouts u

---

a *1914 Elizabeth Boase, 9 Grafton Street, London, W*

b *1914 Laguione et Cie, Soc des Grands Magasins du Printemps, 64 Boulevard Haussmann, Paris. Maison d'enfants, désigner*

c *1914 Butler Brothers, Sonneberg. Exporter of dolls*

d *1914 W. H. Goss Ltd, Falcon Pottery, Stoke, 1858–1944*

e *1914 Carson, Pirie, Scott & Co, Chicago, Ill. Dolls*

f *1914 P. R. Zierow, Berlin. Dolls, and doll manufacture*

g *1914 Etta Lyon, Montclair, NJ. Dolls and dolls' clothes*

h *1914 Martha Köllner, geb. Lotter, Ilmenau, Thür*

j *1914 Richard Scherzer, Sonneberg*

k,l *1914 Marius Rocher, 19 rue Fontaine-au-Roi, Paris. Dolls, dolls' clothes, etc*

m *1914 B. & H. Kahn, Strasburg. Puppenfee-Sportfreund. Freund is friend, fee is a fairy*

n *1914 Gutmann et Schiffnie, Nüremberg, Allemagne. Dolls*

p,q,r *1914 Henry Rostal, 5 rue du Trésor, Paris*

s *1914 Rudolf Schneider, Sonneberg. Doll factory, dolls, dolls' heads, wood & papier mâché*

t *1914 Rehbock et Loewenthal, Fuerth. A doll*

u *1914 Gutmann & Schiffnie, Nürnberg. Dressed dolls*

MON PETIT RIMAILHO a

POUPÉE D'ARGONNE c

MON PETIT TRÉSOR b

LE VICTORIEUX

LA POUPÉE FRANÇAISE e

d

MON DADA f

 g

 h

DURAN MARX j

P&S k

m

n

BÉBÉ GLORIA

Made in Paris l

LUTECIA BABY

Made in Paris p

Baby Bud q

Harald r

Massolin s

---

a,b   1915 Leon Prieur, 19 rue
Michel-le-Comte, Paris. Dolls
c   1915 Mille Suzanne Bonvalet,
8 rue Severo, Paris. A doll
d   1915 D. Le Montréer, 9 rue
Charlot, Paris. Dolls, bébés &
poupées
e   1915 Marius Cornet, 8 rue
Constantine, Lyon. Dolls
f   1915 Laguionie et Cie, 64
Boulevard Haussmann, Paris
g   1915 Mille Gabrielle Verità,

40 avenue de la Bourdonnais,
Paris. Designer of dolls of all
kinds
h   1915 Louis-Aimé Lejeune,
66 Avenue du Bois-Guimier,
Saint-Maur-des-Fossés.
Designer, heads, arms & legs of
dolls
j,m,n   1915 Madame Max
Duran, 25 rue Fourcroy, Paris.
Designer of dolls
k   1915 Mille Marthe Guérin,

301 rue de Vaugirard, Paris.
Designer of dolls
l,p   1915 J-César Koch,
52 rue des Petites-Écuries,
Paris. Dolls
q   1915 Butler Brothers,
Sonneberg, Sachs-meingn.
A doll
r   1915 Wagner & Zetzsche,
Ilmenau
s   1915 M. Winterbauer,
Nürnberg

THE PAPOOSKI *a*   **EXCELSIOR BÉBÉ** *b*   FAVORI-BÉBÉ *c*

La Poupée de France *d*   La Poupée des Allies *e*

La Vraie Parisienne *f*

 g

 *j*

 *k*

Delcourt *h*

L.P.A. *l*

MANOS.
MARQUE DEPOSÉE *p*

 q

„Friedel" *m*

 *n*

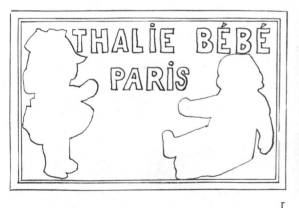

r   *s*

---

a *1916 Robert Sumner Curling, 70 Duke Street, London, W*

b *1916 Joseph Ortiz, 5 bis, rue Béranger, Paris. A doll*

c *1916 Arthur Sadin, 220 bis, rue Marcadet, Paris. Dolls dressed & undressed*

d *1916 Louis Gautier, 68 rue de Rivoli, Paris*

e,l *1916 Mme Perrin, 19 rue Théophile-Gautier, Paris*

f,g *1916 Henry Périer, 1 rue Lincoln, Paris*

h *1916 The Soc Delcourt, near Boulogne in 1916, made porcelain and bisque heads for dolls*

j *1916 A. Noël, 31 rue de Mogador, Paris*

k *1916 Mille Renee Wouilt, 9 rue du Printemps, Paris. Dolls, poupées*

m *1917 E. W. Matthes, Berlin. Dolls, doll parts, clothes, furniture, wigs, everything dealing with dolls*

n,q *1916 Emil Pfeiffer, Wien, Austria. Dolls*

p *1916 Mille M. Fauché, 57 avenue de Suffren, Paris. Poupées*

r,s *1917 Sussfeld & Co, 21 rue de l'Echiquier, Paris c/o G. F. Redfern & Co, 15 South Street, Finsbury, EC2*

M.P.H.L.
Bébé Jeannette
·MARQUE DEPOSÉE·
FABRICATION FRANÇAISE
a

PARFAIT - BÉBÉ
PARIS
MANUFACTURE FRANÇAISE
DE POUPÉES ET JOUETS b

PARFAIT-BÉBÉ
PARIS c

LA PARISETTE d

MONTREUIL-BÉBE e

j

THE CECILY 1700
f

MARQUE MB DEPOSÉE
l

POUPÉE C DÉPOSE "Ma Grand'Mère"
g

BRINGLEE DOLL UNBREAKABLE MADE IN ENGLAND
h

14-18 k

LA MADELON m   LA MADELON n

BÉBÉ BIJOU p

LES POUPÉES DE FRANCE q

"...et si je tombe, je ne casse pas" r

Bébé Bijou
Exclusivement Français
s

ESPIÈGLES t

MUGUETTE v   ROSETTE w

LA MIGNONNE u

JOLI GUY x

---

a 1917 J. Cortot, 51 Boulevard Gambetta au Puy

b 1917 Madame Aline Crosier, 23 avenue de Breteuil, Paris

c,e,j 1917 Edmond Hieulle, 1 rue Marbeuf, Paris. Poupées

d 1918 Mme veuve Coquillet, 14 rue Mandar, Paris. Poupées

f 1918 Edward Joseph Revill, trading as Edwards & Pamflett, 89–90 Milton Street, London EC2

g 1918 Charles Cauvin, 52 rue de Paris à Clamart

h 1919 Models (Leicester) Ltd, Factory Street, Loughborough, Leicestershire. A doll

k 1918 Georges Deleyrolle, 8 et 10 rue du Pont, Neuilly sur Seine

l 1918 Mille Marguerite Brunot, 38 boulevard Bon Accueil, Alger. Poupées

m 1919 Jean-Baptiste Linden, 35 rue du Poteau, Paris. Dolls, Bébés jointed

n 1919 Alfred Francois-Xavier Martin, 47 boulevard de la Reine, Versailles

p 1919 Pierre Lévy et Cie, 67 rue de Turenne, Paris

q 1919 Edmond Levi, 19 rue Saint Paul, Neuilly sur Seine

r 1919 'Les Bébés de France', 14 rue Drouot, Paris. Bébés, poupées, cymbaliers, marottes, folies, pantins

s Label on a Pierre Lévy doll

t 1919 Georges de Roussy de Sales, 22 rue de Lévis, Paris. Designer of dolls' moveable eyes. Espiègle means a frolicsome child

u 1919 'Les Arts du Papier', 168 rue Vercingétorix, Paris. Dolls, notably têtes de poupées

v, w, x 1919 Laquionie et Cie, Soc des Grands Magasins du Printemps, 64 boulevard Haussmann, Paris

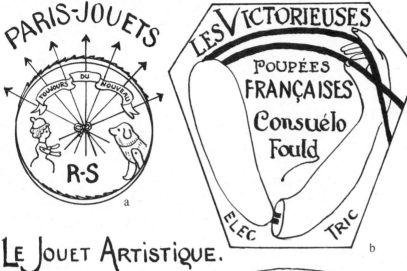

Edelkind

d

Le Jouet Artistique.

F.P.H

e

Hesta

f

A.P.

PARIS.

h

j

E. G.

k

BÉBÉ-SALON   l

m

MIGNON   n

MYSTÈRE

p

q

a   1919 Eugène Sédard, 7 bis,
rue Quesnay, Sceaux

b   1919 Mme Consuelo Fould,
15 rue Treilhard, Paris. Dolls

c   1919 Mlle Renée de Wouilt,
9 rue du Printemps, Paris.
Dolls

d   1919 Hugo Wiegand,
Waltershausen. Puppen, etc.
Accessories, everything dealing
with dolls

e,h 1919 Hirschler et Hirschler,
46 rue de Londres, Paris

f,g 1919 Hesse & Stahl, Berlin

j   1919 Les Arts du Papier,
Paris

k   1919 Edgard Goldstein, Berlin

l   1920 Georges Roncy, 17
avenue Jean-Jaurès, Paris

m   1920 Soc pour l'Exploitation
de Jouets. SAJ. 7 rue Paul-
Baudry, Paris

n   1920 Aréna et Lafond,
16 rue Jean-Nicot, Paris. Dolls

p   1920 Soc de Belleville et Cie,
4 rue Capron, Paris. Dolls,
dolls heads, dolls eyes, moving
etc mechanism

q   1920 Charles Marcoux,
23 rue Buffon, Montreuil sous
Bois

Les Poupées Parisiennes b

LES POUPETTES c

SUNER a POUPÉES DE PARIS e

d

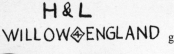

H & L

WILLOW⟡ENGLAND g

JEANNE D'ARC h

j

 k

 l

 n

Welta p

DESSY q Grecon r

m

„Stella" s

Wanda t Dora Petzold u

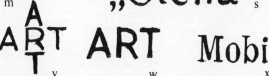

ART v ART w Mobi x

" TANAGRETTE " y

Le plus Bel Enfant de France z

Bébé l'Avenir a¹

 b¹

MY PEARL c¹

 d¹

 e¹

a   1920 Louis Amberg & Son, 101 East 16th Street, NY, USA

b,c,e   1920 Gaston Manuel et de Stoecklin, 137 rue de Vaugirard, Paris. Dolls, dolls clothes, etc

d,g   1920 Hewitt Bros, Willow pottery, Willow Street, Longton, Stoke-on-Trent, Staffordshire

f   1920 Fernand-Paulin Olivier, 26 rue d'Arches, Mézieres. Doll repairs, toys

h   1920 Mlle Marguerite de Raphelis-Soissan, 8 rue Pierre-Blanchet, Poitiers

j   1920 Tersch Kunst, Werkstätten, Berlin. Dolls, doll's heads

k   1920 Groszeinkaufs-Stelle Joseph Salner, Zwickau. Dolls and rooms for dolls

l   1920 G. Neiffe, Nürnberg. Heads

m   1920 Max Seifert, Rodach-Coburg. Toys & ornamental stands for dolls, but no dolls

n   1920 Gertrud Vogel, geb. Cloos, Dresden. Toys, especially dolls

p   1920 Weltal-Vertriebsgell-schaft, Pfantz & Cie, Stetten. Dolls

q   1920 Westel, Allgauer & Co, Wien. Figures, dolls, boxes for them

r   1920 Grete Cohn, Berlin. Dolls, stuffed dolls, and doll parts

s   1920 J. Stellmacher, Steinheid. Dolls

t   1920 Joseph Hermann Sommer, Magdeburg

u   1920 Dora Petzold, Berlin, Wilmersdorf. Dolls, exporter of dolls

v,w   1920 Arthur Blum, Wien. Dolls & dolls' limbs

x   1921 Hermann Schierner, Nürnberg. Dolls, exporter & importer

y   1921 Octave Durand, 72 rue des Gros-Grès, Colombes, Paris. Designer of dolls

z   1921 Thabée Lazarski, 83 rue faubourg Saint-Honoré, Paris. Designer of toys & dolls

a¹   1921 Soc Gutmann et Schiffnie, Nuremberg

b¹   1921 Alexandre Lefebore père, 23 rue Jacques-le-Paire à Lagny, Seine-et-Marne

c¹   Hermann Steiner, Coburger Strasse 16, Sonneberg, Germany

d¹   Drescher & Hirschmann, Nürnberg

e¹   Florig & Otto, Dresden. Spielwaren

„Casadora" a

Hesli

LA POUPEE IDEALE

·FI – FI·

d'une Solidité absolue avec tête lavable d

HUMMEL b

e

„Bobby" f

c

TANAGRA g

„Kleiner Sonnenschein" h

MISS DANCING j

BÉBÉ JEANNETTE k

Peebo DOLL l

Heinrich Tölke Puppen G.m.b.H Bremen m

p

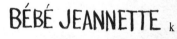

q

AU ROYAUME DE BÉBÉ JOUETS

A.& J. Alexander r

t

Primrose s

n

a   1921 Hüttinger & Buschor,
   Behringersdorf bei Nurnberg.
   Doll manufacturers, especially
   life-like dolls
b   1921 Rosalie Schrader, geb.
   Müller, Mageburg
c   1921 Ernst Schlesische,
   Puppenfabrik. Heinrich
   Schmuckler, Liegnitz. Doll
   manufacturers, jointed dolls &
   stuffed animals
d   1921 Isidore Dreyfuss, 63 rue
   des Vosges à Strasbourg, Bas-
   Rhin. Games & toys, a speciality
   being a doll with a washable
   head
e   1921 Georg Schweiger,
   Nürnberg

f   1921 Herbert Ruhnau,
   Thuringia
g   1922 Albert Leon, Paris. Dolls
h   1922 Catterfelder Puppenfabrik vorm. Carl Trautmann,
   Inh. Franz Kundy, Thuringia
j   1922 Michel Lilienthal,
   9 rue de l'Isly, Paris. Designer
   of a doll
k   1922 Jeanne Cortot, 3 rue
   de la Loi-Liége, Belgique.
   Poupées
l   1922 Arthur Graham, 22
   Highbury Place, London, N5.
   A doll
m   1922 Heinrich Tölke,
   GmbH, Bremen. Dolls

n   1921 Walterhausen Puppenfabrik, GmbH,
   Walterhausen. Jointed dolls &
   bébés
p   1922 Mme Jeanne de
   Kasparck, 11 rue Villedo,
   Paris
q   1922 Paul Jürgel, Nieder-
   Bielau, Oberlaustzer
   Keramische Werkstatten
r   1922 A. et J. Alexander,
   57 rue Saint-Ferréol,
   Marseille. A doll
s   1922 Waltershausen Puppenfabrik
t   1922 Paul Schmidt, Sonneberg.
   Dolls

Herzkäferchen a

„Bärbel-Puppe" b

„Hafraco-Puppe" c

Elfi=Riesling·Puppe d

Elfe e

Mein kleiner Schilngel f

Belinde g

My Fairy h

Puppenfee j

„Henny" k

„My Honey" m

 l

a,f   1922 Bauer & Richter,
Roda. Rodaer Puppen-und
Spielwarenfabrik

b   1922 Bärbel Wichmann, geb.
Emisch, Berlin. Exporters of
dolls

c   1922 Schöffl & Co, GmbH,
Berlin. Dolls, especially
'artistic' dolls

d   1922 Kunstgewerbliche
Werkstätte, Dachau

e,h   1922 Senfarth &
Reinhardt, Waltershausen.
Doll manufacturer, dolls of all
kinds and their accessories

g   1922 Bruno Lindemann & Co,
Hamburg

j   1922 Leo Nordschild, Berlin

k   1922 Clara Böhnke u.Helene
Zimmermann, Königsberg.

Dolls & their accessories,
importer, doll stands, dressed
dolls, dolls' wigs, heads, etc

l   1922 Julia Müller-Sarne
verehl. Moeller geb. Müller,
Dresden. Importer of all kinds of
dolls and dressed dolls

m   1922 Eduard Römhild,
Sonneberg. Dolls dressed and
undressed

a

LA PETITE MÉNAGERE b

LE MÉNAGE ENFANTIN c

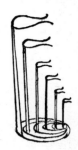
d

„Leckermäulchen"
e

f

g

k

h

MAL'AUTO de ma Poupée j

Ursula l MODESTES m

n

Fee p MON MÉNAGE q

---

a *1892 Heinrichmaier und Wünsch, Rothenburg. Puppenmöbel, ie dolls' furniture*

b,c *1903 Paul Toussaint-Fourot, Paris. Household toys for children*

d *1895 Butler doll stands (also 1904). Chicago, Ill, USA. Mark shows six stands, various sizes*

e *1906 Carl Bierhals, Nürnberg. Dolls' kitchens and children's shops*

f,g *1908 Carl Brandt, jr, Gösznitz'. Toys, especially dolls' furniture*

h *1910 André Hellé, Paris. Toys, furniture, etc*

j *1913 Charles Rouaud, 137 rue du Faubourg Saint Denis, Paris. Dolls' trunks*

k *1918 Emile Merz, 45 rue Sadi-Carnot, Beauvais. Designer of furniture for dolls*

l *1913 E. W. Matthes, Berlin. Dolls, dolls' stands, dolls' furniture, dolls' wigs and all kinds of articles, clothing, etc for dolls*

m *1920 Groszeinkaufs-Stelle Josef Salner, Zwickau. Furniture and arrangement of rooms for doll's houses*

n *1920 Erna Reusz, Berlin. Dolls' furniture*

p *1921 Bruno Ulbright, Nürnberg. Dolls' furniture*

q *1921 Fernand Gratieux, 109 avenue des Moulineaux, Billancourt, Seine. Toy household goods for doll's houses*

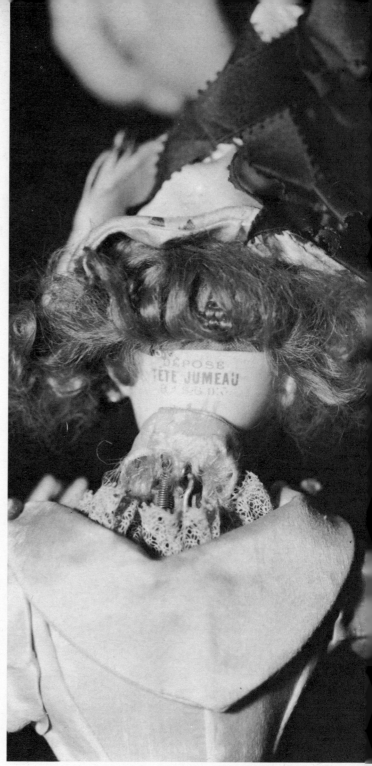

Doll by Jumeau, standing on a musical box base, and wearing her original silk clothes of pink, cream and yellow. Head marked Dépose Tête Jumeau Bte S G D G

French *c.*1878   Doll 15½″ high   Box 4″ high

Lent by Cameo Corner

Doll by Jumeau. Bisque head,
fair hair wig, blue eyes, six
teeth, composition body fitted
with talking machine, winding
key and stop-start lever at back.
Head marked at back, Dépose
Tête Jumeau 11, phonograph
disc marked with Loriot label.

French *c*.1895 Doll 25″ tall

Courtesy of Christie's

JUBILEE a  PALAIS ROYAL c

"PRINCESS"

J.G. e

 ILMOS h

Herk a g

a   1875 Raymond Jenkins,
  Brooklyn, USA. Mrs Jenkins
  made dolls' shoes
b   1886 Alexandrine Deropkine,
  France. Mark stamped on the
  dolls and on their clothes
c   1890 Rosa Lisner, New York.

Dressed dolls
d,f   1909 Union Amicale des
  Négociants de Mercerie et
  Bonneterie en gros, Paris, ie
  haberdashery and hosiery
e   1914 Jacques Gonda, 21 rue
  d'Hauteville, Paris. Designer

of doll's wigs and also for
people
g   1914 Martha Köllner, geb.
  Lotter, Ilmenau. Dolls' wigs
h   1920 Max Burghardt,
  Ilmenau. Augen, ie dolls' eyes,
  registered under porcelain

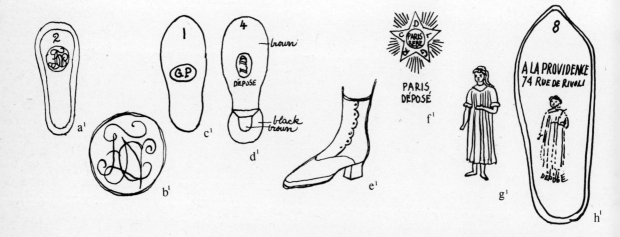

Shoes

a[1],b[1]   1876 Probably the Fischer
  Naumann Co
c[1],d   1878 Dolls' boots exhibited
  at the Paris Exhibition

e[1]   1880 Registered design for
  boots
f[1]   1889 Danel et Cie, fabricants
  a Montreuil-sous-Bois.

*(Stamped or punched in the
middle of the sole of boot or shoe)*
g[1],h[1]   1913 Eugene Alart,
  134 rue du Temple, Paris.
  Designer. See also Jumeau

9. DOLLS IN PARTICULAR

Well known makers of Bisque Bébés

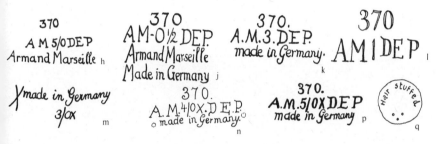

20
A.M. DEP. a

1894
A M O DEP b

1894
AM 1½ DEP
made in
Germany c

A.M.
1895 d

48-94
AM 4 DEP e

600
A.M. DEP. f

AM 1½ DEP
made in
Germany g

a *kid body.* b *doll 15" long
kid body.* c *doll 15¾" long,
kid body.* d *kid body.* e *kid
body.* f *kid body.* g *Doll
15¾" long, kid body*

Armand Marseille, Koppelsdorf, Germany No registered mark, all
rubbings.
The early dolls are marked 1894 AM DEP Made in Germany. Between
AM and DEP is a number. They have fixed or sleeping eyes, wool wigs,
jointed composition bodies, or bodies of kid.

370
A M 5/0 DEP
Armand Marseille h

370
AM-0½ DEP.
Armand Marseille
Made in Germany j

370.
A.M.3.DEP.
made in Germany. k

370
AMIDEP l

X made in Germany
3/0x m

370.
A.M.4/0X.DEP.
made in Germany. n

370.
A.M.5/0X DEP
made in Germany p

Hair stuffed q

h *Doll 15" long, part kid, part
cotton.* j *doll 18" long,
stuffed cotton.* k *20" long,
stuffed cotton.* l *21" long,
kid body.* m *12" long, kid
body.* n *16½" long, unglazed
cotton.* p *17½" long, kid
body.* q *tummy stamp*

Another series is marked 370. In these the heads are in one with the yokes
and therefore do not turn. They have blue or brown sleeping eyes, and wigs.
Some of these have bodies of kid, others have pink cotton, some can be
part kid, part cotton, and some can have imitation kid bodies of unglazed
oilcloth. The lower arms and legs are of composition (a kind which
crumbles easily) and sometimes the lower legs are just stuffed black stockings. The numbers are confusing – 2/0X is 19 inches high, 4/0X is 16½ inches
high, and 12/0X is 8½ inches high.

r   Kid body
s   kid body
t   15¾" high, c1902
u, v   1901, composition body
w   1902, 21½" high
x, y, z   kid body
a¹   c1898, 26" long, kid body

Germany
Kiddiejoy
A   O   M   r

3200
A M O DEP   s

3200
A M O DEP
made in Germany   t

3200
A M O DEP
made in Germany   u

Made in Germany
Florodora
A O M   v

3200
A M 6 DEP
made in Germany   w
3700

Germany
971
A. 8. M.   x

№ 3500
A M 1 DEP   y

A.M. 3/0 DEP
made in Germany   z

3200
A M 5 DEP   a¹

The numbers 3200, 3500, and 3700 frequently occur, and most of these heads have open mouths.

a   c1914, 8¼" high
b, c, d   c1905
d   18" high
e   c1905, 20" high
f   22"
g   c1910
h   c1905

Made in Germany
Armand Marseille
390
A 10/0M   a

Armand Marseille
Germany
390
A O. M.   b

Made in Germany
Armand Marseille
390n
DRGM 2', Gﬁ
3 M   c

Made in Germany
Armand Marseille
390 n.
D.R.G.M. 246/1.
A 1½ M   d

Made in Germany
Armand Marseille
390
D.R.G.M 346/1
A 4. M   e

Armand Marseille
Germany
390
A. 5 M   f

Made in Germany
Armand Marseille
390
A 8 M   g

MADE IN GERMANY
Armand Marseille
390 n
A 9 M   h

The heads numbered 390 have sockets and therefore turn. With these the sizes are easier. No 7 is 12 inches high; 11 is 28 inches, 12 is 29 inches and 13 is 30 inches high. The numbers are incised between the initials A and M.

j   Baby doll with curved limbs
k   Baby doll with curved limbs
l   ditto, 15" long
m   brown baby 13" long

AM
GERMANY
341/3   j

A.M.
Germany
351..5K   k

AM
Germany
5/6/3/2K   l

A ELLAR M
Germany
3½K   m

The baby dolls usually have a K in the mark and those marked ELLAR are coloured brown. Unlike those of Heubach, these babies have sleeping eyes, but they also have bodies of composition. Number 341 is for those with closed mouths and no 351 for those with their mouths open.

Note that none of these signs has an anchor, nor yet a place name. Many are marked Germany, or Made in Germany, and some are marked D R G M as is the case with toys of these dates. All are found at the back of the doll's neck, under the hair.

Baer & Proeschild

a   *1919 Baer & Proeschild registered mark*

b   *1919*

c   *Mark on doll*

d   *Doll mark, 12 indicates the size, 604 the style number Baer & Proeschild, Ohrdruf, Thuringia. Hardpaste porcelain*

C. M. Bergman

e   *1904, registered mark.*
    f 1916, label. g doll, 18" high

C. M. Bergmann, Waltershausen, Germany, see also Cinderella Baby, 1897, and a jointed doll of 1910

BÉBÉ-BAISER m

Paul Girard

1891 Paul Girard, industriel à Paris, agent for Casimer Bru

h   *1891 registered mark, on the dolls and on their boxes*

j   *1891 Girard & Soc Int Inv Mod Registered mark*

k,l   *rubbings*

m   *1894, registered mark*

Casimer Bru of France used Paul Girard as his agent. If anything, his dolls seem slightly more refined than those of Jumeau, the eyes a little further apart and the eyebrows not quite so heavy. The dolls are marked at the back of the head with BRU Jne for junior and a number, they are also marked on one shoulder with Bru, Jne. No 2 is 12 inches high, no 3 is 14 inches, no 9 is 20 inches to 23 inches, and no 14 is 32 inches. The bodies are of jointed kid with gussets, and later of papier mâché. *Bébé Teteur* came in 1879.

Bru won a silver medal at Melbourne in 1880, a gold medal at Antwerp, 1885, Paris and Liverpool, 1886, Paris and Le Havre, 1887, Toulouse and Barcelona, 1888 and also Melbourne and Paris, and a silver medal at Paris in 1889.

1875 *Cuno & Otto Dressel,*
Sonneberg. Dolls, dolls' heads,
wood, glass, porcelain, etc,
basketwork, marbles, slates &
slate pencils
n   1895 registered mark. Doll
p   1903 registered label
q   1907 registered doll name
r   1909 registered label
s   rubbing from back of doll
t   1912 Registered trade mark
u   registered label

Cuno & Otto Dressel

Their impressed mark is at the back of the doll's neck, and in addition a stamped mark on the upper leg. This was in the 1880s. Dolls of the 1912s have the mark stamped on their tummy. The heads are of composition or bisque and many have fair-haired wigs of lambskin.

a   1910 **Catterfelder-**
Puppenfabrik, *rubbing*
b   1920 **Diamond Pottery Co,**
Hanley, England 1908–1935,
rubbing. Doll 17" high
c   1888 **Edmond D'aspres,**
rubbing

D.P.Co were initials used by the Diamond Pottery Co of Hanley, Staffordshire between 1908–35, and by the Dresden Porcelain Co of Longton in 1896–1904. The initials D P were also registered by Hamburger & Co, New York in 1895. Dannin et Paulet of Paris used them from 1908 onwards.

Fernand Gratieux, *82–96*
avenue des Moulineaux,
Billancourt
d   1907, *Fernand Gratieux fils,*
Paris. e   1919. f   1919.
g   1919. h   1919, all registered

Ferdinand Max Schilling,
Sonneberg
j   1893. k   1895. l   1901.
r   1903, all registered marks.
r   is a label. m, n, p, q   are
rubbings. The Z is for Saxony,
pronounced zaxony in German.
In 1895 he registered dolls,
dolls' heads of papier mâché,
paper, wood, rubber, & other
compositions

Ferdinand Max Schilling, Sonneberg

His baby dolls have brush strokes for hair, and moving tongues. Rubbings are taken at the back of the doll's neck.

LES RECALCITRANTES

NOUVEAU JEU

Brevet SGDG

F. & B. PARIS

PAN-MUTUEL

EDEN-BÉBÉ   t

Eden-Puppe   u

Eden-Puppe   v

Eden-Bébé   x

w

A l'enfant sage   y

"BÉBÉ TRIOMPHE"   z

MICHU   c¹

a¹

„Michu"   d¹

b¹

Eden   e¹

Fleischmann et Blodel,

successors to J. Berlin, Fürth
s *1889.* t *1890, Paris.*
u *1891, Germany.* v *1891,*
Germany. w *1895.*
x *1896.* y *1897.* z
1898. a¹ *1903.* b¹ *1909.*
c¹, d¹ *1911.* e¹ *1914, all*
registered marks. x *is for a*
kissing & talking doll

G^br 165K
22
20
Germany   a

G 165K
5
Germany   b

G·K
34–26   c

G·K   d

G K
11
Made in Germany
201 10/0
DEP   e

a *rubbing*
b *rubbing, doll 21" high*
c *rubbing doll 14¾" high*
d **Gebrüder Krauss,** *bisque*
   bébé, 23" high
e *1908,* **Gebrüder Knock,**
   Knock is the German for bone

---

f

g

120   5
Germany   h

B   j

**Wm. Goebel, Deslau.
Porzellanfabrik**

f *registered mark.* g *registered*
   1917. h *rubbing.* j *the B*
   turned up is for Bavaria

ORIGINAL Max Handwerck's BÉBÉ ELITE
EINGETRAGENE SCHUTZMARKE
Made in Germany
no77   grandeur   a

BÉBÉ ELITE   b

MAX HANDWERCK
Germany
4   c

Cornouloid-Doll.
„Madame Butterfly'
MADE IN GERMANY.
Nº _____
Eyes: _____ Hair: _____
EINGETRAGENES WARENZEICHEN.   d

Max Handwerck, Waltershausen

a *1901 registered label.*
b *1901 registered name.*
c *after 1910, a rubbing*
d *1913, registered label*

Herm Steiner
HS
Germany   e

Hermann Steiner, Sonneberg

e *c1921*

145

Heinrich Handwerck, Waltershausen, Germany

At first his dolls were simply marked Handwerck, and later with Handwerck, Germany. By 1898, the word Halbig appeared incised below or sometimes the words Simon & Halbig.

Bébé Cosmopolite came in 1898, and also his Bébé de Reclame. Both models were made with a variety of colour eyes and wigs. They were large dolls, about 20 inches high.

The word Supérieure appears low down on the back of some of the heads by Heinrich Handwerke, and Superior on some by Cuno & Otto Dressel.

Heinrich Handwerck,
Waltershausen

k   1891 Registers his name,
    surname only
l   1895 a rubbing
m   1898 Registers his full name,
    doll factory, ball-jointed dolls
n, p   1895 his 8-pointed star,
    note the word Supérieure and
    the lettering in French
q   1895 Lettering in German
r   1898 registered doll name
s, t, u   1898 registered labels,
    French & German
v   1902 English label. The word
    genuine is added
w   1913 doll name, registered
x   1921 Registered label
y   rubbing, doll 26″ long
z   rubbing

146

Ernst Heubach

Ernst Heubach of Köppelsdorf, Thuringia, made dolls with sleeping or fixed eyes, the majority being blue. The bisque heads are incised on the back with Heubach, Köppelsdorf, and with numbers and sometimes the word Germany. The bodies are of composition and are ball-jointed. No 320, 7 is 20 inches high; 250, 6 is 24 inches; no 250, 7 is 25 inches; 250, 10 is 29 inches, and 230, 6 is 24 inches high.

The bisque baby dolls came later, about 1909 with curved limbs. They have painted hair and painted intaglio eyes. They are between $8\frac{3}{4}$ to $14\frac{1}{2}$ inches high.

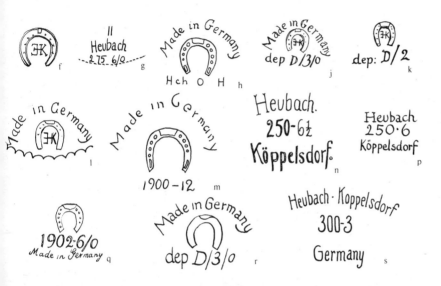

f   1887, registered mark, hardpaste porcelain
g   rubbing, doll 14″ high
h   rubbing, doll, kid body
j   rubbing
k   rubbing
l   c1896 doll with kid body
m   c1900 doll 27½″ high, brown closing eyes
n   rubbing
p   rubbing
q   Coloured doll, 15″ high
r   c1909 rubbing
s   rubbing

Gebrüder Heubach, Lichte near Wallendorf, Coburg, Thüringia

a   registered mark. b after 1909. c c1910. d registered mark. e doll 12″ high. f, g rubbings after 1910

Jumeau

Most dolls around today are those made by Emile Jumeau of Paris, the ones of the 1880s having closed mouths, pierced ears, fixed brown, blue or grey eyes, and blonde or brown wigs. The jointed composition bodies are stamped at the back waist 'Jumeau, Médaille d'Or, Paris'. They are between $14\frac{1}{2}$ inches and 26 inches long. The heads are marked Tête Jumeau with a number. No 9 is 19 inches high, no 10 is 23 inches, no 11 is 24 inches, and no 12 is 26 inches high.

Later dolls, still with closed mouths, have the heads marked Deposé Tête Jumeau Bte S.G.D.G. and after 1885, the bodies will be stamped Bébé Jumeau, Diplôme d'Honneur. The bisque heads marked Tête Jumeau, 5 is the size of a doll $14\frac{1}{2}$ inches high, no 9 is 21 inches, 11 is 24 inches, and 15 is 33 inches high.

Some with slightly open mouths have their composition bodies fitted with speakers which say Mama when a string is pulled, the two strings coming out from the waist. They have fixed blue eyes, wigs and rather heavy brows and are still marked Bébé Jumeau, Diplôme d'Honneur.

Their shoes when original are punched with one of the two Jumeau marks. These dolls are mostly recognised by their enormous glass eyes which protrude when looked at in profile. The iris is threaded.

In 1878, Emile Jumeau added the words 'Médaille d'Or' to many of his products, including the Bébé Jumeau.

Distinctions during the 1880s, include winning gold meals at Melbourne, 1880, New Orleans, 1884, Antwerp, 1885 and a diploma of Honour.

h   *1878 label*

j   *after 1878*

k   *1884*

l   *1884, doll 14" high*

m   *1885, navy blue letters on cream background*

n   *1888, registered mark. Parisian dyer. Mark stamped on the kid leather*

p   *rubbing. Maker of dolls and bébés*

q   *Sole of shoe*

r   *Sole of shoe*

s   *1891, registered mark, stamped in the middle of the sole of boot or shoe*

t   *1896, registered label, Soc. E. Jumeau et Cie, Paris. The background is reddish*

u   *1896, registered label. Gold background, the band is blue, white, red*

v   *1896, registered label. Black letters on white background*

w   *1896, registered label. Gold background, the letters and band white, bordered with black*

Kämmer & Reinhardt

Their star was first used in 1896. The dolls marked 21 are 8 inches high,
28 is 10 inches, 30 is 12 inches, 36 is 14 inches, and 50 is 18 inches high.

Kämmer & Reinhardt, 107 Schlammgasse, Waltershausen

a   *1896 Dolls and doll parts of all kinds, animal figures and papier mâché*

b   *1902 Registered label, my loved one, my darling*

c   *1902, registered label*

d   *1904 and 1906*

e   *1902, registered name*

f   *1903, registered name*

g   *1906, label in England, ie market*

h   *1903*

j   *1907 registered label*

k   *1908 registered name*

l   *1910, registered label*

m   *1907, registered name*

n   *1908 Schelm is a rascal*

p   *1911, my little one*

q   *1912, their sign re-registered*

r   *1915, Unart is the Naughty one*

s   *1920, registered name for England*

t   *1920, registered name for England*

u   *1920, registered name for England*

v   *rubbing, doll 11″ high*

w   *rubbing, doll 20½″ high*

x   *rubbing, doll*

a–u   *are all registered names. Herbert Haddon was their agent in the UK*

J. D. Kestner jun.
Waltershausen

a, b *1889, registered mark,*
       jointed dolls

c, d, e *1896, dolls, leather dolls,*
         jointed dolls, and dolls of
         Nanking

f *1907*

g *1908, rubbing*

h *1915, registered mark, with*
   English wording, and 'Germany'
   added

j *1915, their German mark.*
   Both crowns were labels printed
   in many colours and gold

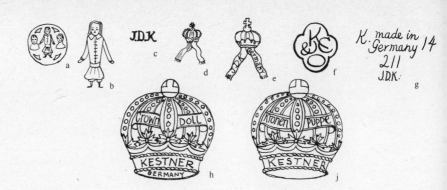

J. D. Kestner

Bisque character babies were made by Kestner junior early in the 20th century. They had blue sleeping eyes, parted lips and short brown hair wigs. Nanking was used for bodies; this was a cotton cloth of a yellowish brown colour, known as nankin or nankeen. It was originally made in Nanking, a town in China.

J. D. Kestner, junior, of Waltershausen, specified many commodities when he registered his crown sign in 1915. His business included the manufacture of dolls, leather skins, stuffed dolls, and jointed dolls. Also papier mâché, pasteboard over celluloid, character babies, dolls' wigs of mohair or natural hair, dolls' shoes, dolls' stockings, biscuit or bisque bathing dolls, dolls' heads with porcelain yokes, paper and celluloid, dolls with turning heads, also porcelain, paper and celluloid.

The crown sign appears as a coloured transfer on the doll's tummy.

A. Lanternier & Co, Limoges

k, l, m, n, p *all rubbings from*
               dolls of c1919

LORRAINE
Nº 0
AL & Cº
LIMOGES k

FABRICATION
FRANCAISE
AL & Cⁱᵉ
LIMOGES
E   l

FABRICATION
FRANCAISE
AL & Cⁱᵉ
LIMOGES
Cherie 5 m

FABRICATION
FRANCAISE
AL & Cⁱᵉ
LIMOGES
Cherie 6 n

FABRICATION
FRANCAISE
FAVORITE
Nº 3
Ed Tasson
AL & Cⁱᵉ
LIMOGES p

Soc. La Parisienne,
39 rue de la Roquette à Paris

q, r, s, t, u, v *doll names*
                  registered in 1911

BÉBÉ EUREKA q

MAGIC BÉBÉ t

BÉBÉ LE RÊVE r

BÉBÉ STELLA u

PARADIS BÉBÉ s

BÉBÉ LUX v

Schoenau & Hoffmeister, Bavaria

These bisque heads are marked at the back of the neck with a five-pointed star with S on one side and H on the other. In the star are the letters P B standing for Porzellan Burggrub. Underneath is often impressed 1906 or 1909 which may be the date of their make, the number below indicating the size and the word Germany. Their dolls marked HANNA are all brown-skinned.

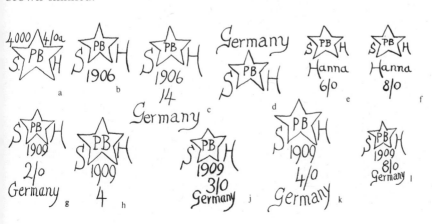

"BÉBÉ PARISIANA" a   LE SÉDUISANT b   BÉBÉ MODERNE c

BÉBÉ PARFAIT d   EDEN-BÉBÉ e

f

g

h

m

BÉBÉ PRODIGE j

BÉBÉ JUMEAU k

BÉBÉ FRANÇAIS l

PARIS-BÉBÉ n

BÉBÉ TRIOMPHE p

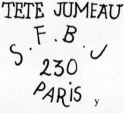
q

LE SEDUISANT r

BÉBÉ PARISIANA s   BÉBÉ MODERNE t   BÉBÉ PARFAIT u

w

LE PAPILLON v

FRANCE
SFBJ
CO
PARIS
G x

TETE JUMEAU
S. F. B. J
230
PARIS y

z

FRANCE
S.F.B.J.
301
PARIS
9/0 a¹

D
S.F.B.J
60
PARIS b¹

S.F.B.J.
227
PARIS
8 c¹

S.F.B.J
236
PARIS
4 d¹

21
S.F.B.J.
301
PARIS e¹

Soc. Française de fabrication de Bébés-jouets à Paris,

a   *1902, registered name*
b,c *1903*
d   *1904*
e   *1905*
f   *1905, monogram. Initials registered in France*
g   *1906*
h   *1910, initials registered in Britain*

j,k,l,n   *1911*
m   *1911, a registered label. Renewing of the department. Registration of the coloured Jumeau bands*
p   *1913*
q   *1917, a sticker label, red, white, blue*
r,s,t,u   *1920*

v   *1921*
w   *1921. Renewing of the department*
x,y,z,a¹,b¹,c¹,d¹,e¹ rubbings
a–w   *are all registered names. The address in the UK was c/o G. F. Redfern & Co, 15 South Street, Finsbury, London*

The S F B J

The Société Française de Fabrication de Bébés et Jouets, 8 rue Pastourelle, Paris, was formed in 1899 by the German firm of Fleischmann & Bloedel, when they took over the following firms of toy and doll makers, – Jumeau; Pintel et Godechaud, Montreuil; Wertheimer, Paris; Frédéric Remignard; Girard; Goutier; and A. Gobert.

In 1903 they were joined by Bouchet, who had taken over Gentil in 1899; Bernhcim et Kohn joined them in 1906, La Parisienne in 1912, and by 1914 the S F B J owned four factories.

Around 1909 bisque babies were made with curved limbs of composition, sleeping eyes and wigs. These have the number 236 incised above the word PARIS, or the number 227, the marks being at the back of the neck.

Another S F B J group bears the number 301. The dolls marked thus are no 9, 5 inches high; no 7 is 19 inches, 11 is 24 inches, and 21 is 26 inches high. Dolls with a deep pink complexion have the UNIS mark above the 701.

In 1921, a change was made in the running of the firm. Apart from toys, they were designers of poupées, dolls' wigs, shoes and all kinds of dress and underclothes.

Simon & Halbig

The initials S & H were registered by Carl Halbig of Gräfenhain, Herzogth, Gotha, Germany, in 1905.

His bisque babies have open mouths showing teeth and tongues and some dolls have auburn hair. His walking doll had a composition body, legs encased in metal with the key in the left side. These dolls had W S K under the S & H mark.

Later dolls, when he had joined up with Kämmer & Reinhardt, could have the S & H either below or above the K star R, or even the complete name Simon & Halbig. It was about 1909 when the two firms combined.

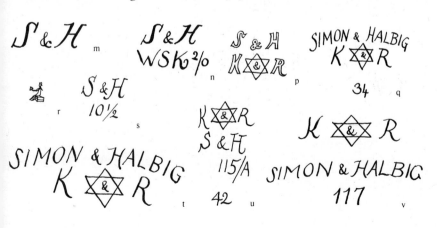

m   1905. Initials registered by Carl Halbig
n   rubbing
p, q, t   rubbings where K & R appears below
r   1914, registered sign for dolls' heads of porcelain fabric, celluloid, wood
s   rubbing, doll 22½" high
u, v rubbings where K & R appears above. v doll 26" high

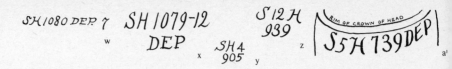
Jules Nicolas Steiner, Paris. Maker of 'bébés-jouets'. Name stamped on the dolls and on their boxes. Unbreakable heads of porcelain or biscuit

a *1862. The first time the word bébé appears in a registered mark*

b,c *1890*

d *rubbing. Fre is for factory, Bte is for Brevette, patent*

e *rubbing, 1889*

f *1896 rubbing*

g,h *registered marks 1889. Mark on dolls & on boxes*

j *rubbing, doll 23" high*

k *rubbing, eyes open & shut by lever at side of head*

l *rubbing from clockwork walking doll. 15" high. Kid torso over cardboard base*

Steiner

Jules Nicolas Steiner of Paris was helped by Edmond D'aspres among others at his factory at Montreuil sous Bois. These dolls are marked E D with a size number between, they have fixed blue eyes and heavy brows.

Those by Steiner are marked Steiner, Paris, Fre A 8 and are 16 inches high; Steiner, Paris Fre A 10 are 17 inches, the Fre standing for Figure. The composition jointed bodies are marked on the front LE PETIT PARISIEN BÉBÉ STEINER. These were made in 1889 and often wear dresses of Broderie Anglaise which was known as whitework. Steiner won a gold medal in the Paris exhibition of 1889.

About 1890, the bisque headed dolls with closed mouths are stamped Steiner Bte S G D G. Bourgoin and impressed Ste C 3/0, and are 10 inches high. Those marked Ste C4 are 21½ inches high, and those marked Steiner, Paris, Frs C4 are 22 inches high. A large doll of 28 inches is marked C no 6 J. Steiner Bte S G D G Paris. There are more dolls with fixed blue eyes than brown, they wear wigs, have heavy brows, and bodies of jointed composition.

The BEBE PREMIER PAS of 1890 has an open mouth, two rows of teeth, fixed blue eyes, and usually a blonde wig, and the heavy brows typical of Steiner. These are walking dolls, they turn their heads, raise their arms and say Mama, Papa. They are wound by a key and the name J. Steiner is marked inside the speaking box.

In 1884 Steiner was represented by Blétry Fréres, boul de Strasbourg, Paris.

BÉBÉ PARLANT a **BÉBÉ PREMIER PAS** b

Le Petit Parisien
BÉBÉ STEINER
MÉDAILLE d'OR
PARIS 1889 . e

LE PARISIEN
Bᵗᵉ S.G.D.G
A 13 f

BÉBÉ LE PARISIEN c

J.STEINER
Bᵗᵉ S.G.D.G.
PARIS
Fre E.9 . d

J.STEINER
Bᵀᴱ. SGDG
PARIS
FIᴿᴱ A 15 j

FIGURE Cⁿᵉ
J.STEINER Bᵀᴱ
S.G.D.G.
PARIS k

g

LE PETIT PARISIEN
BÉBÉ h

J. Steiner Bᵗᵉ SGDG
PARIS l

Edmund Ulrich Steiner,
Sonneberg

m,n   *Two names registered in
1894*
p   *1902 Walking doll registered
by him as citizen of Brooklyn,
New York, NY, USA.
Manufacturer of dolls*
q   *1903. Registered doll name*

Strobel & Wilkin Co.
New York, N.Y.
Also importer

r   *1895.*   s   *1902.*   t   *1914.*
    u   *rubbing, doll 6¾" high.*
    v   *9" high.*   w   *11" high*
*After 1914 Strobel & Wilken
    Co, Cincinnati, Ohio. Dolls*

Wilhelms-feld, Kunstwerkstaten

x,y,z   *Marks registered in 1919*

A. Wislizenus, Waltershausen

a¹   *1902, jointed dolls with hollow
    bodies*
b¹   *1910*

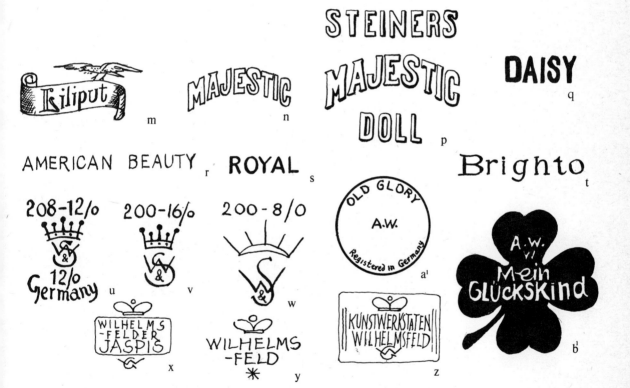

10. CHARACTER TOYS OF ALL KINDS

When a craftsman had made a toy or thought up some character from a book which could be turned into a doll or mascot, the next step was to market it. If not many were going to be made, then the items could be sold privately to a shop, which is what many of the early wax-doll makers did, but if the object was going to be made in thousands then it was necessary to sell to an agent. The whole idea might be sold, the agent thinking up the selling name, and either buying the thing outright or letting the originator partake in the scheme.

George Borgfeldt of Berlin registered marks for dolls and toys in 1896. In 1913 his address in Europe was at 7 Kostlergasse VI, Vienna, Austria, and his agents in England were Abel & Imray, 29 Southampton Buildings, London, WC. His address in France was 43 rue de Paradis, Paris, and in the USA it was at 16th Street, New York.

Borgfeldt handled the character dolls made by Käthe Kruse and the character toys of Margarete Steiff, their own marks being kept on them. In others, the identity of the doll took over, such as the Kewpie and the Happifats, more well known than the originators Rose O'Neill and Kate Jordan.

In some cases these agents or distributors were involved in lawsuits over copyright, sometimes the name was in dispute and sometimes the actual toy was said to resemble that made by someone else.

BÉBÉ MOWIK

MARQUE DÉPOSÉE
J.B
a

KM&C° b

BUSTER BROWN c

Struwelpeter e

KISMI d

E f

WALLYPUG g

THE WISP h

„Little Tich" j

DOLLY
DOLLYKINS l
BOBBY
BOBBYKINS m

GOBLIN GOBBLERS. n

GREEDY CHUGGY. p

HUNGRY GILES. q

MÜNCHNER
KÜNSTLER
KAULITZPUPPEN
k

LE GENDARME s

DUM-TWEEDLE r

PEEK-A-BOO t

SCHNICKEL-FRITZ u

VOTES-FOR-WOMEN y

TOOTSIE WOOTSIE v

SUFFRAGETTE KID z

„Michel" w

x

a 1888 Jacques Berner, trader, Paris

b 1900 Krausz Mohr & Co, Nürnberg

c 1905 Frederick W. Bazley, Highland Park, Mich, USA

d 1905 Stallarde & Co, 37 Commercial Road, London, E

e 1905 Wilh. Anhalt GmbH, Ostseebad, Kolberg

f 1906 Florence Annie Barker, Mirfield, Yorks

g 1906 Constance Mary Chapman, Rodean, Glossop Road, Sanderstead, Surrey

h 1908 Florence Kate Upton, 76 Fellows Road, Hampstead, London

j 1908 S. D. Zimmer, Fürth, Bavaria

k 1909 Marion Kaulitz, München

l, m 1909 Frank Hays, Philadelphia

n, p, q 1910 Katherine Mary Sherwood, 8 Seaside Road, Eastbourne, Sussex

r 1911 Deans Rag Book Co, 18 Paternoster Square, London, EC

s 1911 M. Rouaud, 104 Faubourg St Denis, Paris

t 1911 Bernard Horne Thomson, 44 Queens Gate, London, SW

u, v 1911 A. Schoenhut Co, Philadelphia, Pa. Dolls

w 1911 U. Michaelis, Rauenstein i Thuringia

x 1911 Benjamin Rosetstein, NY. Copyright design of a doll

y, z 1911 Mabel Drake Nekarda, New York, NY. Dolls

Kaulitz

Campbell Kids

SUNSHINE KID c
SUNSHINE GIRL d

RAGTIME KIDS

„Hobby-Bobby"

KEWPIE

PÈRE NOËL

MÈRE FOUETTARD

a 1911 Marian Kaulitz, München	h 1912 Edith M. Miner, Colville, Wash. Ornamental design for a doll	p 1914 Katherine K. Grant, NY. A doll
b 1911 Jos. Suszkind, Hamburg	j 1912 Leon Rees, London, England. Assignor to Monroe M. Schwarzschild, NY. Ornamental design for a Doll	t 1914 Leon A. Searl, NY. Design for a bisque doll
c,d 1912 Bings Ltd, 25 Ropemaker Street, London, EC		u,v 1914 Edith Dayton Titsworth, Greenwich, Conn. A character doll
e 1911 William E. Peck, for E. I. Horsman Co, 365–367 Broadway, New York, USA	k 1912 Hugo Smidt & Hans Kleinschmidt, Hamburg	w,x 1914 Kate Jordan, NY. Character dolls
f 1913 Richard Ordenstein, 17, 18 Basinghall Street, London, EC	l,q,r,s 1913 Rose O'Neill Wilson, Day, Mo. Ornamental design for a doll. Term of patent 14 years	y,z 1914 Mary McAboy, Missoula, Mont. A doll or toy figure
g 1912 E. I. Horsman Co, 365, 367 Broadway, New York, USA	m,n 1913 Gaston-Paul Petiau, 44 Avenue de la République, Paris	1914 William P. O'Neil, NY registers the word KEWPIE for crackers and biscuits

LUCKY-HIPPO

a

THE
HILDA COWHAM
DOLL

H. COWHAM

b

Huberto

c

Kiu-Pi

f

GOO-GOO g

GIGGLY h

THUMBS UP,
HAUT LES MAINS!

TOUCHE DU BOIS!
TOUCH WOOD!

m

Frity

d

"PINKA-BOO"

n

"I'MERE"

p

BATHING JEFF e

LUCKY
BROWNIE j

KISSMY

k

FUMSUP

l

"PET LADDIE BOY"

q

Caprice

r

MUTT & JEFF

s

---

a *1914 Emily J. Shively &
Claire Whitney, both of
San Francisco, Cal. A toy
figure*

b *1916 Hilda Gertrude Lander,
65 High Street, Marylebone,
London, W*

c, d *1917 Emil Pfeiffer, Wien.
Dolls and toys*

e *1919 Art Toy Manufacturing
Co, 46 Fitzroy Street, London,
W1*

f *1920 Ludwig Raisz, Flensburg*

g, h *1920 Edward Hazell Jones,
38 Warwick Road,
Snaresbrook, Essex*

j *1920 Frederick Henry Allenson,
Gerds, 3 Ridgeway Road,
Isleworth, Middlesex*

k *1920 Roger Vormus, 38 rue de
Chateaudun, Paris. A doll*

l, m *1921 Herbert Nalty,
faisant commerce au nom de
Gourdel Vales & Cie, 57 Great
Marlborough Street, Londres.
Fétiches, ie mascots*

n, p *1921 Polmar Perfumery
Co Ltd, 23, 24 Old Bailey,
London, EC4*

q *1921 Lipp & Co, Nürnberg.
President Harding's Pet Laddie
Boy*

r *1921 Emil Bauersachs, Inh
Victor Roth, Sonneberg. Dolls
& character dolls*

s *1922 'Mutt & Jeff'. Germany
Note that the original Kewpie has
wings behind the neck, whereas
the later Thumbs Up has them
on the ankles*

Rag

Käthe Kruse made some of the most lifelike baby dolls, basing them on her own children. They were of washable, unbreakable cloth and her first one, made in 1912, was stuffed with sand. It gives one the feeling of holding a real baby as the sand shifts about and the head lolls if not held as a baby's should be.

The animals and dolls of Margarete Steiff had been made of felt in 1894 but later she used it for the dolls' heads only. Her plush bears were imported into the USA by Borgfeldt in 1906.

Lenci dolls were made in Italy in 1921 by Enrico Scavini, the name Lenci being the pet-name of his wife. These were of pressed felt with child-like faces, eyes glancing towards the side and the dolls have very thick legs. Each one was individually made by an Italian artist and dressed in the style of 1920–25.

a 1892 Arnold Print Works, Mass, USA. Rag dolls & animals printed on cloth ready for stuffing

b 1896 Martha Chase, Pawtucket, Rhode Island. Stockinet dolls

c 1906 Ellen Salt, Hammersmith, London. Rag toys

d 1908 Bach Bros & Katzenstein, USA. Rag dolls

e 1908 Samstag & Hilder Bros, New York. Rag dolls

f,p 1908 Wilhelm Strunz, Nürnberg. Stuff toys

g 1909 Deans Rag Book Co Ltd, 18 Paternoster Square, London, EC

h 1909 Otto Wohlmann. Toys of stuff, felt & plush

j 1910 Max Fr. Schelhorn, Sonneberg

k,l 1910 Josef Deurlein, Nachflg, Nürnberg. Pluschspielwarenfabrik. Stuffed figures in the shape of cats and dogs

m 1912 Käthe Kruse geb. Simon, Charlottenburg

n 1913 Deans Rag Book Co, 2–14 Newington Butts, London, SE

q c1912 Mark of Kathé Kruse on doll 20" high, on sole of left foot

t 1914 Gebr. Grumach, Berlin. Strumpfuraren & Trikotagen. Animals and dolls made of plush, felt and other hairy materials

r 1921 H. Offenbacher & Co, Nurnberg. Stoffspielzeuge und Puppen

s 1922 Enrico Scavini, 5 Via Marco Polo, Turin, Italy. 'Art' dolls for grown ups

Agents and Makers

By 1914, Borgfeldt registered 'Dolls, toys, roly-polies, jumping-jacks, toy paint boxes, and mechanical metal figures'. Later on, in the same year, he added 'Rattles, toy watches, soap bubble outfits, rubber balls, Easter eggs, Cotillion favors, and mechanical toys'.

Eisenmann distributed toy animals and character dolls and again the identity of their makers is lost. His character dolls of about 1913 were similar to the illustrations by Chlöe Preston in the Peek-a-Boo books, and the trade name Tubby referred to a small dog, but unless one actually finds these mascots it is futile to guess what the name conveys.

Hamburgers were exporters of toys from Nürnberg but after 1907 they faded into oblivion.

Hamley's, the famous London toyshop now in Regent Street, were at first in Oxford Street and High Holborn. They sold all kinds of dolls and mascots, which were usually high-class and expensive compared with the trashy toys sold outside on the pavements.

Horsman dolls had composition heads and pink bodies of the material known as sateen, a glossy fabric imitating satin. Their Gee Gee doll was designed by Grace Drayton.

Moses Kohnstam used the first two letters of his name to form the word Moko which was attached to many of his products. Sunny Jim was the best known among these, a bright yellow, red and black printed and stuffed figure advertising Force, a cereal made of wheat flakes.

The Poulbot character dolls were distributed by the S F B J company, who added their initials above the Poulbot mark on the back of the dolls' heads.

From 1900 onwards, the output of J. W. Spear & Son was colossal. All kinds of games, board games, cards, and toys and dolls emerged from their factory in Nürnberg. Spear became the agent for the earlier Happy Family cards designed by John Tenniel, and the popular game of Ludo apart from putting many new things on the market.

Margarete Steiff specialized in toys made of felt and character dolls, all unbreakable. In London, her agent was Herbert Hughes, and Borgfeldt in the USA.

Suszkind was an exporter and importer of games and toys, especially the Daisy Air rifles from the USA, Meccano, and the Erector sets and other construction kits. In 1911 he was agent for the Campbell kids, USA dolls in a variety of dresses, advertising soups.

1908 Offene Handels gesellschaft Moritz Puppe, Leignitz. Doll & toy factory, dolls and stuffed animals

CELEBRATE
a

Elsie
b

Princess
c

Dz. No.
The International Doll.
Made in Germany.
d

Uwanta
e

UWANTA
f

Florodora
k

ALMA
g

Alma

Alma

4
h

13/0
Germany
M 8/0
j

FLORODORA
GERMANY
l

FLORODORA
GERMANY
m

My·Playmate
n

BABY
BELLE
CELSTAR
s

Tootsie
p

KIDLYNE
q

Nuby
r

,,Irvington"
v

Dry Climate
w

My Girlie
x

NORTH POLE
GERMANY
t

NORTH STAR
GERMANY
u

Little Bright Eyes
a¹

,,Fingy-Legs
The Tiny Tot"
y

CELEBRATE
GERMANY
z

Little Bright Eyes
b¹

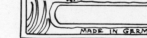
Tiny Tots
Unbreakable Dressed Doll
MADE IN GERMANY
c¹

NIFTY b

Kewpie c

KEWPIE d

KEWPIE e   KEWPIE f   KEWPIE g

MAMMA'S ANGEL CHILD j

SEPTEMBER MORN DOLL k

BUTTERFLY l

PRIZE BABY m

a

Lilly

Made in Germany 8/0 h

Little Sister n

Prize Baby p

CUBIST q

EXELLOID r   PEERO s   **HAPPIFAT** t

„**Nobbikid**" u

KEWPIE v

Jiss-me w

MISS YANKEE y

z

SPLASHME a¹

LOTTA-SUN e¹

ARTISTE b¹

TUMBLE-BO f¹

WINKIE c¹

d¹

HOLLIKID g¹

h¹

j¹

a 1912 Geo. Borgfeldt & Co, New York, NY. Dolls	doll 16¼″ high	s 1914	a¹ 1919
b 1913	j 1914	t 1914	b¹ 1919
c 1913 Berlin	k 1914	u 1915	c¹ 1919
d 1913 England	l 1914	v 1918 France	d¹ 1920
e 1913 Vienna	m 1914	w 1919	e¹ 1920
f 1913 Paris	n 1914	x 1914 Detail of 'Happifat' face	f¹ 1920
g 1914 Borgfeldt's mark	p 1914	y 1919	g¹ 1920
h 1913 Rubbing from doll's head,	q 1914	z 1919	h¹ 1921
	r 1914		j¹ 1921

Pansy b

f

 c

Teenie Weenie d

DANCING KEWPIE SAILOR e

 a¹

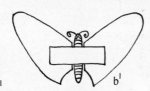 b¹

LITTLE PET c¹

KIDDIELAND d¹

TUBBY e¹

EINCO e

HUGMEE f¹   **TODDLES** g

KWACKY-WACK h   **BEAKY-BA** j

 k

EINCO o

Einco n

Einco 1½ Germany p

m

FIFI q   **BUNNY HUG** r

 s

 t

 u

v

 w

FLOATOLLY x

Borgfeldt

a *1921*
b *1921*
c *1921*
d *1922*
e *1922*
f *1922*

Eisenmann

a¹ *1895 Eisenmann & Co, Fürth. Puppen*
b¹ *1908 Eisenmann & Co, 46 Basinghall Street, London, EC*
c¹ *1908 A doll*

d¹ *1911 Listed as Fancy Goods merchants*
e¹ *1912 A toy dog*
f¹,g,h,j *1912 Four character animals*
k *1912 A toy dog*
l *1912 Mark for dolls*

m,n,p *1912 Three marks from dolls' heads. The 1½ is from a doll 13" high*
q,r *1912 Character animals*
s *1913 Doll head*
t,u,v *1913 Three character dolls*
w *1913 Sailor boy*
x *1914*

Made in Germany *Viola* H.&Co. 2/0 e

SANTA a

Santa b

MARGUERITE c

Imperial H&Co. d

VIOLA f

OLD GLORY g

Dolly Dimple h

BUSTER BROWN a¹

BOLO b¹

NI-NI c¹

ELFIE d¹

POOKSIE e¹

LULU g¹

WUWU h¹

THE BLUESTOCKING DOLLS j¹

CILLYBILLY k¹

FUMSUP f¹

THUMBS UP e¹

FUMS UP m¹

DIDDUMS n¹

BABYBUMPS p

"Baby Bumps" q

BABY BUMPS r

Genuine *Baby Bumps* s

Gee Gee Dolly t

HITCHY KOO u

"Gee Gee Dolly" v

BABY BUTTERFLY w

Hamburger

a *1900 Hamburger & Co,*
   New York. Producers and
   distributors of dolls

b,c,d *1901*

e,f *1903 Two connections in*
   Berlin

g *1902*

h *1907 Nürnberg*

Hamley Brothers

a¹ *1904 Hamley Brothers Ltd,*
   512 Oxford Street, London

b¹ *1910 John Green Hamley*
   (toy merchant), 86 High
   Holborn, London. A toy animal
   in the form of a grotesque dog

c¹ *1911*

d¹,e¹,f¹ *1914*

g¹,h¹ *1916*

j¹ *1917*

k¹ *1919*

l¹,m¹,n¹ *1920*

Horsman

p *1910 E. I. Horsman Co,*
   Broadway, New York

q,r *1911*

s *1912*

t,u *1913*

v,w *1914*

MOKO
b

Gipsy
c

Atlas
d

John Gilpin.
e

Sunny Jim
f

Hidden Treasure
g

h

The Wiggle Woggle
j

MOKO

MOTHERS DARLING
quiet and good
requires no nursing
attention or food
registered
Made in Germany
n

MOTHERS DARLING
quiet and good
requires no nursing
attention or food
p

„Cupid"
l

CUPID
m

FLIP-FLAP.
k

The Duchess DressedDoll
No.
q

r

s

„Sunnÿ Jim"
t

Kohnstam

a 1898 Moses Kohnstam & Co,
   Fürth. Toys, games, musical
   instruments for children, mouth
   organs, accordians, concertinas,
   stationery and household goods,
   hardware, etc. MOKO is
   formed from MOses
   KOhnstam

b,c,d 1900
e 1902
f,g 1904
h,k 1908
j,l,m 1909
n,p 1910. n English.
   p German. The English

address is 21 Milton Street,
London, EC
s 1914 The flag sign registered by
   Rehbock
q 1915
r 1919
t 1922 The return of Sunny Jim

a

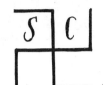
b

c

d

e

f

g

h

PFEIFFER j

k

l

FRITZ m

n

p

HUBERTA p

TORBOLO r

PUPPENPFEIFFER q

s

Oriental agents

a *1890 Taumeyer & Co,*
   Shanghai, China

b *1899 Slevogt & Co,*
   Shanghai

c *1892 A. Meier & Co,*
   Yokohama, China. Dolls &
   toys

d *1914 Pierre Vialard, 24*
   Passage du Havre, Paris

e *1914 Jean-Alphonse Paul,*
   rue Vanoise à Gray

f *1921 MM Viellard, Migeon*
   et Cie, Forges de Mouillars
   commune de Méziré, Boyaux.
   Importées du Japon

g *1919 Morimura Bros, New*
   York. Japanese importers into the
   USA

h *Mark found on Japanese doll*

Pfeiffer

j *1906 Emil Pfeiffer, Wien*

k,l *1916*

m *1917*

n,p *1917*

q,r,s *1922 A Bologneser is a*
   lap dog

UN POULBOT   UNE POULBOTTE
a   b

RINTINTIN   SANSONNET   NÉNETTE
c   d   e

FANFOIS   ZIZINE   MOUTCHOU
f   g   h

Le Petit LARDON   PILEFER   SAC de TERRE
j   k   l

BABA   NINI   COCO   LILI   MOMO
m   n   p   q   r

Poulbot

a,b   *1913 Francisque Poulbot,*
11 rue de l'Orient à Paris

c, d, e, f, g, h, j, k, l, m, n, p, q, r
1918 Madame Poulbot, 54 rue
Lepic, Paris. Designer of toys
and in particular dolls and
mascots of all kinds

Die fliegenden Hüte. _a

Cetro _b

ZILLOGRAPH _c

Hoki-Poki _d

 _f

Blumenflirt _h

Tiny Town _j

Ludo _k Weltgrößen _l Laripino _m Attack _n

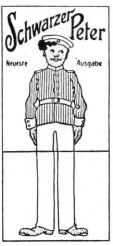

Tiny Tots _p

Toy Town _q

Ri-Ra-Rutsch _r

 _s

Buttercup _t Lebenslauf _v Wer weiß es? _w

Spear

a   *1900 J. W. Spear & Sohne, Nürnberg-Doos*

b   *1903 Paper & toy manufacturers, fancy papers, etc*

c   *1905 Pasteboard toys, etc*

d   *1906 A game. (Hoki-Poki, penny a lump, that's the stuff to make you jump, a contemporary rhyme about ice cream)*

e   *1906 A game*

f   *1912 A spear with a shield put on their boxes etc. Toys & games for in and outdoor use*

g   *1911 A most interesting game*

h   *1912 A doll*

j   *1912* ⎤
k   *1912* ⎟
l   *1912* ⎬ *games*
m   *1912* ⎟
n   *1912* ⎦

p   *1913* ⎤
q   *1913* ⎟
r   *1913* ⎬ *games*
s   *1913* ⎦

t   *1913 Black Peter, a card game*

u   *1913 A doll*

v   *1913*

w   *1913*

Rosycheeks ₐ

Prinzess ᵦ

Buttercup ꜀

Fleur de Lys ₑ

Nations & Flags ᵩ

HAPPY FAMILIES ᵧ

Glücksglocken ₕ

TECHNO ⱼ

Royal Ludo ₖ

Jumpkins ₗ

Gluck Gluck ₘ

Schwuppdiwupp ₚ

Der Wundertopf ᵩ

Hänschen und Fränzchen. ᵣ

Crazy Gussie ₛ

Spear		
a,b,c,e 1914, dolls	h 1914 Fortune-telling clock	n 1917
d 1914, a game	j 1916 An educational game	p 1917
f 1914, a game	k 1916 Board game	q 1919
g 1914 Card game	l 1916	r 1920
	m 1917	s 1921

a

Bouton dans l'oreille. b

c

Steiff d

STEIFF e

f

Sechseck im Ohr g

h

STEIFF j

ШТЕЙФФЪ k

ПУГОВИЦА ВЪ УХѢ l

Ring am Ohr p

Steiff's Prima Spielwaren. m

Steiff's chemisch reine Spielwaren. n

Steiff Original q

„**Billydoll**" r

Roloplan s

Pantom t

„**Steiff**" u

v

Paraplan w

Norost x

Margarete Steiff

a *1905 Herbert Edward Hughes, Long Lane, London. Agent. Button in Ear*

b *1907 Margarete Steiff, GmbH, Giengen-Brenz. Toys of felt & similar materials German registered design*

c, d, e *1907. e, the English entry*

f *1907 France*

g *1908 Six-sided button in ear.*

Animals of felt & similar materials

h *1908 Ring in ear*

j *1908*

k *1908*

l *1908*

m *1908 Stuffed animals and soft, supple dolls*

n *1908 Chemically cleaned toys*

p *1908*

q *1908*

r *1908 Character doll*

s *1909 All kinds of toys, aeroplanes, etc, paper kites, dragon-flies*

t *1910 Soft stuffed animals & marionettes also soft stuffed*

u *1911*

v *1911 Character doll*

w *1912*

x *1914. Toys*

a

Tantalizer b

Ping-Pong c

Whiff-Waff d

SLAZENGER e

BEST IS BEST
TRADE S&S L MARK
THRO THE WORLD
f

Kan-u-Katch g

Bounceola h

Po-Nib-Liz j

Aerotop k

l

CATO m

BOODIE n

Pussy Pippin p

Hippertyhop q

Erector r

Erektit s

Suszkind

a *1897 Jos. Suszkind, Hamburg. Exporter and Importer*
b *1900 Game of endurance*
c, d *1901 Games of table tennis*
e *1902 Balls & articles of sport*
f, g *1903 Balls, sports, games, etc*
h, j *1905*
k, l *1907 Air guns, Daisy Air Rifles made in the USA*
m *1908*
n *1909*
p, q *1912*
r *1913 Construction sets*
s *1914 Construction sets*

Cinderella-
a

QueenLouise
b

MY COMPANION
c

d

Moppietopp
e

Wolf

1892 Louis Wolf, Boston, New York & Massachusetts. Chiefly importers and distributors of dolls & toys

a 1897 Dolls and dolls' costumes. (The word Cinderella used since 1892

b 1910

c 1911
d 1914
e 1914 David Wolf, NY. Dolls and toys

Pedlar Dolls

These belong to the second quarter of the nineteenth century and some are complete with glass domes. Their faces are those of old crones and can be of wax, kid or chicken skin; if of the latter then they are probably made by White of Milton, a district of Portsmouth. Later dolls have faces of composition.

Some have the Grodenthal type body, many have no legs at all, and the stuffed upper body may be supported by a cardboard underskirt. The hands are of wood, china, kid or chicken skin.

A red cape is more usual than one of black and they are made of woollen cloth and hooded. Some dolls wear poke bonnets and a printed cotton dress and an apron, and every pedlar doll is provided with a laden basket or a tray.

There is a mention in *Life among the Troubridges*: 'I asked for a gypsy figure with a tray of tiny toys to sell, that lived under a glass case. I thought it rather like a doll, and Vi set her heart on three little wax babies on three gilt chairs, also under a tiny glass case, that she used to be allowed to play with in my mother's room'. This would be about 1864 from the book by Laura Troubridge. (Published by John Murray.)

This trade label is found on the base of the stand.

Swimming doll by Charles
Bertran. Bisque head, fair hair,
blue eyes, rubber limbs attached
to cork body, with mechanism
patented by E. Martin. Blue
bathing dress with collar
marked Ondine.

French   1876   Doll 13″ long
Courtesy of Christie's

Porter, bisque head, metal body, blue cloth uniform. Cart yellow, wheels red, Hotel Metropole painted on each side. The clockwork mechanism is underneath and connected to the porter with two rods actually pulling the man along, who walks and moves his head from side to side. This toy when marked is by Rouillet & Decamps.

French   *c.*1876   Height 12½″

Courtesy of Christie's

11. AUTOMATA IN GENERAL

About 1535, a hollow image was erected near the shrine of Saint Alban in the cathedral and a person placed within who would work the necessary wires. The eyes would move and the head nod according to whether it approved of an offering. At certain times this image would be carried round the town by two monks and set down by the Market Cross, where the monks pretended that they could not move it. Whereupon the Abbot came, laid his crozier upon the image and said 'Arise, arise, Saint Alban, and get thee home to thy sanctuary', then the monks came and bore it away. An awe inspiring spectacle for both children and grown-ups. (The Antiquarian Repertory, Vol III, 1688.)

At the beginning of the seventeenth century, Robertus de Fluctibus, a doctor, made working models in England, and in Germany Kaspar Schott made musical automata. In France, Salomon de Caus used hydraulics for his models.

In 1716, 'costly and ingenious dolls which display *actiones* by means of concealed clockwork' were made in Augsburg and Nürnberg, and were shown in the streets of France. Picture them in New Bond Street which was built about 1721.

In 1738, Jacques de Vaucanson of Grenoble became famous for his automata featuring the flute player, the duck and the drummer. Toy monkeys dressed and imitating humans amused the French court at the end of the reign of Louis XIV, and became very popular during the Regency.

At parties it was fashionable to amuse one's guests and in the year 1734 'the Duke of Wirtenburg gave a dessert in which was a representation of Mount Aetna, which vomited out real fireworks over the heads of the company during the whole entertainment. The Intendant of Gascony also celebrated the birth of an heir by a magnificent festivity . . . the dessert concluded with a representation of wax-figures moving by clockwork, of the whole labour of the Dauphiness and a happy birth of an heir to the monarchy'. (The World, No. VI, by Adam Fitz-Adam, 8 February 1753.)

Some of the earliest automata were those exhibited to the public throughout Europe at the annual fairs. Forgotten makers of these were Jos Tschuggmall and Matthias Tendler towards the end of the eighteenth century.

176

Their figures were complete with scenery and the 'movements natural'.

A London spectacle in 1802 was Maillardet's Automaton at Spring Gardens, Charing Cross. This exhibition consisted of a 'musical lady who performs most of the functions of animal life, and plays sixteen several airs upon an organized pianoforte, by the actual pressure of the fingers'. In 1827 Schmidt, in London, bought the automata of Henri Maillardet.

The *Phantasmagoria* was shewn at the Lyceum. It was a new application of the common magic lanthorn; where images are thrown upon a transparent screen, which is hung between the lanthorn and the spectator. To prevent the passage of extraneous light, the sliders are painted black except on the part on which the figures are painted. The motion of the eyes and mouth in some figures, is produced by double sliders.

In 1806, children could be taken to the Tower of London to see an exhibition of shell-work, 'the model of the Pagada (*sic*) at Kew is particularly curious'. Also they could be taken to the Lyceum in the Haymarket 'where Mr Cartwright occasionally exhibits his philosophical fireworks, accompanied by performances on the *musical glasses* by Mrs Ward, (late Miss Cartwright). Boxes 4s, Pit 2s.'

Another amusement was *Merlin's Mechanical Museum* in Princes Street, Hanover Square. Among the exhibits were a newly invented clock, the hydraulic vase, a band of mechanical music, the Temple of Flora, a mechanical cruising frigate, Merlin's cave, the juggler playing with cups and balls, an aerial cavalcade and an artificial flying bat.

It is a long list and at the bottom appears 'besides the various public exhibitions we have noticed, there will always be, in such a vast metropolis, some too contemptible, and others too evanescent, for notice; of this kind may be mentioned ventriloquists, slight-of-hand performances etc.'

In 1808 a new amusement appeared in New York. This was the *Theatre Pictoresque & Mechanique*, with 'Fontoccini or Artificial Comedians, animated pictures, Arabesk fires etc.'

About 1809, Geisselbrecht, who had come to England from Vienna, made marionettes which could move their eyes and cough, and these were regarded as the finest in Germany. However Italy was considered to be the home of marionettes and also the founders of the Christmas Cribs and in these some of the figures were animated.

Amongst simple moving toys for children there are several ways of producing an animated effect. First there was the wind as in windmills, or by blowing down a pipe as with warbling birds and many fairground toys. Bellows were used to produce squeaking noises, the squawking of birds, whistles and the dancing movements of small figures.

The Egyptians used threads for opening and closing the jaws of toy animals and for nodding heads. Much later, threads were used as in the pecking chicks of Russia, the Italian puppets, the French pantins and the various jumping-jacks. Lead weights were placed in the tumbler toys from

China and Japan and on the tails of paper perching parrots.

Pull toys were made to produce extra movements and sounds when the wheels rotated, handles could be turned or hand-cranked as in the simple musical boxes. The twirling around of poupards or marottes produced music and the compressed springs in the rather frightening Jack-in-the-boxes made them jump out towards the onlookers.

Andreas Müller of Neukirch in the Black Forest made clocks with moving figures on the top of them and there were other makers of watches in the forest by the name of Müller. Toys worked by clock mechanism were made between 1820–1860 and among the most popular were the Potato Eater, the Shoemaker at Work and the Peasants Quarrel, all coming from the Black Forest and with the figures worked by ingenious clock movement.

Pictures with moving ships and windmills could be as early as 1820. Mechanisms behind painted canvases and known as Picture Clocks were advertised by Abraham-Louis Brequet in 1822.

Nuremberg was the centre for the European clockmakers, while in the USA Connecticut became the chief town. However, although clockwork toys were on show at the Great Exhibition of 1851, it was several years before they became popular and cheap.

In Vaucanson's duck there had been over four hundred articulated pieces in one single wing. After the intricate automata of Vaucanson and of Droz it was a relief to turn to the less complicated specialities of the mid-nineteenth century. Among these were the handmade products of Lucien Bontems, and his beautifully dressed ladies worked by clockwork and standing on cube bases which concealed a musical box. Towards the end of the century these dolls could be surrounded by singing birds. The musical boxes were covered with cloth or velvet and edged with braid. They were wound by a key on which were the initials L B.

Boxed sand-toys depended on gravitation for their movement. The picture at the front was worked by sand falling on a wheel at the back of the box, the wheel being similar to a water-wheel and the box being about one and a half inches thick. Cats with kittens were favourite subjects and monkeys performing as humans dressed in the clothes of the period of around 1830.

Apart from gravity, toys could be animated by the twisting and untwisting of rubber bands or by pulling a string to set spinning a heavy fly-wheel as in a top. Butterflies flew by the rubber band method and mice scuttled across the floor. Sometimes the rack and pinion method was used in place of the string and on the other hand, a simple method was by just rubbing the toy's wheels on the floor, a means which incidently returned during the Second World War.

In the middle of the nineteenth century scraps of tin-plate were turned into small articles for children, particularly furniture for dolls' houses. The less complicated toys were made from the left-over pieces of pressed tin from other articles. Poor folk would take the discarded tin and beat it into flat shapes and then cut it to a pattern. The tin was often coloured in bulk and by the slot and tab method could start life afresh in the shape of humming-tops, cyclists, horses, carts and delivery vans.

In Europe, Decamps made a stalking panther and an elephant which could suck up water and blow it out again. He also made automatic rabbits which were covered in plush and sent to many parts of the world. Other automata were walking dogs with clockwork motors and wheels concealed beneath the paws. The dogs were of metal covered with papier mâché and kid.

The Automatic Toy Works in New York, famous between 1870–80 for wind-up toys, was later bought up by Ives. The tin toys of George Brown were all well-known; moving mice, fire engines with bells ringing, waltzing figures and circus wagons, all typically American.

Quite often the keys for clockwork toys have become lost, but they were sometimes marked with the monogram of the maker. Power for a toy did not have to come from a spring unwinding but could come from a flywheel which wants to go on turning. One method of setting the flywheel in motion was to pump a ratchet as in some humming tops, or more simply by pulling a string wound round a thin axle. In 'friction drive' the axle of the flywheel rubbed on the wheels of the toy thus carrying it some distance, but often with a jerky motion characteristic of the cheaper toys.

Expensive mechanical toys were on sale in the Lowther Arcade besides the cheap ones for which it was noted. There were whirling dolls in tulle ballet dresses, monkeys blowing trumpets or beating drums, toy soldiers, and dolls which opened and closed their mouths while playing the piano. All these novelties were to be found here and also some of the first toy balloons, mentioned in 1893.

At the turn of the century the most well-known makers of clockwork toys with figures were William Britain in England, Fernand Martin in France, and Ernst Paul Lehmann in Germany.

Early in the twentieth century Ferdinand Strauss in the USA was known as the Toy King. He made wind-up toys such as Dapper Dan, the Coon Jigger, and a tin monkey which could climb a string. Later on, about 1920, he was bought out by Louis Marx who began life as his office boy and became a millionaire before he was 30. The Marx Company continued making metal toys including merry mice and ambulances with sirens.

In the following marks many of the firms listed under Metal also made automata, but unless mechanical toys are especially mentioned by them at the time of registration, their names appear here under Metal.

1913 Strauss, Man & Co,
Rutherford, NJ & NY.
'Duckie Doodles', the duck that
quacks. As it is pulled along,
the beak opens

179

a

L'ATALANTE
Marque P.L. Déposés
PARIS

b

Marque Deposée c

"LOYAL" d

"Schlaumatz" e

M.&K.
MADE IN GERMANY

f

Le Lunatic g

h

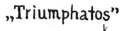

"Triumphatos" k

Le Magadis

MARQUE HM DÉPOSÉE

j

MARQUE DÉPOSEE l

m

Ki. Co.

n

VOLVOX

Perplex p

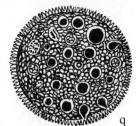

q

S.Günthermann's
Saltomortale

r

a   *1907 Ernst Döbler, Dresden-Löbtau. Mechanical metal toys*

b   *1907 L. Paillet, Paris. 'Jouets giratoires'. Mechanical toys & others*

c   *1907 Aubert et Papin, Versailles. Mechanical toys & others*

d   *1908 Leon Brock, Berlin. Automatic toys of all kinds*

e   *1909 Athenia Neutechnische Industry, Berlin. Toys, games, automata*

f   *1909 Mohr & Krausz, Nürnberg. Metal toys*

g   *1909 Constant Georg, Paris. Automatic toys*

h   *1909 Vergnes et Fontaine, Paris. Designer of toys & scientific models*

j   *1909 Georges Haran, Lavallois-Perret. Electrical toys & articles of morocco leather*

k   *1910 Fritz Wiegel. Construction toys and electrical layouts*

l   *1911 Lavieuville & Le Roi, Montmagny. Mechanical toys*

m   *1910 Mme Legrand, née Mathieu, Pesmes. Designer of a scientific toy*

n   *1911 Kienberger & Co, Nürnberg. Clockwork toys*

p   *1911 S. Günthermann, Nürnberg. Mechanical metal toys*

r   *1914 S. Günthermann, Nürnberg. Mechanical metal toys*

q   *1912 Wilhelm Götze, Hambourg. Designer of mechanical toys & automata*

b

c

d

e

f

Orobr

g

h

Orowerke

j

RAYLO

k

ULGO

n

„Sherlock=Holmes"

l

P A X

q

Sanofix

m

p

r

Gundka

s

t

u

GRESHA

v

w

---

a   1904 Lünerhütte Ferd.
Schultz & Co, Lünen a d
Lippe. Iron foundry and
machinery

b   1905 Saupe & Busch,
Radebeul. Metal toys ie sheet-
metal, tin

c   1906 Hans Eberl, Nürnberg.
Toys of tin & other metals

d   1908 J. A. Bäselsöder,
Nürnberg. Tin toys

e   1908 Hans Krausz,
Nürnberg. Sheet-metal toys

f   1910 Banneville et Aulanier,
Paris. Designers of metal toys

g,j   1911 Oro-werke Neil,
Blechschmidt & Müller,
Brandenburg. Sheet metal toys

h   1908 H. Fischer & Co,
Nürnberg. Sheet metal toys

k   1912 Frank Hornby, 274
West Derby Road, Liverpool.
Designer of toys

l   1911 Neudewitz & Co,
Nord-deutsche Metall und
Spielwarenfabrik, Berlin

m   1912 Georg Brunner,
Nürnberg. Metal toys and
goblets

n   1914 Bruno Ulbricht,
Nürnberg. Metal toys

p,q   1917 Ludwig Wohlbold,
Fürth. Toys, highly polished
metal

r,s   1919 Greppert & Kelch,
GmbH, Brandenburg.
Gundka-Werk Vereinigte
Blech-Spielwaren. Toys,
sheet metal toys etc

t   1920 Christian Götz & Sohn,
Fürth. Metal toys

u   1920 O. Schener & Co,
Nurnberg. Dolls, wooden toys,
sheet metal toys, ie iron or tin

v   Greene & Sherratt Ltd,
84 Hatton Garden, London,
EC1. Metal workers

w   1920 Gustav Fischer,
Zoeblitz. Sheet metal toys,
ie tin

Battleship called Mars, by
Gebrüder Bing. Clockwork and
painted a grey-green with red
stripe, and flying four British
flags, complete with stand.
Marked G B N.

German   c.1910   24″ long

Courtesy of Sotheby's

Car by E. P. Lehmann.
Clockwork with key at side,
the car and front wheels driven
by an eccentric. The fat man
driving the car blows a horn,
the tooting sound produced by
bellows. The toy is called
Tut-tut.

German *c.*1910 7″ long, 7″
high

Courtesy of Sotheby's

Automatic Figures

a *1823 Jean Maelzel, Paris. Mechanician to the Austrian court. A doll which could say Mama and Papa*

b *1862 Sketch of the Autoperipatetikos*

c *1878 Charles Bertran, 4 rue des Archives, Paris. Toys. Manufacturer of the 'Swimming Doll' or 'Poupée Nageuse' called Ondine*

d *1891 Couturier, Paris. (May be related to Alice Couterier). A doll of French bisque*

e *1890 Charles Rossiguol, Paris. Toy maker*

f *1898 Pierre Bois Gill'o, artiste peintre à Lyon, designer of an automatic figure*

g *1901 Bousquet, France*

h *1912 Volvex Company mbH, Hamburg. Dolls driven by clockwork*

j *1893 Roullet et E. Decamps, Paris. A walking doll*

k *1910 Edmund Boehm & Co, Berlin. Various toys, automatic figures, wax heads, etc*

l, m *1920 Badin et Guibert, 233 Grânde-Rue, Ouillins.*

Magnetic toys

n *1919 Otto Günzel & Co, Gittersee. Toys, mechanical etc, especially gymnastic figures*

Charles-Abram Bruguier, working in London in 1815, made a little doll which could walk like an ordinary person, that is putting one foot in front of the other, and she could turn her head at the same time. All the mechanism was inside the body.

The most famous of these dolls are those stamped Theroude & Cie, Paris, a mark which comes on the platform base. These dolls have three wheels and when wound up, move along, turning their heads from side to side, and raising and lowering a posy of flowers. Made about 1860, they are $10\frac{1}{2}$ inches high.

The Autoperipatetikos was one of the first walking dolls and although made over a hundred years ago, many examples today are found to be in good working order. She was patented 15 July 1862 in the USA and in Europe on 20 December, and is wound up by inserting a key into her left side. Names on the original boxes can be Joseph Lyon & Co, Martin & Runyon, Munn & Cobb, and the communication to England regarding this patent was sent by Enoch Rice Morrison.

The doll's height is usually 10 inches, her head can be in china, parian or bisque, or papier mâché, with painted eyes, and her hair, fair or dark swept back and held in a snood. Some have very beautiful heads of glazed china with gilt-decorated snoods with more glazed ribbons and flowers. The arms are usually kid, the hands having five fingers. The original dresses are of silk varying in colour but all are trimmed with lace either black or white.

The Autoperipatitikos must not be confused with the Toy Automaton walking doll patented a year later by J. S. Brown. In 1868 a wind-up toy of a doll pushing a baby-carriage was patented by William F. Goodwin, and walking figures pushed bath-chairs; Newton patented such a one in England. Other dolls pushed small go-carts and doll carriages of the three-wheel type. Wooden dolls rode on painted metal tricycles worked by clockwork motors. In the USA, clockwork tricyclists were patented by A. M. Allen in 1870.

About 1865 Jean Roullet specialized in mechanical dolls and in 1867 he won a bronze medal at the Paris Exhibition. H. Vichy, another Frenchman, made dolls which appeared to play music or shake tambourines to the tune of a musical box hidden in the cube-shaped platform on which they stood. As early as 1860 the firm of Jumeau supplied doll's heads which were used for the dancing dolls on the top of the Swiss musical boxes.

Charles Bertran's swimming doll came in 1878, the same year as the phonograph doll of Thomas Edison. Bru's musical doll was in 1872 and there are other mechanical dolls such as these which can still be classified as dolls to play with rather than automatic examples as things to watch. The swimming doll known as *La Poupée Nageuse* had a bisque head marked Halbig, and under were the initials S & H Germany. The word Ondine appears on the collar. The bodies are of cork, the limbs of wood or rubber and the winding key is at the waist. The original dolls are dressed in red or navy-blue bathing dresses trimmed with braid, and they wear caps. This swimming doll by Martin was exhibited for the first time at the Paris Exhibition of 1879. It appeared again in 1929 when it was mass-produced by a descendant of the original firm. The swimming frog was also a great commercial success. This Martin is not to be confused with Fernand Martin, maker of tin toys.

The name of Lucien Bontems stands out amongst the true automata and maker of Parisien specialities. In 1880 he had made a waltzing doll on a platform, and apart from singing birds in cages, he made dressed figures worked by clockwork. These, together with the musical boxes on which they stood would be about fifteen inches high. They were hand-made products, beautifully dressed in silks and satins; some were flower sellers, others played mandolins.

Decamps, of Paris, who later made polichinelles and dolls with kettle-drum sticks had many drawings of his items in his 1880 catalogue. At this time Roullet worked with Ernst Decamps making performing dolls on stands, dolls doing conjuring tricks, smoking, dancing or drinking and others which were fixed to platforms with wheels as pull-along toys. In order to save time the dolls' heads came from Jumeau or Simon & Halbig, but every doll was dressed with great care and with fussy details.

Luke Fildes, the RA, wrote that when his parents returned from visiting the Paris Exhibition in 1885, they brought with them a doll dressed as a ballerina. She was perched upon a platform mounted on a handle. When this was rotated, the doll pirouetted to the strains of Gounod's Faust, for there was a musical device inside the toy. She was knicknamed the 'Fairy' and the one I drew in the museum at Bethnal Green for Antique Toys answers to this description.

In 1892 a clockwork walking doll was patented by Roullet & Decamps and mechanical toys with music were still being made up to the First World War, marked with the initials R D, and sometimes a sign with a child pushing a two-wheeled cart. These initials R D must not be confused with the R D used by Rabery & Delphieu for their dolls who usually inserted the size or pattern number between the R and the D. They made talking dolls and unbreakable jointed dolls which is rather confusing.

Henry Vichy, rue Montmorency, Paris, made a soldier playing a bugle with phonograph music about 1900, and dolls which appeared to play music or shake tambourines to time. A more recent automatum was the 'Equilibrist' designed by G. D. Decamps which was a clown figure dressed in white and doing a hand-stand. This was worked by an electric motor.

Musical Toys

Sometime around 1730 in the Black Forest, some of the first *toy* automata appeared. These were the little singing cuckoos on the wooden clocks shaped like Swiss châlets. Later came small wooden figures pulling bell-ropes, musicians and marching soldiers. The toy-like clocks were made near Nuremberg, whereas the more complicated and scientific ones were made at Augsberg.

Among the most beautiful and intricate automata are the gilt cages containing singing birds. Like the snuff boxes, the cages were not made as playthings for children and much care went into their making. The mechanisms inside the bases of their stands whereby the birds could sing were kept secret within the family concerned. The maker's wife would supply the bird with beautifully arranged plumage carefully spread out to hide the metal cases, and the nests were sometimes set with rubies and turquoise.

In Geneva, Charles Bruguier, his two sons and his grandson Jacques were well-known makers and in Paris the family of Bontem began with Blaise Bontem in 1868, his son Charles and his grandson Lucien with a partner named Clavel. Their address was 72 rue de Clery, Paris. Early in the nineteenth century, the Frères Rochat were famous makers, marking their products with F R in a circle or oval followed by a number.

Jerome B. Secor made mechanical toys and mechanical birds in cages with musical boxes in the base in 1880. He lived in Bridgeport, Connecticut, USA.

The Magasin Pittoresque gives a description of a musical toy in 1880. This was 'a little golden rabbit mounted on pins, who holds between his front paws two drum-sticks, with which he plays a swift tattoo on a microscopic drum placed before him'.

In 1890 the German polyphons had changeable discs of perforated metal, but it was the invention of the gramophone which upset the musical box industry.

A musical fishing game was on the market in 1888 published by L. Saussine of Paris. As the music played, a pond revolved under a bridge, and the cardboard fish fitted with brass rings were caught by magnetized rods.

Poupards, Follies, or Marottes

Half toys, half dolls with music, these curious playthings belong to the end of Queen Victoria's reign. They were popular especially as the Queen gave two to her grandsons when they were babies. They are not true rattles for a baby to hold but are more to amuse a child who can twirl the doll around by holding the handle. Music plays a tinkle tune, the bells jingle and the jesterlike clothes swirl outwards as the circular movement increases.

The doll-part is mostly the upper half only, but some can be complete with legs. Jumeau, Halbig, F.G., and Schoenau & Hoffmeister have all supplied dolls' heads for these rather French toys and at the turn of the century many were supplied by Armand Marseille. The earlier heads were of bisque with closed mouths, the later ones had parted lips showing teeth.

The tiers of overlapping petal-like clothes often ended with a bell at the tip, many dolls wore pointed caps or elaborate hats with feathers. As usual, the incised maker's mark will be found on the lower part of the back of the doll's head.

a

MUSICAL PNEUMATIC TOYS

b

c

g

Revotina.

d

e

Musketeer.

f

The Zingara

h

Arionette

j

HUMPTY-DUMPTY

k

EUREKA

l

L·B

m

n

p

q

Jig=A=Jig

r

s

t

u

a *1800 Ludwig Wessel, Popplesdorf, Bonn*

b *1888 William Henry Brown, England*

c *1895 L. Chr. Lauer, Nürnberg*

d *1897 M. Kohnstam, Fürth. Musical instruments for children*

e *1899 Felix Schlunper, Berlin. Small musical toys of paper and tin*

f *1899 M. Kohnstam, Fürth. Musical toys*

g *1897 Horster & Kluge,*

Dresden. Toys and apparatus for jugglers

h *1900 M. Kohnstam, Fürth. A musical toy*

j *1902 Carl Emil Fiedler, Klingenthal i S. A child's trumpet*

k *1904 Jos. Süszkind, Hamburg. Toys and musical toys*

l *1903 H. O. Kratz, engineer, Paris. A toy phonograph*

m *1900–1905 Lucien Bontems, 72 rue de Clery, Paris*

n,p *1910 G. A. Dörfel, Brunndöbra i. Sa. Musical toys*

q *1909 Ad. Richter & Cie. Talking machines, phonophones, ringing sounds*

r *1910 Jos Süszkind, Hamburg. Toy musical instruments, etc*

s *1912 Mary E. Grieves, Iona, Mich. Games*

t *1919 Les Bébés de France, Paris. Makers of marottes, dolls, etc*

u *1922 Donny et Cie, 29 boulevard Saint Jacques, Paris. Musical toys*

a

b

c

CINÉBAROSCOPE
d

Climax
e

h

THEATROSCOPE
f

LE PROTÈE
g

Sperroculos.
j

TINTOSCOPE
k

DIDA
l

m

n

p

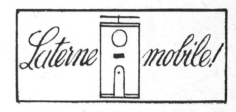
q

AU SOU BB DE 1855
r

RADIMA
s

Sélecta
t

POLARIS
u

PROJECTOR MAGICA v

PROJECTEUR MAGIQUE
w

---

a   *1876 T. H. McAllister, optician, 49 Nassau Street, New York. Parlour kaleidoscopes, graphoscopes, magic lanterns. In the same street, Peck & Snyder imported magic lanterns, comic slides, nursery and fairy tale slides from England and Germany*

b   *1897 Joseph Falk, Nürnberg. The sign is a camera obscura*

c   *1897 Max. Uhlfelder & Co, Bamberg. Fabrik Physikalscher Spielwaaren*

d   *1897 C. A. Watilliaux, Paris.*

Toy maker

e   *1898 Jean Schoenner, Nürnberg. Model toys, projections and magic lanterns*

f   *1899 Alfred Bréard, Paris. Scenic effects obtained by an optical manner*

g   *1899 Pierre Louis Rousset, Paris. 'Le Protèe', a scientific toy with multiple transformations*

h   *1898 Max Dannhorn, Nürnberg. Metallwaarenfabrik. A magic lantern*

j   *1901 Maximilian Hoch-kirch, Berlin. A toy where different colours of variegated glass are*

seen with surroundings

k   *1902 E. L. Moreau, trader, Paris. A scientific toy to teach an arrangement of colours*

l   *1904 Carl Rosenfeld, Berlin. Illusion Apparatus*

m   *1904 Zay, Paris. Toys of tin or pewter, mandrils, phonographs, bidons*

n   *1905 Fritz Neumeyer, Nürnberg. Mechanical & optical toys. The motto is 'opus coronat laborem'*

p   *1906 Albersdörfer & Co, Nürnberg. Mechanical & optical toys*

q   *1908 Albert Hauptvogel, Klosysche b. Dresden*

r   *1908 Ange-Jean-Marie-Gilles Morel, Paris. Talking machines & accessories, cylinders, discs, etc*

s,v,w   *1909 A. Deperdussin, Paris. An optical toy, magic lanterns etc*

t   *1907 Etienne-Jean-Baptiste Ratelle, trader, Paris. Optical games & toys*

u   *1909 Itzen & Bauthieu, Hamburg. Optical toys*

Milton Bradley, Springfield,
Mass, USA
1860, All kinds of toys
including optical

Optical Toys

In 1876, T. H. McAllister, optician, of 49 Nassau Street, New York, made parlour kaleidoscopes, graphoscopes and magic lanterns. In the same street Peck & Snyder imported magic lanterns, comic slides, nursery and fairy tale slides from England and Germany. Milton Bradley was interested in Zöetropes apart from the many games he made and in France Zöetropes and Praxinoscopes were made by Emile Reynaud.

In 1880 cardboard cut-outs were made for shadow shows in which the wheels were cut out and pinned on separately in order to give movement.

E P is for Ernst Planck and A L for the French firm of Auguste Lapierre, who made magic lanterns between 1890 and 1910. Aubert of Aubert & Papin, Versailles, made magic lanterns with slides in 1895 and 1900. The initials M D are for Max Dannhorn who made a Thaumatrope about 1890 and a magic lantern in 1898.

In the Commemoration volume of James Clerk Maxwell, born in 1831 it says 'another toy which attracted him in boyhood and to which later on he also gave a scientific application was the zöetrope or wheel of life. Long afterwards he used it to represent the way two circular vortex rings play at leap-frog with each other. This is I think the first application of the principle of the cinematograph to scientific purposes'.

Milton Bradley produced his Zöetrope or wheel of life, patented in 1867, and the pictorial strips to go with it.

„Reflorit"
a

Skandikado
b

c

d

a *1909 Josef Lipp-Kalthoff,*
   Berne, Switzerland. Toys,
   phonographs, music, optical etc
b *1909 Patent und technisches-*
   Geschäft Heliophor, GmbH,
   Hannover
c *1914 Imre Warga, Long*
   Island City, NY.
   Kaleidoscopes
d *1921 Jacques de Chivre,*
   12 rue de Herel à Granville
   (Manche). Toys (Phare is a
   lighthouse)

Vehicles

Carriages and carts and all the numerous horse-drawn vehicles were made at home or by carpenters and coachmakers. They were beautifully constructed but naturally do not have registered marks though sometimes initials or even a crest might be painted on the doors.

Horse-drawn dog-carts had a small wheel placed centrally underneath the horse. Among the vehicles in the USA were clockwork street cleaners, iron circus wagons containing wild animals and many fire-engines.

'Bought' toys could be worked by friction where a heavy wheel rotated against the axle when set in motion. On the omnibuses made in Germany, the destinations were named according to the importing country, thus a bus for England might have Coventry or Piccadilly painted on it. Parts for cars were exported by the leading firms such as Bing, Carette, Hessmobil, Lehmann and Märklin, all in pressed tin which was joined by the slot and tab method before the First World War.

In 1912, Charles Roitel, famous French toy manufacturers, made cars such as the De Dion Bus which were marked with his monogram C R, but production ceased about 1918.

The French cars were of stronger sheet metal than those from Germany and had soldered joints. Naturally they were more expensive being hand-painted and with such luxuries as padded seats. Ettore Bugatti, in Italy, made a car in which a child could sit which was driven from a car battery, and Citroën also made cars of this size. By giving children these, Citroën hoped that when they grew up the first real car that they would choose would be a Citroën. His firm was the Jouets d'André Citroën.

In the USA models were made of cast iron, for which the country was noted, by such firms as that of Wilkins, Kingsbury, and Arcade. The Thompson Manufacturing Co who made 'Structo' in 1912 also made cars, and in Britain model cars were made by Dowst. In France the most well-known were those made by the Jouets de Paris, that is J de P, and commonly known as Jep. Their motor cars and char-a-bancs came about 1914.

Later on, toy cars were often reconstructions of early models which became known as veterans.

Boats

Very few toy boats are to be seen in museums though there are plenty of models including the bone models made by French prisoners of war and the little boats in glass bottles which are most attractive.

A French firm of scientific instrument makers, Radiguet & Massiot, Paris, made steam boats, warships and locomotives between 1880 and 1895, Arnaud made clockwork boats in 1890 and Clément in 1895 made toy submarines.

Limousine by Georges
Carette. Clockwork car of
tinplate, painted dark brown
with red and yellow lining,
bevelled glass windows,
removable lamps and liveried
chauffeur. Marked G C N Co.
This car was sold for £480 in
May, 1973, a record price.

German   c.1905   12½″ long
Courtesy of Sotheby's

Omnibus by Gebrüder Bing.
Open upper deck and outside
staircase, painted red, grey and
yellow, and finished with
advertisements for the English
market. Clockwork, with trade
plaque G B N.

German c.1910 10″ long
Courtesy of Sotheby's

In Germany boats for export had their names chosen for the various countries to which they were going. In general, those of Märklin were wide and heavy with much superstructure, whereas those of Bing were narrower and duller in colour. Carette's boats were as attractive as their cars.

In London, Bassett Lowke made scale models and in the USA the Walbert Manufacturing Co. Bing made boats from about 1890 to 1914 and Ernst Planck around 1905 and steam launches in 1910; both these makers exported from Germany. The firm of C.B.G. in France was one of the first to make boats which were sold in boxed sets; this was in 1916.

In the 'Shops and Companies' of London by Henry Mayhew is a description of the goods in the Model Ship Shop in 1865:

'Here is every variety of craft, from the little model of a frigate to that of a hay-barge, and here may be obtained everything for the rigging and fitting of a baby ship.

'Really this shop is enough to drive a boy mad, with a limited supply of pocket money, wild. Just look at the little marine engines with their bright steel pistons, green bearings, and red paddle wheels, exactly like the hundred-butterfly power engines which you could fancy the fairies to use. Cast your eye over those patent anchors, no larger than a good-sized fish hook, but which are nevertheless complete models, down to the very rivets and staples . . . and in the shop window there is popgun artillery and doll-house-like furniture for the elfin pleasure boat.'

Engines

In Germany, in 1859, the firm of Märklin were making their famous toy locomotives, and some of the first toy steam engines were made in 1860. In the USA George W. Brown became a well-known maker and Ives in Massachusetts became the largest clockwork toy maker around 1868. By the 1870s, Beggs made steam engines which worked on wooden rails. These USA dates are more or less contemporary with those of Germany where Märklin was in Göppingen and Bing and Planck in Nüremberg in 1865 and 1866 respectively.

Many of the makers of tin toys registered their marks with addresses in Nüremberg for the tin mines were not far away, whereas the makers of wooden toys came from around Sonneberg.

The early steam engines had bodies of brass and iron and the best were sold in the scientific instrument shops. The later ones were made of tin and were more suitable as toys but they were by no means cheap. Steam engines led to other toys which could be worked by these engines, and were sometimes constructed at home.

Georges Carette, a boy from France but living in Germany, started making his engines about 1886.

In 1888 a reversing clockwork locomotive was made by Garlick in the

L.G.ₐ

b

C.R.ᵤ c

TRANSSIBÉRIEN
d

LE TRANSMANDCHOURIEN
e

f

C.R.
g

Maja
h

A.R.O.
j

EXPORT-AVIATION
k

ANTOINETTE ᴅᴇ LATHAM
l

m

AERO-TANDEM
n

ANTOINETTE
p

GNOME
q

r

s

t

u

C.R.
v

---

a   1880 Monogram found on locomotive

o   1887 Louis Bourgaie, Paris. Mark stamped on mechanical horses, vélocipèdes etc

c   1890 Charles Rossignol, Paris. Toy maker

1896 E. Escher, jun, Sonneberg. Trains

d, e   1904 Soc du Louvre, Paris. Designers of toy railways

f   1904 Daguin Géraud et Porcabeuf, Paris. Designers of scientific electric toys

g, v   1905 Veuve Rossignol, (Widow of Charles), Paris.

Renewing of the depôt

h   1907 Carrosserie et Sellerie, Maja-Verkaufsgesellschaft G. H. Schoenleber & Co, Stuttgart. Toys, cars, etc

j   1908 Réné Arnoux, Paris. Toys and parts for engines on sea or air and all things connected with them

k, l, n, p   1909 Vergnes et Fontaine, Paris. Toys & scientific models

m   1910 Alfred Leblanc, Paris. Scientific toys, engines, boats, aeroplanes

q   1910 Moteurs Gnome, Paris. Automatic toys

r   1910 Doll & Co, Nürnberg. Mechanical toys of sheet metal

s, u   1910 William Ritzmann, M. Ettinger's Nachf. Nürnberg. Mechanical sheet-metal toys

t   1912 Charles Roitel, France. Mark found on French army truck

v   1920 Soc Veuve Rossignol et Cie, 110 avenue de la République, Paris

USA where the important engine makers were Ives, Lionel and Knapp. The first electric street-cars were made in France by Carette in 1893 and by Carlisle and Finch in 1897 in the USA. By the 1900s both Ives and Haffner had become the chief makers of clockwork trains.

On the continent tin-plate trains were made by Bing, Bub, Carette Krauss and the Märklin Brothers. Stefan Bing showed his toy steam engines at the Paris Exhibition in 1900, along with clockwork, steam, and electric railways. These left a great impression on all railway enthusiasts especially those visiting the exhibition from England.

It seems appropriate here to state that a true model is made to scale whereas in a toy the scale does not always matter.

The first known catalogue of Bassett Lowke of England is from the year 1901, and in 1903 they advertised their locomotives as being in the correct railway company's colours. In 1908 their shop was at High Holborn, London and in 1910 it was at no 112. When Gamages sold these trains they added their own stamp to them.

Where there is smoke there is fire and steam engines did not appear in English nurseries till about 1904 where they were frowned upon as being highly dangerous and were more likely to find a place in the fathers' workshops. Actually many of them did blow up with dire results.

In 1907 the American Flyer Co produced clockwork trains, another maker was Edmund Metzel of Chicago. From 1914 up to about 1951 Haffner made 'O' gauge tin-plate clockwork trains. Electric toys running off the mains began to appear in 1909; nevertheless there had been toy trains worked by electricity before the real electric trains appeared in 1891.

Frank Hornby, the inventor of Meccano, made engines and train sets about 1915. He made his clockwork engines of light tin-plate and rolling stock like the real thing, adding names where suitable, and all true to scale.

The tin-plate clockwork models of Bassett Lowke went out of production when the firm was on war work between 1914–18. During this time they sold pre-war stock, and later on they made those large locomotives seen in playgrounds where a man, usually very fat, sits on the engine and the children pile into the trucks behind.

Well Known Makers, Metal Toys & Automata

Gebrüder Bing, Nürnberg

Early in the nineteenth century Stefan Bing made street cars and in 1866 when there were steam engines, he made several toys which could be worked by them. However, his speciality became boats and locomotives.

In 1900, he made a sand toy, more street cars and a stationary steam engine in 1905. Among toys worked by these engines were windmills steam rollers, boats, locomotives, cars, and lighting for the interiors o

BOSCO a

Bavaria b

Ferrit c

MONNA d

VANNA e

 f

 g

Fotobing h

Aëroulette j

KINOGRAPHON k

 l

STRUCTATOR m

Bing Constructor n

 p

 q

 r

Pilz im Pelz s

Pilz im Filz t

Attatroll u

Zoo im Fussring v

Talo w

zoola x
Zoolo y

Astralot z

 c¹

Über Fels und Firn a¹

Durchs Sternenreich b¹

Bing

a 1900 Gebrüder Bing,
Blumenstrasse 16, Nürnberg.
Metal toys with lacquer finish.
Magic lanterns, optical toys,
projectors, mechanical &
instructive toys

b 1903 Machine models

c,d,e,f 1904. The words
Monna and Vanna can be used
together or separately

g 1906 Used on locomotives, etc

h 1907 optical

j 1909

k 1910 optical

l,m,n,p 1913 Construction sets

q 1918 A sign for building
bricks used in Germany &
England. Importers & exporters

r 1918

s 1918

t 1918

u 1918

v 1918

w 1918

x 1918

y 1918

z 1919

a¹ 1919

b¹ 1919

c¹ 1919 Book publishing was
added to their list

a 1919
b 1919 *Building bricks made of artificial stone*
c 1919
d 1919
e 1919
f 1920 *Dolls are added to their list*
g 1922

dolls' houses. In 1910 came sawmills, forges, stations, ticket offices and signals. In 1912, Bing exported boxed locomotives to the USA. Carriages and clockwork double-deckers came in 1914, to be followed by aeroplanes during the First World War. His toy gramophones with conical horns attached to sound boxes were known as Pigmyphones.

His mark was G B N, the G B for his name and the N for Nürnberg all placed within a diamond. His locomotives were marked Bavaria. He also exported toys and games but in 1925 the firm was taken over by SHUCO.

a

BING-B₿ WERKE

b

c

f

Pitti-Bum

g

d

Carette, Nuremberg

Georges Carette of Georges Carette et Cie was a Frenchman who had lived in Germany nearly all his life. This may account for the decorative coloured details which give distinction to all his toys.

In 1893 he made an electric street car, a steam locomotive in 1899 and other locomotives during the early part of the twentieth century. By 1910 and 1912 he had turned his attention to cars, beautiful little cars complete with side lamps like the early models which appeared on the roads at this time. The address in Nuremberg was 5/7 Schillerstrasse.

h

G.C.&C°

N. j

k

FLAMMOTOR

l

h 1898 *Georges Carette & Co, Nuremberg. Dampf-Spielzeuge, Dampf-Lokomotiven. Dampf= steam*

1909 Soc Georges Carette & Cie, Nuremberg. Engines

j,k 1909 *Georges Carette & Co, Schillerstrasse 5/7, Nuremberg. Phonographs, talking machines*

& discs, optical articles, stereoscopes, electrical articles & accessories

l 1913 *Optical, mechanical, electrical toys*

a

b

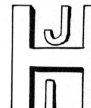

c, g

Hessmobil d

Spielzeug-Autos gibt es viel,
aber nur ein „Hessmobil". e

„Hess" f

I-EL-HA h

„Dreadnought" j

„Dynamobil" k

„Lloyd" l

„Flirt" m

Peary q

Eskimobil n

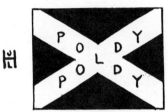

p

„Kismet" r

Red-Cliff s

Nimrod t

„Tippu-Tipp" u

HESS-ROLLER
"PUSSPET"

Hess-Auto v

Hess-Racer w

x

Furor teutonicus y

---

a   1895 Math. Hesz,
    Nuremberg. Tin & sheet-metal
    toys, railways, locomotives, and
    cannons
b   1896 Math. Hesz. Ditto
c   1899 Joh Leonh Hesz,
    Nuremberg. Metal engine &

train
d,e   1906 Spielzeug-Autos
    gibt es viel, aber nur ein
    „Hessmobil"
f,g,h,j   1907 games & toys
k,l,m   1908
n,p,q,r,s   1909 Their new sign

on the left, and their old sign
on the right are incorporated in
mark p
t   1910
u,v   1911
w,x   1912
y   1915

Clown and Cart with Zebra by
E. P. Lehmann. Tinplate
painted, clockwork with key
at side of cart. A toy called
Zikra, this one after 1927.

German 1913 Zebra and
cart $7\frac{1}{4}''$ long

From the Bethnal Green Museum

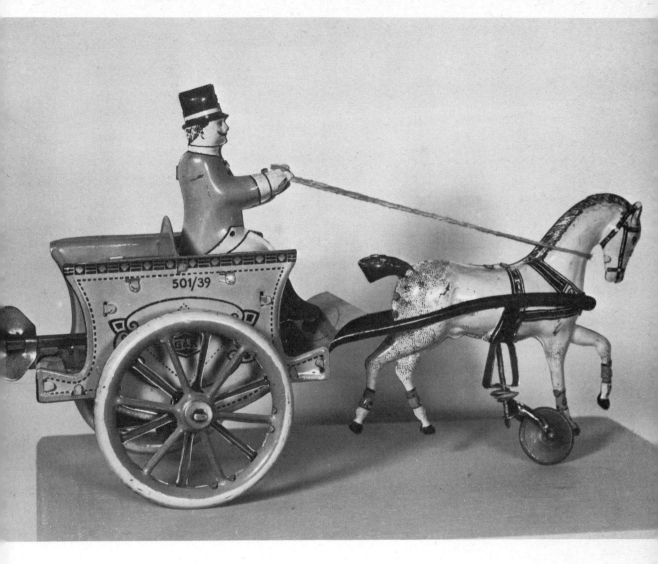

Jaunting cart by Greppert &
Kelch. Painted tinplate cart with
clockwork inside and key at
back, single wheel under the
horse. The mark G & K on the
side of cart.

German   before 1922 $7\frac{1}{2}''$ long

From the Bethnal Green Museum

a *Gnom* b   c   d SEKTOR e

LEHMANN f   g HIE GUET BRANDENBURG ALLEWEGE h TUT j

Lehmann k   l (mark) m  n (mark) p TAP q

Gustav r Paul s

Ernst t Otto u BISMARCK v Mandarin w

OHO x MA-MA z PA-PA a' OROH b' VINCENT c'

 y ZICK-ZACK d' GERTRUD e' AM-POL f'

EPLI g' HAVEL h' NANNI j' WIKING k'

T-AKU l' ORRO m' UNDA n' ROTA p' EVA q' ROON r'

SPREE s' BEROLINA t' OH-MY u' EPELE v' VELLEDA w'

---

a *1890 Ernst Paul Lehmann,*
   Brandenburg on the Havel,
   Prussia. Toys
b *1895 Blechspielwaren und*
   Kreisel beliebigem material
c, d, e *1896*

f *1898*
g, h *1902*
j, k, l, m *1903*
n *1905*
p, q, r, s, t, u *1906*
v, w *1907*

x *1909 Plauerstrasse,*
   Brandenburg/Havel, Germany.
   Sheet metal toys
y *1910*
z *1910 z, a¹, to r¹*
   1911 s¹ to w¹

ADAM _a MARTHA _b TAMTAM _c PARDUIN _d

ITO _e ATA _f ITI _g HOP _h ONO _j

KNÜPPEL _k HOHENZOLLERN _l NA-OB _m ATOM _n

TRUDE _p LANA _q TERRA _r ILTIS _s HALLO _t

HALLO _u TOMMY _v TOM _w PERLE _x OH-MY _y

HIP HIP HURRAH _z

KINTOP _{a¹} KADI _{b¹}

SNIK-SNAK _{c¹}

PRELLE _{d¹}

DUO _{g¹} EMGEH _{h¹} APPAM _{j¹} „Futurus" _{k¹}

---

a, b, c, d, e, f, g, h, j, k, l, m, n, p,
  q, r, s, t *1911*
u, v, w, x, y, z *1912*
1912 Ernst Paul Lehmann,
  Brandenburg-on-the-Havel,
  Germany. Sheet-metal toys

mounted on wheels, or con-
structed to walk, climb autos
etc. Aeroplanes, entered in the
USA
a¹, b¹ *1913*

c¹, d¹ *1914*
e¹, f¹, g¹ *1915*
h¹, j¹ *1916*
k¹ *1920. This mark was also*
  entered under porcelain

·ZIKRA· MARKE

1913. Mark from tinplate, clockwork toy, of clown driving a zebra cart. 7" long. USA patent

Ri-Ka-Ko

1919 Max Lehmann, Leipzig. Toys

MÄRKLIN
c

a,b *1910 Gebruder Märklin & Co, Göppingen. Metal & clockwork toys*
c *1919 Especially states that the firm does not make dolls*

Ernst Paul Lehmann, Brandenburg, Prussia

The firm of Ernst Paul Lehmann was founded in 1881 in Prussia and amongst other things it specialized in cheap clockwork toys, playing cards etc. both exporting and importing a variety of goods.

Figures playing diabolo, dressed porters and boys on motor bikes worked by clockwork were made at the end of the nineteenth century, motor cars in 1905, and toys which were worked by means of weights. In 1906 there was a balloon and in 1909 a clockwork car with three wheels.

By 1910, Lehmann toys were the hits of the world markets. Clockwork figures, clowns, mandarins and skaters were amongst his rather exotic automata and there were many kinds of vehicles. Cars, tricycles, hansom cabs, carts pulled by donkeys or ostriches and driven by clowns were among the seventeen names registered in 1910 alone. In 1914 there were more clockwork cars, tin buses, beetles four inches long which crawled along the ground, and wonderful tap-dancers.

His zeppelin, patented about 1906, was made of tin and celluloid.

By 1913 childrens' pistols and cannons were added to his extensive list, also cinematograph apparatus. Often the Lehmann toys consisted of pairs such as his figures with vehicles and his dancers, the people having heavily painted eyebrows and other details which might be lithographed on the flat tinplate before the toy was assembled.

Lehmann used his initials E P L embossed or painted on the toys and incorporated the press design in many of the trademarks. Toys by this firm were still in production in 1925 and many, many names were registered up to this time.

Gebruder Märklin & Co, Göppingen

The Märklin firm founded in the nineteenth century made soldiers in 1865. By 1900 they specialized in boats, steamboats, locomotives and street cars. In 1903 a steam pump was made, and by 1905 they made stationary steam engines and toys to be worked by them. Boats were exported to the USA, cars, metro-cars, level crossings, ticket offices, a tinplate swimming pool with hollow dolls to swim in it, and even one of those lavatories which are to be seen in the public places of France.

Märklin excelled in boats and locomotives with all the accessories. Their steam engines worked threshing machines, and they also made automata

1905 Märklin. Toy Car

which was operated by coins. By 1910 guns and other military toys were added to their lists. However their name is mostly associated with locomotives, railway signals etc. As many firms used parts made by other firms it is difficult at times to decide by which firm the actual toy was made.

Their mark is a shield with the initials G M & Cie.

Fernand Martin, Menilmontant, outside Paris

At first, about 1878, Martin's toys were worked by rubber bands, such as the one in which two men are working a saw, and the one of a tin fish which could swim. He used sheet metal with the tab and slot method and his figures had their arms and legs made of wire. He weighted the feet with lead and in some dolls he placed a spiral spring. The metal figures were dressed simply in cloth materials; his lavender seller and chestnut vendor were popular and in 1880 a clockwork peacock was a great success.

In 1895 Martin had a dressed butcher, a dressed porter and other figures dressed in flimsy cotton clothes which hid their joints. By 1900 he had clockwork piano players, musicians, a man with a concertina and a boy playing diabolo. His clockwork performing bear was covered with furry material and all his tinplate toys had the clockwork within the bodies.

About 1908 these tin and coloured varnished toys were sold in the streets for a few pence, being about six inches high. Among these was a Messenger boy, a man breaking plates, Father Francis' pigs, the Barber shampooing, the little pianist and the violinist, and a toy called the Mysterious Ball.

There was a negro who pushed a cart along with his feet, and another negro had a barrow load of pomegranates and there was also a clothed policeman. The clothed soldier was made about 1910 and the man on a horse and the preacher about 1911. Also at this time came the man stealing the Mona Lisa, the delivery man seen on the cover of my *Antique Toys*, and a clockwork spiral. When carts are used, the mechanism is within the cart.

Martin's toys were marked F M, the usual words Schutzmarke or Marque-Deposée, Article Français being added. In 1912 the firm of Fernand Martin was taken over by Bonnet & Cie. Among the toys still being made in the 1930s were the Tippler, the Drunkard, the Goal keeper, the Orange seller, the Policeman with a baton, and the Fireman with a ladder.

Ernst Planck, Germany

Ernst Planck or EP of Germany made an early locomotive about 1875, and in 1880 he was making clockwork metal figures and musical boxes. The platforms were of tin and the musical box was in the base.

Between 1885 and 1890 Planck's interest was in magic lanterns and optical toys such as the Zoëtrope. He also made stationary steam engines, street cars, boats and about 1895 he made a model distillery. In 1908 he made clockwork penny toy aeroplanes and more aeroplanes and steam launches in 1910. Many of his toys were made to work by steam engines.

Noris e

Evening Star f

Diogenes g

Ernest Planck, or Plank, Germany,
 Magic Lanterns
e, f   1898
g   1900. A magic Lantern

Chor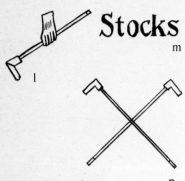

Charles Roitel, France

Roitel used a monogram made up from the initials C R, whereas Charles Rossignol, and later on the widow, both used the letters C R side by side.

In 1880 Roitel made clockwork toys. In 1890 there was a clockwork circus, firemen, milk floats and toys to be worked by steam engines, Locomotives, knife grinders, soldiers and guns came later, street cars in 1910, cars and army trucks in 1912.

E. R. Ives, Plymouth, Conn, USA and later at Bridgeport

Ives first toys were made about 1866, tin toys wound up by keys. His clockwork figures, often coloured people, were dressed in cloth and muslins. In 1869 he made a clockwork rowing boat with a man and oars, and in 1870 he marketed the well-known boy on a tricycle which was patented by A. M. Allen.

This was followed by a doll in a clockwork swing and a lady sitting in a cart and driving the horse. Other toys were clockwork see-saws and dancers, and a figure of a woman on a platform shouting for womens' rights. In 1880 he made a negro preacher.

During the 1880s, Ives took over the Automatic Toy Works in New York city, which had been started in the 1870s.

American Makers

Here are just a few of the numerous firms in the USA who made automata, the most well-known being Schoenhut with his musical instruments and toy pianos, and Carlisle & Finch with their electric trains.

1843   J. & E. Stevens Co (Noted for toy pistols)
1856   Don Evaristo Peck, Burlington, Conn. Mechanical toys
1857–80s   George Brown, wind-up toys
1868   Stevens and Brown formed the American Toy Company
1872   A. Schoenhut & Co Philadelphia. Toy pianos, musical instruments, dolls etc
1873   J. A. Pierce, Chicago, Illinois. Mechanical toys, steam engines, steam boats, locos etc
1875   Leo Schlesinger, Inc NY
1880   Standard Manufacturing Co New Haven Conn. Mechanical toys
1880s   Charles Bailey, metal and mechanical toys
1885   Home Music Co Providence, Rhode Island. Mechanical and musical toys
1887   F. O. Wehoskey, Providence, RI. Mechanical toys
1890   Knapp Electric Co NY. Electric toys
1890   James Fallows, Philadelphia. Mechanical tin toys
1894   Kingsbury Manu Co Keene, New Hampshire. Wind-up toys
1896   Carlisle & Finch. Electric trains

h, j   *1906 Walter Stock, Solingen. Maker of metal goods and exporter, also toys, christmas goods such as candle holders, cribs & Nativity scenes for which he registered a great many drawings*

k   *1908 A Hexenschlösschen is a witches castle*

l, m   *1909 Stock is the German for a walking stick or cane, on which he based his sign*

n, p   *1910*

q   *1912 Toy manufacturer*

Initials on Metal Toys

A L	Auguste Lapierre	J	William Jerger, Villingen
A P	Aubert & Papin, Versailles	J A B	J. A. Bäselsoder, Nürnberg
A R O	René Arnoux, Paris	J A F	Jouets et Automates Français
B & S	Blomer & Schüler, Nürnberg	J B	Josef Bishoff, Nürnberg
C K	Kellermann Co, Nürnberg	J F	Joseph Falk, Nürnberg
C R	Charles Roitel, France (monogram)	J F N	J. Haffner, Nürnberg
		J L H	Joh. Leonhard Hess
C R	Charles Rossignol, Paris	J & P	Le Jouet de Paris
D C	Doll & Co, Nürnberg (monogram)	K B	Karl Bub, Nürnberg
		L B	Louis Bourgaie, Paris
E B A	Banneville et Aulanier, Paris	L G P	Alfred Poux, Paris
		L S M	L. S. Mayer & Co, Berlin
E D	Emile Dandrieux, Paris		
E D D	Ernst Döbler, Dresden	L W F	Ludwig Wohlbold, Fürth
E P	Ernst Planck, Germany		
E P L	Ernst Paul Lehmann, Brandenburg	M B	Milton Bradley, Springfield, Mass, USA
E X A	Vergnes et Fontaine, Paris	M D	Max Dannhorn, Nürnberg
F M	Fernand Martin, Paris	M & K	Mohr & Krausz
F N N	Fritz Neumeyer, Nürnberg	M U	Max. Uhlfelder
		P F	Pean Frères, Paris and Creil
G B N	Gebrüder Bing, Nürnberg	R & G N	Oscar Egelhaaf, Biberach a Ritz
G C & Co	Georges Carette, Nürnberg	S B R D	Saupe & Busch, Radebeul
G & K	Greppert & Kelch, Brandenberg	S G	S. Gunthermann, Nürnberg
G M	Gebrüder Märklin, Göppingen	V B	V. B. & Cie, Paris, known as Vebe
H E N	Hans Eberl, Nürnberg	V M	Victor Maillard, Paris
H K	Hans Krausz, Nürnberg	W R	William Ritzmann, Nürnberg
H M	Georges Haran, Lavallois-Perret		

Indexes

INDEX OF MAKERS, AGENTS ETC WITH ILLUSTRATED MARKS

Ihlee & Horne 26t, 27h
Illfelder, B 124w
Illfelder, M 68l,m, 123n, 124b, 125u
Indiarubber, guttapercha & Telegraph
    Works 54m
Int Inv Mod 143j
Issacs, A & J 119z
Ismenau 22w,x
Italo, I 71q
Itzen & Bauthieu 191u
Ivens, T E 49b
Ivimey, A A 124c[1]
Izon, T 31w

Jackson, P 56f,g,h,j
Jacob, H 105k
Jacob, L E 28h
Jacobshon, L 79b
Jacobsohn, A 59p
Jacquier, A J B 76n
Janssens, J F 74b,c
Jaques, J 69c, 86a, 87a,h, 89q, 91s, 92x,
    104m,n, 108a
James, A W 32j
Jary, J 76m
Jean, E 40w
Jeanson, J 120y
Jefferies 66a
Jeidel, J 33s,t,w
Jenkins, R 140a
Jerger, W 180t
Jewitt, H 86c
Joanny, J 40e, 125c
Jones, A S 180b
Jones, E H 159 g,h
Jones, W H 41g
Jordan, K 158w,x
Joseph, H 107e
Joyce, R J S 26d,e
Juilla, A 42p
Jumeau, E 120c[1], 148
Jung, J 56c
Jürgel, P 135q

Kaempfer, J G 128j
Kaestner, F 20j,k,l, 23c
Kahn, B & H 129m
Kaiser, H 60e
Kallista, E 50
Kalthoff, J L 192a
Kämmer & Reinhardt 56p,q, 149, 153
Kann & Co 95
Kaulitz, M 157k, 158a
Keilich, B 101f
Keim, P D 110c
Keller & Co 57d

Keller, Gebr 96n
Kelson, G M 31e
Kempe, A 62e
Kennard Novelty Co 48g
Kermik Manufactur 23b[1]
Kersten, H 41b
Kestner, J D 150
Kienberger & Co 181n
Kindler & Briel 41e
Kirby Beard & Co 70c
Kirch, H 72g
Kirchner, H 53m
Kirn, H 27x
Kister, A W F 46b
Kleefeld, L 97e
Klein, J A 91r
Kleinig & Blasberg 29j
Klen & Hahn 123p, 126a,l, 127e, 128p
Klimke, O 41a
Kling & Co 22c[1]
Klob, T 106n
Kluczyk, I 62r
Knoch Gbr 145e
Knoop 107l
Knorpp, J N 52d
Kobrou, C 68e
Koch, J C 130l,p
Koeber & Co 27a,e
Koenig & Rudolph 128h
Köhler, A 106s
Kohn, G 31n, 72e
Kohnstam, M 166, 190d,f,h
Köllner, M 129h, 140g
Kölner Stoffwäsche-Fabrik 104k
Konsbrück, H 44m
Korbuln, J 99a
Krampe, O 123m
Kratz, H O 190l
    see also Boussac, K
Krause, K J 78d
Krause, W 92t
Kraus Mohr 30f
Krauss, Gbr 145a,b,c,d
Krausz, H 183e
Krausz, S 26f
Krenkel, F R 26g, 30n
Krieg, G 73h
Kriege, J 124v
Kriszner, J 62b
Kronheim, W 69l, 96k
Kruse, K 160m,q
Kuërs, M 92z
Kühnert & Co 34v, 51m
Kunst gewerbliche Werkstätte 136d
Kunst, T 134j
Kunzel, H 57j

Kurtz, H 36e

Laboureyras, E C 100e
Lacmann, J 17l
Lafosse, M 121e,n
La Francia 39h
Laguione et Cie 129b, 130f
Lallement, H 58h
Lambert, C 41t
Lanagnère, T 119t
Lander, H G 159b
Landrieu, P 59j, 102n, 109c,d,e,g
Landsberger, A 125l,q
Landshut, H 121u
Langguth, P 92c
Langsel, G 44k
Lanternier, A 150
Lapp, L 40v
Laquionie et Cie 132v,w,x
Lasker, E 30d
Lauer, L C 190c
Laupheimer, A 41k
Laurent, A 47j
Laurent, G 68d,h, 108r
Laurent, G E E 53n
Laurent, J 82c,d,e
Lauterburg, E 89c
Lavieuville & Le Roi 181l
Lavignac, E 104j
Lavy, C 71l
Lazarski, T 134z
Lebel, R S 39k
Leblanc, A 197m
Lebourdais, A 91a
Lebreton, P A F 42k
Le Comte, E 42n
Leconte, M 119e[1]
Lee-witz, A 101k
Lefebore, A 134b[1]
Legener, F 66w
Legrand, Mme 181m
Legros, M D 120a
Lehmann, E P 204, 205, 206
Lehmann, M 206
Lehnert & Co 44h
Leibenger, G 89t
Leibenger, M 102b
Leichmann, H C E 49c
Leischener, J 91g
Lejeune, L A 130h
Le Jouet de Paris 74k, 89m, 180n
Lelievre, Y 100j
Lemoine, Y M E 23s
Le Montréer, H, 37m
Le Montréer, D 130d
Lenoir, G 39a

von der Linden, T 40d[1]
von der Meden, C A 80a
von Hasperg, G 50b
von Hirschberg, M F 30p
von Neyheiten, F 59m
Vormus, R 159k
Vuillaume, E 73n

Wagner, F A 99c
Wagner & Zetzsche 130r
Waite, F 14a[1]
Wallace, F C 92r
Waltershausen Puppenfabrik 135n,s
Walton, T 103f
Wakenphast Ltd 27j
Wannez et Rayer 120d[1]
Ward, S H 40a
Warga, I 192c
Warmuth, H W 53j
Warncke, A 27w
Warne, W 53b
Wasmuth, A 104l, 105a to g
Waterman, L 104f,g
Watilliaux, C A 29a,b,m, 30q, 54d,
    98a, 120z, 122g, 191d
Watris, M 72m
Wedeses 121c,d
Wehncke, E 30c
Weigel, A 180p
Weill, A 36s
Weintraud, J 26b, c
Weiser, Ignatz 32d
Weiss, A 34h, 62k

Weisz, H 121x
Weisze, A 27m
Welfling, A 92d,e
Wellhöfer, J A 180g
Welter Gebr 49f
Wendland, W 103d
Werner, M E 97b, f
Wernicke, C 29n, 182l
Wessel, L 22f,p, 190a
Westel, Allgauer & Co 134q
Wheeler, J 118e
Wheelhouse, M V 40b
Wheelock, L D 110k
White, C & H 173
Whiteley, W 14b[1]
Whyte, R 26l
Wiart, G 103a
Wichmann, B 136b
Wicke, F 60b
Wiederholz, O 32a, 41q
Wiegand, H 133d
Wiegel, F 181k
Wielers, H 90d
Wilhelmsfeld 155x,y,z
Wilkinson, W H 88n
Williams, R S 30x
Wilson, R O'N 158l,q,r,s
Windsor, E S 87r
Winkler, E 127d,f
Winkler, F E 122p
Winterbauer, M 32c, 46m, 59k
Wislizenus, A 123t, 127a,b, 155a[1],b[1]
Wohlbold, L 183p,q

Wohlmann, O 37j
Wölber & Co 23n
Wolf, D 173e
Wolf, J P G 89d
Wolf, L 173a to d
Wolff & Co 67n
Wolfgang, M M 41r
Wolgemuth & Litzner 39l
Woodham, H 67r
Worsnop, A 102a
Wouilt, R 131k
Wunsch & Pretzsch 77d
Wurt: Porzellan 23z
Wuzel, L 38u

York Novelty Co 78e

Zahren, H 93f
Zay 191m
Zeife, R 96g
Zeigler, B 36a
Zero-spiel-vertriebs 91d
Zeuch & Lausmann 28m
Zierow, P R 126k, 129f
Zimmer, S D 35s, 81z, 157j
Zimmermann, M 46e
Zink, H L 31v
Zipper, E 108
Zitzmann, E 17m
Zocher & Semmler 103n
Zuber, Y 38v
Züllchower Anstalten 38b, 62p, 107j

INDEX OF PERSONS, MAKERS AND TRADE NAMES, MENTIONED IN THE TEXT

INDEX OF TRADE NAMES, ILLUSTRATED MARKS

Tap, 204q

Tausendschönchen, 126d, 151t

Techno, 170j

Tecla, 37k

Teddyball, 66b¹

Teddy Bear, 46g

Teenie Weenie, 164d

Tellus, 66r

Temco, 107d

Tennisa, 67n

Terra, 205r

Tessella Royale, 87p, 96b

Tete Jumeau, 148p

Thalie Bébé, 131r

Thauma, 66c

The Acme, 63g

Theatroscope, 191f

The Demon, 67c

The Dolls' Home, 13a¹

The Dolls House, 13y,z

The Fairy Kid, 127m

The Flirt, 149k

The Genteel, 67k

The Grace, 87g

The Irrgarten, 169g

The Kings of Em All, 49y

The Little Mindbuilder, 103b

The Metropolitan, 63j

The Newleywed's Baby, 126m

The Papooski, 131a

The Princess Doll, 124f¹

The Rattlum Snakorum, 48c

The Real Dolls House, 28a

The Soldier's Baby, 129a

The Tiny Tot, 162y

The Toy House, 14g¹

The Tri-ing Try-angles, 103e

The Wide-Awake Doll, 129c

The Wiggle Woggle, 166j

The Wisp, 157h

The Zingara, 190h

Thumbs up, 159m, 165l

Tic, 93p

Tiddledy-winks, 87q

Tiger, 28f

Time, 88x, 110k

Tinkertoy, 98n

Tintoscope, 191k

Tiny Tots, 32m, 162c¹, 169p

Tiny Town, 169j

Tip, 72a

Tipple Topple, 73e,j

Tip-Top, 72h

Tippu-Tipp, 201u

Tir des Alouettes, 57v

Tir des Apôtres, 57l

Tir des Bécasses, 57u

Tir des Grands Chevaux, 57r

Tir Mécano-Electrique, 57s

Tir Mouche, 57g

Tir Olympien, 57n

Tir des Patriarches, 57p

Tir des Perdrix, 57w

Tir des Pigeons, 57t

Tir des Rois, 57m

Tit, Tat, Finger, 92g

Ti tu, 34t

Titus, 60r

Toddles, 164g

Togo, 89s

Tom, 205w

Tommy, 205v

Tom Tiddler's ABC, 101a

Tootsie, 162p

Tootsie Wootsie, 157v

Top, 61s

Torbolo, 167r

Torpill's, 80j

Toton National, 91a

Toto-Tip, 41c

Tottie, 129g

Toupies Turf, 72k

Tout va Bien, 144h

Toy Town, 107g, 169q

Transsibérien, 197d

Tree the Possum, 92k

Treis kai deka, 105h

Trepidus, 33j

Trésor, 129q

Trëugolnick, 55g

Triangulo, 99e

Triumph, 111y

Triumphatos, 181k

Trixyl, 28x

Trolley, 89m

Trude, 205p

Tru Life, 100r

Trust, 108r

Trutza, 45b

Tsäh, 67v

Tubby, 164e¹

Tuff-a-Nuff, 126t

Turbo, 40d¹

Turn Over, 100p

Tut, 204j

Twee Deedle, 127p

Twinwin, 32k

Über Fels und Firn, 199a¹

Ubra, 93c

Ulgo, 183n

Unda, 204n¹

Un Poulbot, 168a

Une Poulbotte, 168b

Union, 90e

Unis, 152z

Universal, 96d

Universal Provider, 14b¹

Ura, 61e¹

Ursula, 128y, 137l

Vanna, 199e

Vantage, 110b

Vauen, 106j

Velleda, 204w¹

Véloplane, 82e

Velvokin, 126v

Veritas, 30m

Vestris, 49q

Victoria, 62d, 80w

Victory, 39q

Vierkleur, 88c¹

Vigoro, 88y

Vincent, 204c¹

Vingt et un, 90k

Viola, 165f

Volafix, 35t

Volksfreund, 111f¹

Volo, 76k

Volvox, 181q, 186h

Votes for Women, 157y

Vox Populi, 33x

Wallypug, 157g

Wanda, 134t

Weko, 34h

Welta, 134p

Weltgröszen, 169l

Wer weisz es, 169w

Whiff-Waff, 172d

Whitely, 71l

Wibolo, 33s

Wig, 105l

Wiking, 204k¹

Wild-West, 60c

Willow, 134g

Windikus, 49r

Wonderscope, 192c

Wood Street Ball, 67s

Woody Tiger, 47e

Woollybambolly, 35d

Wunder-Ei, 112p

Würfel = Piano, 104r

Wuwu, 165h¹

Wyn-kah, 106h

Yak-yak, 41b

Yankee, 127u

INDEX OF ILLUSTRATED MARKS WITH INITIALS